To my soon-to-be fa

Words cannot express how grateful I am
to you for your incredible support as
well as to you and your dearly departed
beloved wife, may she forever rest in peace,
for having raised a very special young lady.

I am looking forward very much towards
the meeting of our families and I pray
that Hashem bless us all with lives of
joy, health, peace and happiness and the
strength to do always what is right in
His eyes and fulfil the mission for
which we were placed on this earth.

                    May we know only simcha
                                    Baruch

Ostrow fam.

WESTWOOD

HEAVEN ON EARTH

HEAVEN ON EARTH

Down to Earth Jewish Spirituality

EDITED BY

NECHEMIA COOPERSMITH

AND SHRAGA SIMMONS

FROM THE AWARD-WINNING WEBSITE, AISH.COM

TARGUM/FELDHEIM

First published 2002
Copyright © 2002 by Aish.com
ISBN 1-56871-206-5

Published by:
TARGUM PRESS, INC.
22700 W. Eleven Mile Rd.
Southfield, MI 48034
E-mail: targum@netvision.net.il
Fax: 888-298-9992
www.targum.com

In conjuntion with:
AISH.COM
1 Western Wall Plaza
P.O.B. 14149
Jerusalem, Israel
e-mail: heavenonearth@aish.com
www.aish.com

Distributed by:
FELDHEIM PUBLISHERS
202 Airport Executive Park
Nanuet, NY 10954
www.feldheim.com

Printed in Israel

This book is dedicated to

Rabbi Noah
and
Rebbetzin Dinah Weinberg

whose tireless dedication to sharing
the beauty of our heritage
has brought so much heaven
down to earth.

Contents

DARKNESS AND LIGHT

THE INNER STRUGGLE

Acknowledgments

When Aish.com was launched in February 2000, we set our goal unrealistically high — to reach 1 million visits each month.

We've surpassed that and more. And for that we thank our loyal readers. Your encouragement, criticism, and raves ensure that the site thrives.

It is clear that none of this would be possible without the Almighty's unceasing care and orchestration. We are humbled by His undeserved blessings and thank Him for enabling us to be a part of sharing His infinite wisdom.

Rabbi Noah Weinberg, the dean of Aish HaTorah International, has been instrumental in guiding the overall direction of Aish.com and its maintenance through his ongoing financial support. His depth of wisdom, indefatigable efforts on behalf of the entire Jewish people, and palpable love of God and humanity have profoundly impacted our lives, and those of every Aish.com reader.

We thank all the supporters of Aish.com for their generous financial assistance and invaluable guidance. In particular we thank Yuri and Deana Pikover for their unwavering commitment and trailblazing vision, and Art and Sally Klein, Bob and Michelle Diener, Dov and Nancy Friedberg, Mitch and Joleen Julis, Meir

Vaisman, and Rabbi Sholom and Leah Mark for their tremendous support and dedication.

Behind the scenes at Aish.com is a dedicated and incredibly talented team of people who have become a second family. David LeVine takes our raw content and masterfully turns it into web reality. Yitzhak Attias produces stunning graphics that enhance every aspect of the site. Rabbi Shmuel Silinsky planted the seeds of Aish online and continues his keen input. Rabbi Kalman Packouz is the mastermind behind two of our most popular features, Shabbat Shalom Weekly and the Western Wall Camera.

We are also grateful for the unique skills, remarkable vision, and good fortune of working with Seth Aronstam, Emuna and Nachum Braverman, Binyamin Buxbaum, Mike Cooper, Dovid Gross, Tuvia Hoffman, Shmuel Kaffe, Rabbi Jack Kalla, Chavi Miller, Uriela Obst, Stefanie Pearson, Chaya Richmond, Malkie Sender, Chaya Sorcsher, Mike Waldman, Rabbi Pinchas Waldman, Yedidya Weil, and Chaya Gitty Wolpin. We also extend our gratitude to the Aish HaTorah administrative and executive offices.

We also thank the staff at Targum Press and Leviathan Press for helping make this book a reality.

We especially acknowledge the writers and contributors to Aish.com. Without their insightful, high caliber content, neither this book nor the website would exist.

And finally, our deepest gratitude goes to our wives and families, for their endless support, feedback and willingness to endure our long hours in the office, on the phone, and glued to the computer screen. In the merit of their helping bring Torah to our people, may they be blessed with all of God's goodness.

Nechemia Coopersmith and Shraga Simmons
Jerusalem, August 2002/Elul 5762

Introduction

For many of us, the depth of Jewish spirituality that has nourished Jews throughout the generations has been locked away. This book opens the door, exploring the myriad paths within Judaism to spiritual fulfillment.

The Torah tells us of Jacob's arrival at the holy spot of Mount Moriah:

> [Jacob] had a vision in a dream. A ladder was set on earth, and its top reached toward heaven. And behold — angels of God were ascending and descending on it.
>
> *(Genesis 28:12)*

Jacob's vision depicts a ladder reaching the uppermost heavens — while staying firmly rooted to earth.

This is a metaphor for Jewish spirituality. Spirituality does not require that we renounce the physical in order to dwell in the celestial. Accessing Jewish spirituality means grappling with the mundane world in a way that uplifts and elevates. We climb the ladder, step by step, in order to bring pieces of Heaven down here on earth.

Aish.com personifies the concept of "Torah shall go forth from Zion" in its most modern application — through the melding of ancient wisdom with state-of-the-art technology. The website attracts over 1.4 million visits each month and 80,000 e-mail subscribers, providing practical, inspiring wisdom for leading a more fulfilled life.

This anthology, the first in our virtual wisdom series, brings together Aish.com's best essays on spirituality, written by some of the top Jewish educators and writers around the globe.

We hope the book contributes in some small way to your journey toward bringing the spiritual heights of heaven... down to earth.

SPIRITUAL ODYSSEYS

SARA YOHEVED RIGLER

Arriving at Sinai

I was sitting cross-legged on the floor of my guru's receiving room amidst a dozen or so other disciples, all Indians. A few meters in front of me, on his divan, sat my octogenarian guru, the renowned pundit Sri Gopinath Kaviraj, retired principal of the Varanasi Sanskrit College.

I had come to say goodbye. After a year in India, I would be leaving the next morning. My guru had taught me about the different levels of reality: physical, emotional, mental, astral, and spiritual. He had also taught me to meditate, which was the way to access the highest, spiritual level of reality.

Having been raised in a Judaism where God and soul were never mentioned, I approached the spiritual world like an awestruck tourist whose guide had led her to a fantastical domain

SARA YOHEVED RIGLER is a featured writer on Aish.com. After 15 years practicing and teaching Eastern philosophy and meditation, she became a Torah-observant Jew and moved to Israel, where she now lives in the Old City of Jerusalem with her musician husband and two children. Her articles also appear in *Chicken Soup for the Jewish Soul* and *Jewish Women Speak about Jewish Matters*. She is currently working on a biography of "Rebbetzin Devorah Cohen," entitled *Holywoman*.

not included in the standard guidebooks. Meditation was the key to the otherwise impenetrable gate of that world. I would rise at 4 o'clock in the morning, when the predawn stillness lent wings to my not-yet-cluttered mind, and meditate for an hour, sometimes experiencing an ecstasy which made me loath to return to the plodding heaviness of the physical world.

Innately spiritual, I loved to meditate, and believed, as the Eastern way taught, that someone meditating behind cloistered walls could uplift the vibrations of the whole world.

On the other hand, the Jewish activist in me could not be silenced. It was the heyday of the Sixties. As a college student at Brandeis, I had been active in S.D.S. — Students for a Democratic Society, and the anti-Vietnam War struggle, until I read a quote by Zen teacher Alan Watts: "Peace can only be made by those who are peaceful."

Put off by the hatred of our S.D.S. leaders for each other, I had come to India for my junior year to seek a deeper, truer way to save the world.

Now, in my last audience with my guru, I was eager to ask a question that tormented me. That year I had found a goal to which to dedicate my life: God-consciousness. Yet how was I supposed to navigate my life in such a way that I would not get sidetracked or lost in the maze of problems and choices which surrounded me?

For one, I had wanted to remain in India, but my father insisted that I return to Brandeis to finish my final year. And then what? Should I go on to Psych Grad School, as I had always planned I would? The academic world now seemed vapid and supercilious compared with the profound light of the spiritual world. And what about my handsome Indian boyfriend? My parents had always insisted that I marry a Jew. Was marrying my Hindu love worth the anguish it would cause my family?

After 15 minutes of answering questions in Bengali, my guru finally turned to me and asked in English, "So you are leaving tomorrow?"

I nodded glumly and fired my question: "When choices present themselves to me in life, how will I know what to choose?"

I was asking him for a compass. I was embarking on a long, perilous journey. How would I find my goal when the clouds of confusion obscured the stars?

I had too many friends who ambled aimlessly through their lives, bumping into disastrous consequences along the way. Their lives were splattered with false starts and failed relationships, and they changed their college majors as often as they changed their shirts — every month.

I abhorred the modus vivendi of trial-and-error. Back on the college campus the debate was raging about whether LSD caused permanent brain or chromosomal damage. At that point in the Sixties, the drug was too new to study its long-term effects. How many of my brilliant and creative friends experimented with it, as if their future mental acuity (or that of their children) was worth the gamble! I was more goal-oriented, with too scrupulous a sense of efficiency to waste years of my life or my emotional well-being on wrong turns. I wanted a compass.

My guru fixed me with his gaze and replied, "Let the scriptures be your guide."

"The scriptures?" I thought, incredulously. "What scriptures? I have no scriptures!"

I knew that Sri Kaviraj-ji himself was an orthodox Brahmin, who followed the injunctions of the Vedas. But in the year I had been studying with him, he had never once mentioned the Hindu scriptures.

Did I have any scriptures? I wondered, quickly canvassing my life. Surely he couldn't mean the Bible! Growing up, I used to attend my synagogue every Shabbat and read the boring commentary on the weekly Torah portion. Surely there was no wisdom for living, no compass there.

"I have no scriptures," I replied meekly.

"You have no scriptures?" he commiserated, as if I had told him I lacked a pancreas or a kidney. "Well, then, you'll have to be guided by your inner voice."

My inner voice. He had handed me a compass, but clearly, in his mind, a second-rate one, cheap, imprecise, the kind they sold at the five-and-dime — not the state-of-the-art compass they sold in the Hammacher Schlemmer catalogue.

The trouble with the inner voice, I was to learn, is that the ego is a great ventriloquist. What sounded like the inner voice was often no more than the voice of base desire pulling off a good impersonation: "I must do that. It is my destiny. It is God's will for me." And I, hoodwinked, would march off into a bramble patch from which I would manage to extricate myself only with great difficulty, emerging scratched and bleeding.

Intellect versus Intuition

I got my degree from Brandeis and, the very next day, joined an ashram in the woods of eastern Massachusetts, a mile from the ocean, where I stayed for the next 15 years. The guru was a 64-year-old Indian woman whom we called Mataji. She had been teaching Vedanta philosophy and meditation in the U.S. since 1927. Mataji herself was like an embodiment of one of India's goddesses — alternately loving and demanding, gentle and fierce, merciful and merciless.

Mataji was as enlightened a human being as I had ever met. She moved, and guided all of us, by Divine direction received through meditation. Intuition was the apparatus by which she tuned into the divine will.

Intellect, on the other hand, was disdained as a flawed and limited tool that could probe no higher than the physical world. The intellect, according to Mataji, was a charlatan, which claimed infallibility while in fact it was incapable of transcending the barriers of logic to soar up to the greater truth of paradox, the mystical world beyond the limits of physical reality.

I had grown up in a middle-class Jewish milieu where intellect, distilled into academic achievement, was everything. Sri Gopinath Kaviraj, too, had spoken to me on the level of intellect, although explaining concepts beyond the grasp of my spiritually untrained mind, like a physicist expounding on the intricacies of atomic structure to a high school freshman.

At the ashram, however, the intellect was an unwelcome

intruder that interfered with the quest of pure intuition. When I would ask Mataji questions about Eastern philosophy, she would refuse to answer, deriding me as her "question box."

Over the years, I realized that the guru-as-compass had two drastically opposite features. On one hand, the guru system had worked for centuries in India because it took the direction of the seeker's spiritual life out of the control of the wildly subjective inner voice, and placed it in the more objective control of a presumably enlightened guru. Even if the guru was not totally enlightened, he or she was likely wiser than the seeker, and almost always more objective about issues that faced the seeker. Thus, even if the guru's advice did not come directly from the fount of divine wisdom, at least it did not come from the subjectivity of the seeker's own ego or desires. Obeying the guru required discipline and self-abnegation, an exercise that was always beneficial to the spiritual aspirant.

On the other hand, the guru, however enlightened, was still a human being, with his or her own subjectivity. While Mataji occasionally ascended in meditation to the ethereal realms and brought back messages for which she was merely the transmitter, most often her direction came from her own intuition, which was filtered through the circumstances of her particular life and culture.

Where were her scriptures?

Social Activism

When a devastating blizzard struck New England one winter, 45-foot tidal waves demolished dozens of homes in the neighboring town of Scituate. Those who had no place else to go, including many elderly people, were put up on army cots in the local high school. The radio issued constant calls for people to take into their homes these traumatized disaster victims. Since the ashram retreat cottages, which housed visiting retreatants during the summer, were empty, I was eager to offer them for the rescue effort. While Mataji was in California at our other ashram, I was the administrative head of the East Coast ashram. Almost as a technicality, I telephoned Mataji for her approval.

She refused. Housing strangers of questionable spiritual vibrations, she insisted, would damage the rarified atmosphere of the ashram. I argued with her. How could she let elderly people, who had just lost their homes, sleep on army cots in a school building? Mataji was adamant. Devastated, I realized that my Jewish social activism had banged up against the wall of Mataji's Hindu social passivity. Her made-in-India compass had swung to the magnetic pole of her own background and conditioning.

When I hung up the phone, I stood there and wept.

I was not a good disciple. I clashed with Mataji often. Sometimes I was in awe of her ethereal vibrations and genuine humility, and I strove mightily to surrender my arrogant ego to her guidance. At other times, I saw only her human frailty. As her personal secretary, I was in daily, close contact with her. "Familiarity breeds contempt," she often quoted sadly when faced with my rebellion and obstinacy.

As for meditation, the means to achieve my own direct access to the divine, I found it as erratic as drugs. At the ashram we used to say that the difference between drugs and meditation is that drugs will make you high, but the high lasts only as long as the drug. During 17 years of practicing meditation, I had experienced many ecstatic highs, complete with revelations of the ultimate Oneness — only to land with a thud as soon as someone intruded into my altered state of consciousness by speaking to me.

Objective Compass

In 1984, when I was 36, the book I had been working on for five years, a detailed historical biography of my guru's guru, was published. As a gift, Mataji gave me a two-month leave of absence and $2,000 to go anywhere in the world I wanted. I went to New York City to study Jewish mysticism.

There I found, to my utter astonishment, that the Torah was not, as I had thought, a history of the Jewish people, nor an antiquated compendium of ancient rituals. The Torah, my teachers claimed, was the God-given instruction manual to go with planet

Earth. It was, they claimed, God's will for how human beings should conduct their lives, revealed to the entire Jewish nation at Sinai. According to my teachers, even the Oral Law, the commentary that makes the written Torah intelligible, was deduced by the Sages according to definite exegetic principles also given at Sinai.

If their claims were indeed true, then the Torah, I realized, was the ultimate compass — objective, directly from God, as immune to human subjectivity as was possible for anything in this finite world.

It seemed implausible to me. How could the infinite God reveal His will in a finite book? But there was something about the sheer objectivity of a book that goaded me to investigate further.

A month later my search took me to Jerusalem. There I studied Chumash, halacha, Maimonides, and the weekly Torah portion. Something started to stir inside me. My intellect, which so often at the ashram had been scolded and sent to sit in the corner, was now set free to run and do cartwheels. We were invited to question, challenge, demand proof, pick apart every argument. My intellect was engaged as an ally in the search for spiritual truth, rather than shunned as a subversive element.

Further, as much as I valued the path of Eastern spirituality and meditation, I was uncomfortable with its subtle scorn for the physical world. Many distraught souls came to our ashram, and Mataji usually welcomed them into the uplifting, healing atmosphere of our wooded retreat. But the help proffered was spiritual, not physical. The purpose of all our spiritual endeavors was to transcend the world, not to become embroiled in the lowly level of physicality.

In Jerusalem, during my first week of studies, I noticed that when people emerged from the restroom, they would stand for a minute with their eyes closed, muttering something. When I inquired what they were doing, I was told that just as there is a blessing to say when eating or drinking, there is also a blessing to say after using the toilet, acknowledging the Divine source of all the bodily functions.

I was blown away.

The more I studied, the more I was struck by how deftly Judaism straddles the paradox of the spiritual and the physical. Without a doubt, spirituality is important in Judaism — just as important as in any Eastern religion. But physicality is not abandoned. Rather it is embraced and made a part of the spiritual path.

The most vivid illustration of this is Shabbat. In the Torah, God commands: "Six days you should work." Read: fix the world, get your hands dirty. "On the seventh day you should rest." Read: let the world go, immerse yourself in spirituality.

Helping other people is mandatory in Judaism, and considered more important than indulging in a spiritual experience. The Torah relates how Abraham, the first Jew, was experiencing a vision of God when three travelers passed. Abraham broke away from his rapture in order to attend to the guests. The Talmud comments: "From this we learn that receiving guests is greater than receiving the face of God."

Where Intellect and Intuition Converge

Everything I learned, I loved. I battled with several issues, principally Judaism's ostensible opposition to universalism and feminism, but the depth of my teachers' approach left nothing outside its ken. Here was intellectual brilliance aligned with spiritual profundity. The way of life enjoined by the Torah fit me like a dress that had hung in my closet for decades, ignored as too tight and too old-fashioned; only when I actually tried it on did I find that it fit me perfectly.

Still, my leave of absence from the ashram was drawing to a close, and my former life beckoned. In the end, all the intellectual proofs in the world could not fortify me enough to leap off the precipice into an unknown future.

I was 37 years old. The ashram was not only my physical and spiritual home, but also my place of employment and the residence of all my friends. Accepting the dictates of the Torah would require a radical change of lifestyle — a repudiation of so much I held dear, an estrangement from my friends, and the forfeit of whatever standing and prestige I had acquired in the New Age world. I would have to start from scratch as a neophyte Jew. The very idea overwhelmed me.

One night, sometime after midnight, I went to the Kotel, the Western Wall, Judaism's holiest site. There I meditated. What was God's will for me?

We speak of the Torah as being given to the Jewish people, like a present that appears on our dining room table one day. Yet in actuality, the Torah was offered with the free choice whether or not to accept it. The Torah records that the entire Jewish people, "like one person with one heart," responded to God: "*Naaseh v'nishma* — We will do and we will understand.*" Our ancestors unconditionally, wholeheartedly, sight-unseen, committed themselves to following the manifold dictates of the Torah.

Sinai, for every Jew, is the moment of saying "yes" to God: "Yes, I'll do it on Your terms. Yes, I'll live the way You want me to. Yes, I'll accept Your Torah as my guide, even when it is inconvenient or downright difficult."

Late that summer night at the Kotel, I stood at Sinai. I had reached the point where intellect and intuition converged. I meditated and I chose. "Yes," I told God, "I will accept Your Torah, wherever it leads me, whatever it costs me."

That night I fairly floated up the steps from the Kotel to my room in the Jewish Quarter. Instead of feeling saddled by the mitzvot to which I had just committed myself, I felt free and light. After searching for 17 years, I finally had my Scriptures.

RABBI NACHUM BRAVERMAN

Falling in Love with Judaism

Growing up, I always knew I was a Jew. I felt proud when our people were strong, and I was crushed when we were threatened. But I never lit Chanukah candles, and I wasn't bar mitzvah-ed.

Judaism, I knew, had something to do with monotheism — a pale, unemotional word which never conveyed much to me. Synagogue interested me for a sense of belonging, but the actual experience was never sufficiently compelling to look inside.

I grew up in New York, studied philosophy at Yale, and in 1978 went to Israel for the summer. In Jerusalem for a weekend, I was issued a strange invitation by a friend. "How would you like to meet a Jewish philosopher?" my friend asked. It was a good line, and I accepted. That meeting led me into a yeshiva — a world more similar to my imagination of Plato's academy than to any academic environment I'd ever experienced.

RABBI NACHUM BRAVERMAN is the author of *The Bible for the Clueless but Curious*, and co-author of *The Death of Cupid*. He lives in Los Angeles with his wife and family, where he is the West Coast Director for the Jerusalem Fund of Aish HaTorah.

At Yale, mealtimes had been dominated by discussions of grades and deadlines and Rhodes applications. In the yeshiva there were no grades, no deadlines. Just a pure and ruthless intellectualism.

Is there a God? What makes life meaningful? Can you define love? These were the questions — the core issues of life — I'd hoped to answer at Yale, and here at last I was finding provoking answers.

At times, staying wasn't easy. I heard ideas that shocked and frightened me. I confronted parts of myself I would have liked to avoid. My family did not understand what I was doing, and I felt estranged, alone, and far from home.

I stayed because I defined myself as a truth-seeker, and I felt I'd have to change that definition if I left a place where there was insight, simply because the answers I found were new and troubling.

I also learned a great deal that I'd never known about Judaism, particularly the Jewish view of God. In the pagan concept, we serve the gods, appease their wrath. In Jewish understanding, God wants only our pleasure. "God our Father" wants what a parent wants for his children — their growth, their happiness, their pleasure.

Creatures of Pleasure

Pleasure has to be distinguished from another concept, comfort. Comfort is the absence of pain — a warm bath, sleep. Pleasure is energy and excitement. Pleasure is purchased at the price of effort and of pain.

There are five classes of pleasure and they differ in their yield of energy.

Class five, the lowest class of pleasure, is made up of things like wine, intimate relations, and lying in the sun — and Judaism endorses their enjoyment. Shabbat is a time when we put on our best clothes, eat fine food, and make love with our spouses. Old men should sit in the sun, says the Talmud, to remember the simple feeling of well-being that physical enjoyment brings.

The physical pleasures are available for money, and many develop their appreciation to a fine art. The connoisseurs of food and clothing, stereo and cars, are experts in the enjoyment of physical pleasure.

Onward and Upward

Class four, love, has a much higher yield of pleasure, transcending food, wine, and marital relations. Love surpasses physical pleasure as well in the effort needed to achieve it. Commitment, loyalty, and patience are necessary for love. Many are unwilling to pay the price. The rich enjoyment of children can't be had without a stern payment of effort.

There are few connoisseurs of love. Many can't even recognize it. They confuse it with that cheaper product, infatuation. That's the moment on the beach when, with the sun in her hair, she was so beautiful and everything seemed so perfect. Love, by contrast, is the appreciation of another's character traits. When we see kindness and honesty, the pleasure it yields is love.

There are limitations on the pleasure of love, just as there are limitations on physical pleasure. A partner can't give meaning to life. You can't live for love; it's not enough. Parents anxiously struggling to feel needed by their children when they've grown and gone away; the stress on a romantic relationship when it's called on to give purpose and self-respect; and the crisis of identity we feel when love relationships fail — all these testify to the fallacy of "living for love."

Class three, the experience of "meaning," is a greater pleasure than love. When we feel our lives have a goal and purpose, it gives a sense of deep-rootedness. Meaning yields energy and strength. We long for the ecstasy of committing ourselves in the service of some great mission. We may even risk death, so nourishing is the experience which gives our life ultimate purpose.

Class two is a pleasure which surpasses meaning — the enjoyment of power and the ability to create. The Talmud directs every person to say "the world was created for me." It is my world to shape and to define. The pleasure of social and political action comes from creating and molding the world. Kindness, too, is an aspect of creativity. When I nurture another to discover and express his potential, I bring meaning out of clay. The pleasure of teaching and of parenting as well derive from this deep and God-like creativity.

Class one, love of God, is the top of the pleasure scale. In Jewish understanding, the Almighty created mankind to enjoy the rich experience of life in its awesome depth of pleasure.

Ours is a world with the opportunity to love, to validate with a cause our brief span, and to create in God-like imitation. The appreciation of that great gift is love of God.

Instructions For Living

To help us achieve these pleasures, the Almighty gave us the Torah — *Torat Chaim*, literally, "instructions for living."

We license today the exercise of many professions. In the issues of living, which are infinitely more complex and more important, many receive no education. Who understands clearly the principles on which a stable marriage or a lifetime of happiness are built?

The Torah teaches us crucial definitions and distinctions: the difference between love and infatuation, pleasure and comfort. It's all found in the five classes of pleasure.

As the years passed, my feelings of estrangement and discomfort toward Judaism have faded. I fell in love with Israel, with Jerusalem, and with the Torah. It's been a never-ending love affair.

TZVI GLUCKIN

Knee-Deep in the Funk

"The secret to driving in New York is to tailgate cabs until you're good enough to cut them off."

We were doing 70 mph as we hit the sharp right at the end of the Brooklyn Bridge going into Manhattan.

"The next thing is to watch the 'Don't Walk' signs. Hit the gas when they start flashing."

Botz was driving and talking. He felt it was important to teach me about the practical things most people overlooked. I'd soon learn about garlic and the wonders of the digestive system.

Our banana-yellow 1978 Dodge Aspen wagon was moving cross-town at breathtaking speed. Somebody honked.

"New York cops will never bust you for a moving violation. In New York we have real crime."

Botz was expounding on the never-ending list of advantages to New York living. I was a newcomer from Boston. These insights

TZVI GLUCKIN has a degree in Jazz Studies from the New England Conservatory of Music, has worked professionally in music, traveled extensively, and spent eight years with Aish HaTorah in Jerusalem. He now lives with his wife and children in Boston, where he is director of Aish HaTorah's campus initiative.

were crucial for my development.

Botz and I shared an apartment in Park Slope with another guy. The three of us played music, but we weren't making any money. Botz sold life insurance. I did surveys over the telephone.

An old acquaintance called out of the blue. He was now booking a club in Hoboken. He offered me a Thursday night for $200 and a $30 bar tab. I took the gig. I hired my roommates as the other musicians and a band was born. Soon we were playing regularly with an occasional road trip. Botz turned me on to Frankie Valli and AM radio.

The Hoboken gig evolved into a fairly steady weekend job. We'd start around 11:30 and play into the wee hours of the night. We were a decent band, but there were times when we went beyond ourselves. In most bands, the members need constant eye contact and body gesticulations in order to communicate musically. By us, this was unnecessary. If I wanted to create a certain mood or texture, Botz would telepathically anticipate what I was going to do and be right there with me. It was amazing.

There were times, usually around 1 A.M. when the beer began to affect us, that we'd hit a level of extra-sensory communication and go intergalactic. The walls would begin to pulsate. The lights would grow dim. The usually packed crowd would stop everything and just listen. Everyone there was aware that something bigger than all of us was happening. I never wanted it to end. This was why I played music! This was why I was living! I was tickling the soft white underbelly of existence, and I loved it. Yes, I was wading knee-deep in the funk of life.

Looking for a Perpetual High

I wanted it to go on and on and on and on.

But it always ended. Inevitably the club would close. We'd have to pack up our gear ourselves and head back to Brooklyn alone. The feeling was gone by the time we got all our equipment back to our space and went out for breakfast before going to bed. The great transcendental high just hours before was fleeting and fading.

"The parasystolic effects of coffee are quite remarkable," Botz would say looking up from his fried eggs and hashbrowns. "Just the mere sound of the percolator gets my body rumbling."

I began reading Henry Miller and hanging out in Prospect Park. I grew depressed. Why wasn't life as real as those moments when the band was plugged-in?

I shaved my head and became a conservative. Nothing.

I wrote lyrics and poetry. I thought I was Charles Bukowski. I was miserable. Nothing could cheer me up. Something was missing.

On my 25th birthday, the World Trade Center was attacked for the first time. I took this as a sign — it was time to get out of New York. I figured I'd go to Paris. I could be like Henry Miller. Maybe if I lived like a real artist I could recreate that on-stage feeling off-stage. I'd live on French bread, drink cheap white wine, and scam free rooms. I left my band, quit my job, said goodbye to my apartment, and bought an open-ended ticket. Something big needed to happen.

I spent the next five months moving east across Europe. I stayed in cheap hotels. I crashed on people's floors. I played guitar in the streets. I read voraciously. I was open to everything. I stayed up all night talking art, politics, religion, whatever it was with whomever cared to listen. I was becoming the most pretentious person alive. I felt electric. I was free.

Suddenly Jewish

For some reason the outside world began to take an interest in my Jewishness. Total strangers and fellow travelers would approach me and ask if I was Jewish. I couldn't figure out why this was happening. Maybe Europeans, who've hated us for so long, had a keener sense of who was a Jew than Americans did. It began to occur to me that maybe being Jewish meant something.

I went to Poland and wandered through the old Jewish ghost towns. What could it be?

I went to Turkey. I heard about the Oslo Accords. I could smell history in the making. I had to go to Israel.

I ended up in Jerusalem. I danced at Damascus Gate with the newly independent Palestinians.

I stayed in Israel for about a year. I began to explore my Judaism. Something was happening to me. The culture, the people, my heritage, everything overwhelmed me. I couldn't get enough. I lacked the ability to articulate what I was feeling. I was connecting to my people in a way I couldn't describe. I was plugging into something bigger than myself. For the first time in my life I stopped playing music, and I didn't care.

I began to get lost in my new Jewish world. I grew a beard. I wanted to live in the desert and meditate all day. I wanted to be Abraham. I was the "Earth Jew." I was one with my new cosmic Jewish Earth culture. I was on fire. I was in heaven.

And then I was back in New York. My cousin was getting married and my mother insisted I come.

Nobody could understand me. My family thought I was a space alien. I looked for Botz. He'd spent the last year on the road touring with an old blues musician. He was in town visiting his mother.

We met downtown. "You're one of them beanie-wearing Heebs," he told me wryly.

We roamed the streets looking for kosher food. I tried to explain what I was going through. He was interested but distracted. It was summertime and the living was easy.

I fled uptown. I took three days' refuge in the house of an old abstract painter I knew. We talked nonstop about everything. Avant-garde records played continuously in the background. We talked about music. We talked about the blues. We talked about Fuzzy Walter.

Fuzzy Walter versus Life

"If Fuzzy Walter offered you a gig, would you take it?"

"Sure I would," I said.

"Isn't that a contradiction?"

"How so?"

"On the one hand you want to be 'Earth Jew' and yet you'd go touring with Fuzzy Walter?"

He was right. I didn't know how to answer him. I'd left my whole world behind but I still wanted my old life. And then the question hit me: What was wrong with playing with Fuzzy Walter?

I went back to Israel a mess. Months went by. I couldn't sleep. Fuzzy Walter? Earth Jew? I was going crazy.

My eyes were pulled open a few months later. The question was all wrong! Of course there was nothing wrong with playing with Fuzzy Walter. The real question was, "Would I want Fuzzy Walter as my dad?"

Inside the world of Fuzzy Walter, nobody could touch him. He created a special energy. He brought people to a higher level. But what about the rest of his life? Womanizer, drug addict, never at home. His music was fantastic, but what about him?

I realized that my goal as a musician and my goal as a Jew were exactly the same. I wanted to be knee-deep in the funk 24/7. The only difference was that music was limited to music. When the music was over it was over. What about the rest of the time? How did it offer transcendence in real life?

Instead of getting lost in the world of music or art, instead of tapping into the cosmic fabric via a canvas, Judaism was telling me: Let life be your canvas.

Torah was a system to help me tap into the groove-energy thing all the time. Every moment in life became an opportunity for transcendence.

Music is great, but it is limited. Life is unlimited. Every moment is thick with potential.

I walked into my new world a new man. I picked up my guitar and played. I had never sounded this good before.

JENNA ZIMAN

My Moment of Transformation

I waded in the waters of the *mikveh*, anticipating the rabbis' entrance. For more than two years I had pictured this moment, this last phase of my conversion journey when I would finally become a Jew. My patience endured as I moved around the small pool; a white soaked terrycloth robe anchoring me into the profundity of the moment. Indigo blue-and-white Moroccan tiles blanketed the walls around me. A hum from the room's heating vents buzzed in the moist air, lulling me into an eager peace. The waters were kind and soothing and much warmer than I had expected.

I found myself repeating a passage from the Torah over and over again in my mind, "Go for yourself from your land, from your relatives, and from your father's house to the land I will show you." This was God's call to Abraham. I, too, had gone on a journey — in order to find the woman I longed to become. She had told me she would wait for me to cleanse my life and that it would take much more than time.

A *mikveh* is a tiled reservoir, minimally two square feet by six feet deep, containing about 200 gallons of water derived directly from

JENNA ZIMAN is a Los Angeles-based freelance writer, reporter, and fine arts painter.

natural resources, such as accumulated rain water or melted snow or ice. Ritual immersion, *tevilah*, is the total submersion of the body and is a core component of the Jewish conversion process.

The ritual of immersion is not something a convert can do on her own. Since it involves a major change in personal status, it is treated as a community function. Therefore, the immersion is administered in the presence of a *beit din*, a rabbinical court.

Amazon Entertainer

The rabbis entered the room.

They were all in their 40s, with full beards and dispositions of solemnity. Only one of them was a familiar face. Rabbi David Rue and I had spent numerous hours together, as he counseled me emotionally, intellectually, and even politically in preparation for this day. He acted as head of the Los Angeles Beit Din. I looked upward, hoping to find safety in his confidence and control over the moment. I did. He asked if I wanted my friends to join us for the ceremony, and to my delighted nod, he left to fetch them both. I took a deep breath, reminding myself to remain present in the moment, and to breathe.

They are my closest female friends, Elizabeth and Storm. Elizabeth is a photographer and Jewish. Although not observant, Elizabeth's visceral sense draws her time and time again back to Judaism's most poignant and moving moments: Kol Nidre services, candle-lighting on Shabbat, a conversion ceremony. She has a strong intuitive attraction to life's precious occasions, which she captures with precise timing behind a camera lens.

Storm is a singer, performer, model, and non-Jew (or "shiksa" as she likes to say with a hearty chuckle), though she knows more about Judaism than most Jews I know, from watching me attentively in my studies over the years. Upon first-time introductions to a Jewish man, Storm has no qualms about asking him if he wrapped tefillin that morning, and she's been known to chastise Jewish folk for being out-on-the-town listening to her perform during the Nine Days of Av, a traditional mourning period when we refrain from listening to music.

Coming from a six-foot-tall, three-colored dyed long hair, tattooed, Amazon-like entertainer, her haughty reprimands are great shocks for their poor recipients. I'm sent reeling every time. Little did I know that while I waited in the *mikveh*'s waters, Storm waited in the adjacent room complaining to a group of religious women about how much she was craving a nice, juicy, freshly caught crab.

For Myself, a New History

My two friends hesitantly followed the rabbi and crept into the room with wide eyes, beaming nervously. I looked upward at the group of five and recognized this linking of secular and religious worlds, all bound together in this solitary ceremony. Yes, it can be done, if only for an instant, I thought to myself.

Rabbi Rue began to speak. He directed me to repeat aloud after him...

"I, Jenna Erin Ziman, do hereby solemnly swear, in the presence of the undersigned members of the *beit din* and in the presence of the Almighty God, that I accept all the mitzvot of which I am aware, and those that I will learn in the future, both scriptural and rabbinical, as binding upon me personally from now and forever..."

The air around us became thick with meaning. Internally I began to panic and looked to Rabbi Rue again for solace. His gaze became a porthole to a different space entirely, and I locked-in, desperate to continue. My voice began to weaken and quiver.

"Specifically, I undertake to observe the Shabbat, festivals, the laws of family purity, kashrut, both in my home and outside, and the laws of charity among others. I do solemnly accept the God of Israel as the sole, indivisible Lord of the universe..." I paused, and began to cry. "All this I do declare after due deliberation and in perfectly sound mind. So help me God."

Rabbi Rue continued without regard to my emotional swelling. He spoke of the limitations I would have to face, from this moment on, with respect to adhering to the laws of Shabbat and keeping kosher. He asked me why I was choosing this path.

"This path had already been determined for me," I told him. "It was just a question of when, through the exercising and expression of my own free will, I would unlock the reality of this path for myself. It was my free choice, but it had already been decided."

All the weight of the ceremony intensified, and with a degree of seriousness I had yet to see from Rabbi Rue, he said, "If you were to go to Israel right now, there would be people there who would want to kill you." I nodded in understanding. "And if one of them put a gun to your head and told you that you had to choose between giving up your faith or your life..."

"My life," I said, without taking a breath. "I would give up my life."

My answer injected into me a burning sensation that could only be called Fear. I fought to ready myself for this emotion's steady descent. My body was motionless, as the rabbis watched me being cradled in the arms of stopped Time.

From uncertainty and panic, to thinking, thinking, thinking, to flow, and then finally to being, I turned my back to the rabbis and lowered my body into the water. And there she was, the woman I had so longed to become — this woman who had tried my wisdom, anchored my ignorance, topped my dreams, determined my path, and who had waited so long for me to find her. I reached out for her and found my heart in a moment of sacred illumination, elevating us upward in time and inward in space as she kissed my essence in a place called home.

The equation was solved, alongside the knowing that it was neither of us who had done the math, in a union allowed only under the sight of God. It was a moment of surrender without the consciousness of vulnerability — a true mating of souls. Heaven and earth changed places, our mingled beings caught in the median of their exchange. It was larger than silence. A panicked dive into the one-second of my self's past and future. A call to life.

In a locked open gaze, I could see that she was weeping for this faith and for those who had loved and died for this faith before us. And so I took on her tears, awoke from my frivolous dream, and emerged from the waters with a new history and a new name: Yael.

KATHARINA VON KELLENBACH

Confronting My Family's
Nazi Past

In contemporary Germany, there is considerable interest in the history of the Holocaust and its Jewish victims. But there is little detailed knowledge about the perpetrators. While the Holocaust is taught in schools, portrayed in the media, and discussed in public life, it continues to be a taboo subject in most families. Young Germans generally have no idea what their parents, grandparents, aunts, and uncles did during the period 1933–1945. Many laudatory speeches — at birthday parties and eulogies — simply skip over this time and construct biographical outlines without these years.

KATHARINA VON KELLENBACH was born in Stuttgart, Germany in 1960, studied evangelical theology in Berlin (West) and Goettingen, and entered the graduate program in religion at Temple University in Philadelphia in 1983. As a fellow of the Alexander von Humboldt Foundation, she is currently completing a book, *The Politics of Christian Discourses of Forgiveness and the Prosecution of Nazi Perpetrators*. She is associate professor of religious studies at St. Mary's College of Maryland.

I was "lucky" that one of my uncles decided to show me a newspaper article during a family gathering that reported about a trial in the early 1970s involving Nazi crimes. I was about 13 when I read that my uncle, Alfred Ebner, was accused of killing 20,000 Jews, and that his trial was to be discontinued because of health reasons.

Alfred Ebner was sitting across the table from me while I was reading this news release. He was a regular guest at family gatherings, and I had often visited his family's house in Stuttgart before my family moved to Munich. I remember my confusion and inability to make sense of this information while he sat peacefully (and apparently healthy) among my family. What was I to make of the fact that my family did not censure him? Would my family not ostracize him if he had killed one person, or two? The fact that he sat among us unperturbed seemed to imply that these murders never happened. I wondered, how does one person kill 20,000 people? Where did he do it? Who were his victims?

My attempts to find out more were brushed off: "Of course he didn't do these things. It's all lies. Leave this old man his deserved peace, he has suffered enough..." The newspaper article was taken from me and my questions ran into stony walls of silence. For years, I pestered family members with questions about this subject, but to no avail. Eventually, I "forgot" (repressed?) this incident.

Years later, as a graduate student in religious studies, and in conversation with Jewish survivors and their children in the United States, I "remembered." As I saw myself through the eyes of my Jewish dialogue partners, I realized that my ignorance was not innocent. My lack of precise knowledge colluded with the perpetrators' desire to conceal their crimes. In order to interact with Jewish peers, I had to break the "conspiracy of silence" and become much more deliberate in my search for the truth.

Since my immediate and extended family continued to resist any inquiry into "the past," I turned to historical archives. Strict privacy laws protect German archives, and I had to show my academic credentials before gaining access to the indictments against Alfred Ebner. When I began reading the charges, my initial sense of triumph at having broken through the wall of silence soon disappeared. As his crimes became real to me, I too did not want to be burdened with this knowledge. I had to force myself to continue reading, and for the first time, I understood the temptation of denial. Maybe this was not true after all?... How could the old man of my childhood be identical with this fanatical killer?

A Past Unveiled

After his early enrollment and steep career in the National Socialist party, Alfred Ebner was appointed deputy area commissioner (*stellvertretender Gebietskommissar*) to the city of Pinsk in Byelorussia in September 1941. He was the responsible official for the Jewish inhabitants of the entire region of Pinsk and in control of the lives and deaths of approximately 20,000–30,000 Jews who had survived the first mass killings in August 1941.

Between the fall of 1941 and December 1942, Alfred Ebner oversaw the systematic expropriation of Jewish property, the exploitation of their labor, and their methodical starvation. He organized the ghettoization of Jews in May 1942 and helped implement the mass execution of the entire Jewish population between October 29 and November 2, 1942. Based on the historical record, Ebner was directly responsible for the implementation of Nazi extermination policies, and he killed both by virtue of his position as well as on personal impulse. Yet he was never convicted and, as far as I know, never regretted his actions.

My quest to collect information about Alfred Ebner in archives in Germany, Israel, and the United States was often circuitous and accompanied by ambivalence. On one hand, I felt driven to learn as much as I could about his activities as deputy commissioner of Pinsk, a major center of Jewish life since the 16th century. I wanted to understand the depth of anti-Semitic hatred that justified his murderous activities in his mind. And I wanted to learn about his victims, whose lives and culture have been destroyed so completely — Pinsk was once 80 percent Jewish, but today there is only one small synagogue — by people who knew next to nothing about their victims.

On the other hand, this knowledge is painful, because it brings profound evil and the horrors of mass murder close to home. Most families like to think of themselves as essentially "good," and it is not surprising to me that German families engage in far-reaching strategies of evasion and denial. We tend to project evil onto others and assume that the "bad guys" live over there, in a different time, a different place, and a different family. To acknowledge evil in one's own family raises disturbing questions. Does this evil contaminate me? Am I like him? Would I have done what he did? What (if anything) makes me different from him?

Although I sometimes feel disloyal, like a traitor to my family, I consider it my responsibility to "own" this past. This story of anti-Semitic hatred, of supremacy and greed, is as integral to German history and identity as Goethe and Mozart. There can be no future without a truthful account of the past.

DAREN FRIEDMAN

The Secret Formula

Siberian pines towered over thousands of Russian teens dancing in mist and siren light as an American techno DJ mixed
hyper-tribal sounds. My client, a representative of Coca-
Cola, stood by me and smiled at the work my company had
produced.

I have a winter memory from early childhood of a pine tree-
like image formed from hundreds of people holding candles and
singing in one voice: "I'd like to teach the world to sing in perfect
harmony... I'd like to buy the world a Coke..." And the memory
fades.

Around that time, my preschool teachers spoke of a sweet,
giving old man with calm, joyful eyes and a long, white beard
visiting all the families in our Texas neighborhood. He'd visit mine
if we'd put up a Chanukah bush for him. I made the Jewish star
that hung above it, and opened, with my brother and sister, all our
Chanukah presents the morning after his visit.

Coca-Cola may be the only company in history whose

DAREN FRIEDMAN, originally from Texas, is the founder of Conceptual
Entertainment Ltd, a trend strategist advising multinational corporations
and ad agencies in Russia and its republics.

advertising successfully featured an old man. Coke's version of Santa in a red suit became the icon of joy the world over. Usually, old people in advertising is depressing.

"We're not just brown fizzy water," my client explained to me. "Authenticity! Refreshment! Joy! This is what we are about." I had been hired to link these values with Coca-Cola in the minds of Russian teenagers.

The Real Thing

Brainstorming, I turned to my own Coca-Cola memories and was frightened to find what was stocked up there layer upon layer: "The Real Thing," "Always," and an element of mysticism — "The Secret Formula." Even an association with an omniscient being flying through the clouds to reward children with gifts according to whether they were naughty or nice.

I wasn't sure if I was describing a soft drink or my confused childhood image of God as Santa; I experienced Coca-Cola almost as powerfully. Other Americans I asked fondly recalled similar memories. Coca-Cola was a real part of our collective childhood.

With Santa on contract, Coke could draw on two powerful ideas — tradition and giving. This is unlike Ronald McDonald, who reigns unconvincingly in his plastic childhood utopia under a universal yellow-and-red banner, offering every child an equal portion of happiness in a box (which incidentally includes a Coke). The power of Santa, even over adults, is that he is the ultimate giver, granting each boy and girl whatever they really want.

With Coca-Cola as my client, the money was good, but I became depressed. It started me off on a tangent. Authenticity, joy, refreshment, giving, and tradition were qualities I'd craved, not only in a soft drink, but in something more substantial — life. Christmas was not my holiday and Santa Claus was somebody else's grandpa, probably long since sitting in an old folk's home. What had I been bonding with all these years — sugar and carbonation?

I spent six years in Russia creating a parade of pleasures, marketing to emotions that inspire people: fashion shows with

Bolshoi ballerinas pirouetting down the podium in Versace; rave parties stretching from Siberia to the Black Sea beaches; prestige events covered by leading cultural magazines; concerts off Red Square. I created special atmospheres and messages and brand links so people could think that when they were using various products, they were experiencing whatever it was they needed to experience in life.

Checking Out

Then one day as New Year's festivities approached, I experimented. Burnt out from events and parties, from figuring out lucrative ways for people to enjoy themselves ("Enjoy" is the current Coca-Cola motto), I decided to retreat from my lifestyle — to search out my version of Hedonist's Anonymous. I narrowed it down to a month studying in either a monastery or a yeshiva. I opted for the more exotic — a yeshiva in Jerusalem.

I was looking forward to spending day after day stared down by millions of strange black squiggle letters and stranger black-hatted Jews rocking back and forth, who I thought had revoked the physical world.

I was not so lucky.

A few evenings after arriving, a nebbishe-looking character approached me in the study hall and asked me to join him for his cousin's wedding. I grabbed a yarmulka from my sock drawer and prepared myself for a long night sitting among men who spent their entire day looking at books written for people living thousands of years ago.

The wedding was sheer madness. Twirling black coats, hats on fire, acrobatics, unicyclers, spinning in circles, singing and dancing. And not a woman in sight except the bride and her grandmother.

An ancient white-bearded rabbi smiled at me, nodding knowingly: "It's a mitzvah to give the bride and groom *simchah* on their wedding night."

"Where does one get *simchah*?" I asked, feeling embarrassed for not bringing any.

"*Simchah*...happiness," his eyes shined as his gruff voice continued. "An Eskimo has 35 words for snow. He recognizes each one. *Rinah, sasson, gilah, simchah* — we have many Hebrew words for happiness. Stick around and you'll begin to feel how a Jew experiences each. You'll get to be a connoisseur of happiness!"

I pondered this, as a man with his son on his shoulders tap-danced slapstick for the newlyweds.

Pursuit of Pleasure

The greater part of my adult existence has been spent pursuing pleasure. It was, therefore, this particular aspect of God's genius that I recognized in Judaism first. The studying I got done between all the weddings, brises, and bar mitzvahs, the wild dancing, and an endless surplus of religious holidays no one ever informed me about growing up as a Jew in Texas, led me to one obvious conclusion:

The ultimate giver is not Santa, but God. Aside from life and all those other neat necessities, He also invented Shabbat (a concept later copied by the T.G.I.F. restaurant chain) — a weekly reward dispensed equidistantly toward infinity.

Shabbat, like a vacation or a party, is a distraction-free zone. As far as I could tell, God's plan was to bless Jews every weekend with short-term amnesia and bliss — comparable to a weekend in the Bahamas — and then return them by Monday fired up for the world of action and responsibility.

We were meant to be like Adam in Eden. Before he was cursed with the four-letter word W-O-R-K, Adam had the ideal leisure lifestyle — no work, and infinite meaning.

Shabbat is a piece of paradise passed down. A day "to be." No work, no last-minute phone calls, bank transactions, bills, cooking. Just sun-tanning in the light of God.

A Jew is commanded by the Infinite to be happy, to focus happiness within time, especially Friday night and all day Saturday, connecting with the full force of life by doing what many Jews love best — eating and talking.

God is the Divine social planner. The social life of the

observant Jew is well-arranged: no standing in club cues behind red ropes waiting to be picked out of a crowd, no scurrying around to find the ultimate party, no singles' bar approach/avoid tactics, no struggling to act confident but relaxed, no stress of being left out, no entrance fees.

And if Shabbat was not enough, God threw in theme parties throughout the year. Purim's drunken masquerade, an eight-night Festival of Lights during the shortest and most depressing days of winter, and the Rosh Hashana New Year's extravaganza. And then the parties I'd never heard of: Shavuot (an all-nighter with cheesecake), Tu B'Shvat (a holiday for ecologists), and Sukkot (a week of camping!).

Shabbat in Jerusalem

After four weeks of Shabbat in Jerusalem, I recognized all the parties I ever threw, but with an open door policy and minus the extravagant outer trappings: the nutty randomness of guests mingling; the sudden affinity of strangers recognizing some part of themselves in one another; the atmosphere; the amazing catering; the dancing; the interaction which pierced superficial courtesy; the sweet drunken excitement.

I felt like an idiot. All this time Shabbat had stood quietly among the days like a princess waiting in line, too humble to announce her own stature, as I rushed by failing to notice her.

The lengths to which we go — frat party spring break, bungee jump, swinger's lounge, celebrity cocktail — are the extent to which intense emotional satisfaction eludes us.

Coca-Cola's secret formula is the company's recognition that true bonds and emotions build in strength over time — ad after ad evoking warmth, giving, tradition, joy. Marketing ploys aside, I think of Coca-Cola and smile.

Shabbat is the secret formula that has been keeping Jews happy for millennia. It has power to quench real inner needs as it builds its bond, memory upon memory.

I can almost conceive of building my own family one day. If I do, I will want at least one day each week to unabashedly experience shared emotion. To concentrate all my happiness on those who mean the most to me. To sense, even in silence, the energies of love from a grandfather, a brother, a child, a mother, an aunt, a friend. To savor over the years the flickering subtlety of each stage of life bound in its happiest moments.

No doubt, until then my craving for novelty will still lead me around the world, to rooms full of people whose only common language may be expressed through singing voices. I am a social animal. Even when I'm settled and old, I know I'll want a house open to guests changing every weekly episode — travelers with bizarre stories, visitors not quite sure where they've ended up but happy to be there, and a tumult and lull of impassioned discussion.

Shabbat is a secret formula worth smiling about.

RABBI SHRAGA SIMMONS

Daredevil on the Bridge

S an Francisco. A chilly November morning. My friend and I stood at the midway point of the Golden Gate Bridge. We both looked down. Then he climbed over the three-foot-high fence, slithered onto the catwalk below, and jumped.

No, this was not a suicide. My friend was attempting to set the world record for the longest Tarzan swing.

I had met Steve a few months earlier, on the day that he'd gone over Niagara Falls in a barrel. Steve was trying to attract attention in order to boost his career as a Hollywood stuntman. I found him down at the local TV station, fielding reporters' calls from Melbourne to Tokyo, and making a deal to sell videotape of his barrel ride.

Good-looking, vivacious, age 25, Steve became an instant celebrity. He was the youngest person ever to survive a barrel ride

RABBI SHRAGA SIMMONS, originally from Buffalo, New York, received rabbinic ordination from the Chief Rabbi of Jerusalem and a degree in journalism from the University of Texas. He is now co-editor of Aish.com and a contributing writer for America OnLine, About.com, and Ya-hoo.com. He lives in the Modi'in region of Israel with his amazing wife and children.

over the Falls, and the first American in 25 years to do so. The next morning, Steve was a guest on *The Today Show* and was hailed by banner headlines in *USA Today*, the *New York Post*, and hundreds of newspapers around the world.

I, too, was attracted to Steve's courage and charisma, and we became fast friends.

The momentum continued unabated. By week's end, Steve's photo had appeared in *Newsweek* magazine, and he was in LA as the guest of Johnny Carson on the *Tonight Show*. Then it was back to New York and the studio of a posh New York fashion photog, having been selected by *Mademoiselle* magazine as "one of the 10 coolest men in the world."

Birthday Thrill

A few weeks later, the phone call came.

"My birthday is coming up soon, and I want to celebrate it with a high-profile stunt," Steve told me. "I'm going to do a Tarzan swing off the Golden Gate Bridge."

He explained how it would work: Since the water of San Francisco Bay is 260 feet below the bridge, Steve planned to tie a 250-foot-long rope to the center of the span, and then position himself at the end of the rope — 250 feet away from the point of attachment. He would jump off the bridge and swing in an arc, reaching just above water level — almost like Tarzan swinging from a vine. (The only difference being that Steve would swing back and forth, eventually coming to a standstill.)

I tried to discourage him. "What do you need this for?" I asked. "You've already achieved enormous public acclaim, and no other stunt can compare to the Falls. This will be a step backward in your career."

But Steve would not be dissuaded. "I'm going. I want a special thrill for my birthday," he said.

I figured I might as well go along for the ride.

Helicopter Video

Two days before Steve's 26th birthday, when our plane

touched down in San Francisco, we headed straight for the hardware store. Hooks and rope, that's all Steve needed.

Our biggest problem was how to film this momentous event. Since the Golden Gate Bridge is over a mile long, the center of the bridge — where Steve planned to perform the stunt — was too far from shore for photographers to get a good shot. The only option was a boat (positioned in front of the bridge), or a helicopter. We chose the latter; it was much more hi-tech.

Because Steve's stunt involved illegal trespassing, everything had to be ready before the workmen came out to paint the bridge at 7 A.M. So the night before, we drove to the midway point of the bridge, where Steve got out, climbed over the fence, and attached his rope to the catwalk on the underside of the bridge. Phase one accomplished.

The next morning, we got up at the crack of dawn, drove to a spot near the toll booths, and took the long walk out to the center of the bridge. Steve descended to the catwalk, found his rope, and pulled it 250 feet along the catwalk, leaving the other end still attached to the center of the bridge.

The rope had to be taut so that when Steve jumped he would swing in a perfect arc. Otherwise, he would be freefalling at 70 miles an hour and would likely snap his bones.

Steve also had a small wooden disk attached to the end of the rope to serve as a seat. Otherwise he could never have held onto the rope; the centrifugal force would have sent him crashing into the waters of San Francisco Bay.

We waited for the helicopter to arrive, and I had a few minutes to think. Here we were, about to perform a stunt that would be reported the next day on the front page of newspapers around the world. I was struck by the absurdity of it all. Is this actually the most important event in the world today? Does this hold value in the greater scheme of things? Is this what society should be glorifying?

The chopper came into view, the sound of its blades cutting through the crisp morning air. The videographer hung precariously out the window straining to get the best angle.

I felt sick to my stomach. Is this where I want to be putting my time and energy? Have I been consigned to a life of promoting trivial acts of entertainment?

My soul ached for something more meaningful, more genuine, more eternal.

At that moment, I made a commitment to find a better way.

Steve jumped, swung in a magnificent arc for a few minutes, and then dropped down into the water. Unscathed, he was taken ashore by the Coast Guard and turned over to the police for questioning.

The Accidental Mug

I followed through on my commitment, and a few weeks later I was in Jerusalem. (Being Jewish, I figured that was the logical place to start.)

One day I was looking at a bulletin board, casually reading some of the postings. One in particular caught my eye:

> *I accidentally broke a blue coffee mug. If it's yours, please see*
> *me so I can compensate you. Signed, John Doe.*

Those few words hit me hard. I had come from a world of material pursuit, dog-eat-dog, get what you can and don't get caught — and now I found something quite different. The contrast was stark.

John could have broken the mug, kept quiet, and nobody would have known. But he was determined to set things straight.

This is interesting, I thought. What matters here is not the bombastic display of ego-boosting hype, but taking responsibility for one's actions, fairness to others, and a clear conscience.

I wondered: With effort and commitment, why couldn't the whole world work this way?

Or at least, maybe *my* world could work this way.

I pursued the source of this innocuous note, and it led me to a college of Jewish studies. There I found a group of young people, like myself, who sought to nourish their spiritual-ethical yearnings with the intellectual idealism of Torah values. The backgrounds were varied, but the common denominator was a longing for truth, and a striving for personal perfection.

Bigger Boosts

There's more to the story. A week later, I passed by that same bulletin board and noticed something that impacted me immensely. Whoever broke the coffee mug had crossed out the word "accidentally" and wrote instead "negligently." His conscience could not rest until he acted with total integrity.

I thought back to tattered, yellowed photographs of my European ancestors, and began to understand why a long line of generations had clung so tenaciously to their Jewish values in an often-turbulent world.

And what about Steve? His Hollywood career never got off the ground. The stunts, I came to realize, were less a professional pursuit and more a way to bring thrill to his life. The brush with death, apparently, gave him a momentary feeling of life. But it was all artificial, and ultimately could never satisfy. And like an addict, Steve constantly needed newer, bigger boosts.

Over the years, Steve and I lost contact. I heard his name mentioned on the news twice: Once when he went over Niagara Falls in a barrel (again), and once when he fell out of a tree and broke his neck.

As for me, I am grateful for that chilly November morning on the bridge. Steve was a daredevil, but in a way he became my angel. Fifteen years later, I have never looked back.

DAVID CARASSO

The Jewish Haiku

Recently my wife and I began taking a creative writing class together at the local community college. We have three young wonderful children, thank God, but sometimes we need a little adult time away. This class was nothing I took seriously; just a pleasant diversion to share with my wife.

In the class I planned to write some innocuous poems, and not wanting my every word to somehow be mistaken for "Jewish wisdom," I always had a baseball hat over my yarmulke.

But behind the scenes, Someone had plans to take that baseball hat off.

One particular night the class was learning about the haiku, a type of short poem originating in Japan. There are several specific and essential qualities that make a poem a haiku. Most people know that the structure consists of three lines, with a 5-7-5 syllable pattern. I had seen haikus before, usually in a humorous context, such as in David Bader's *Haikus for Jews*:

Would-be convert lost —

DAVID CARASSO lives in Northern California with his wife and three children.

thawed Lender's Bagels made a
bad first impression.

Monarch butterfly,
I know your name used to be
Caterpillarstein.

While these poems are funny, and follow the 5-7-5 pattern, that night in class we learned about other qualities needed to make a real haiku.

Haikus should express something about nature. They use very concrete terms, never generalities. They deal with the here-and-now. They are composed of strong nouns and verbs, and rarely use modifiers such as adjectives or adverbs. The three lines are often split into two parts, by a colon or a dash, with an imaginative distance between the two sections. Each line, however, should contain a complete thought.

And finally, the whole haiku should have a twist that offers some spiritual insight by juxtaposition.

Clearly these poems aren't just rattled off by counting 5-7-5 on your fingers!

Moment of Revelation

That night, driving home from class, I noticed the darkness in the sky and the few stars out. I started thinking about the Shema — the most important Jewish prayer, the Jewish "pledge of allegiance," which testifies to our belief in one God.

Some neurons thinking about class, and some neurons thinking about the Shema, must have greeted each other, because my heart started racing and my fingers went up in the air to count the syllables:

She-ma Yis-ra-el   Hear O Israel
A-do-nay El-o-hei-nu   The Lord our God
A-do-nay E-chad   The Lord is One

I gulped hard. 5-7-5 in the original Hebrew! I counted it in my head a few more times to make sure.

At times like these, when certain mundane things click together and form a Divine experience, I often think of the words *Ani Yosef* — "I am Joseph." In the Torah, Joseph uttered these two words upon reuniting with his brothers (Genesis 45:3). They finally understood that the prime minister of Egypt was none other than their long-lost brother. All their confusion and doubt vanished, and God's master plan became clear.

In other words, my baseball hat was coming off.

Simplicity and Twists

The more I thought about the Shema as a haiku, the more I was amazed at how it jumps through the definitional hoops. It has the 5-7-5 syllable pattern. It is about nature, or rather the nature of the universe. It is very concrete, and consists of strong nouns and a strong verb, with no modifiers. It deals with the here and now. Its three lines each express a complete thought. There is an imaginative distance between two distinct sections: The first section (Israel) is finite, and yet connects with the second section, God the Infinite.

Finally, the Shema's six simple words have many twists, offering spiritual insights by juxtaposition. Here are three:

- *Elo-him*, the God of monotheistic Judaism, is a plural noun, signifying the seemingly many forces that are spread throughout creation. Yet these worldly forces are One.

- "*Ado-nay* is our God" — the God of the Jews; but in the future, *Ado-nay* will be acknowledged by all as the One God.

- *Ado-nay* is used to denote God's Attribute of Mercy, while *Elo-him* is used to denote God's Attribute of Justice. But no matter whether we perceive God as kind, angry, merciful, or judging, He is One, and His Truth and Purpose are One.

Profoundly Zen-Like?

So there it was: The Jewish Haiku, the ultimate Jewish Poem. No jokes about bagels or gefilte fish. Here were all the key issues: who are we, who is God, what should we be doing.

I told some friends about my discovery, and it reached one woman who's much more into Japanese poetry than into "Old World" Judaism. But framing the Shema as a haiku made it modern, "Zen-like," poetic, and deep. She said it affected her more profoundly than anything else she'd encountered in Judaism.

Indeed, Judaism is not Old World. It is timeless, applicable, and relevant at every moment.

I proudly submitted the Shema for my haiku homework, giving the Almighty full writing credit.

The baseball hat came off.

Was this the real reason I took the creative writing class?

Ani Yosef?

TOVA SAUL

Thank You for Assateague Island

S uddenly I was an adolescent, lost at sea in a Pittsburgh public high school of 3,600 students. Suddenly I was surrounded by teenaged girls who obsessed about their clothes, make-up, hair, nails — in short: how to beat their competition to impress the boys.

Boys and looking good seemed to be all that mattered in life. One gained social points by being beautiful, having a cute walk or giggle, and dancing well — none of which described me.

I loved exploring the woods. I admired the horses at the riding stable and worried about the world's injustice and cruelty. I felt there was something very wrong with me. I didn't belong. I did not have the faintest idea of what to talk about with my peers. They yakked constantly to each other. What on earth did they have to

TOVA SAUL, originally from Pittsburgh, Pa., has been living in Jerusalem's Old City for 18 years. She works as a licensed tour guide, specializing in Israel's natural history and hiking trails, and also volunteers for Magen David Adom as an emergency medical technician.

say, while I could think of nothing?

If I ever did venture to say anything, I would rehearse it at least five times in my head before saying it aloud. It was in this state of bewilderment and loneliness that I spent my high school years.

Upon graduation, someone asked if I could be a chaperone for a small Girl Scout troop, whose Jewish den mother was named Mrs. Roberta Hoechshtetter. It was to be a 500-mile trip to camp out on the Assateague Island Nature Reserve for a few days. I had read about this wild windswept island in a children's book, a long narrow strip of land off the coast of Virginia. The eastern side had clean beaches facing the Atlantic, while the western side had lush marshes with shaggy-maned wild ponies.

I tried to tell myself not to expect anything too beautiful, so as not to be disappointed if the island didn't live up to its mythical allure in my imagination.

Off on an Adventure

We set off in two vehicles — Mrs. Hoechshtetter, her daughter Wendy, two other chaperones, and 11 Girl Scouts who were almost my age. The girls were wholesome and down-to-earth — nothing like my high school peers. There were people in the world I could relate to, after all.

By the time we reached the island and pitched our tents, I simply forgot about any social discomfort. Before I knew what was happening, I was experiencing joy with a group of fellow human beings for the first time since pre-adolescence. Feeling a new, warm life in my veins, my excruciating shyness melted, and I became the acknowledged comic of the group.

No matter that we never saw a wild pony. We swam in the sunny waves and just had fun.

One afternoon, a ranger came to our campsite and told us that everyone had to leave the island because a hurricane was on its way. Indeed, we could see in the distance that others were already packing up, and cars were slowly making their way on the one road over the water to mainland Chincoteague.

We paid no notice. As far as we could see, all was serenely calm.

Even the insects and birds were nowhere to be seen nor heard. This was, of course, the "quiet before the storm."

That evening, we were smugly the last on the island, preparing dinner. Mrs. Hoechshtetter had suggested that we make a stew on a Coleman camping stove. We put it up to simmer, covered by its very heavy lid. I will never forget the sight of that lid being blown off the pot by a sudden gale, fluttering off as light as a butterfly! As our tents were wildly ballooning and contracting, Mrs. Hoechshtetter gave orders to tie them down, pack up whatever we needed for the night, get into the two vehicles, and evacuate to the mainland.

In the short time it took to secure the camp and pile into the two vehicles, it had become pitch dark, and we were cold and drenched from the driving downpour. Negotiating the slick, unlit black road over the marsh to the mainland was not a simple matter. It was hard to see where the roadside ended and the marsh began. The windshield wipers were on full speed, and the radio obligingly played The Doors' "Riders on the Storm," which is accompanied by thunder and rain in the background, and Paul McCartney's "Uncle Albert," with its chorus of "Hands across the water, hands across the sky." It was these two songs that accompanied us as we carefully crawled on that slippery marsh road and made our way to a motel in Chincoteague.

The next morning was glorious sunshine and blue skies once more. We arrived back on Assateague Island to unbury and set up our sand-covered tents, and continue our merry vacation until its end back in Pittsburgh.

Life after Assateague

I entered my freshman year at college much more relaxed and outgoing — not the withdrawn, socially frightened person I was in high school. It was the direct result of Mrs. Hoechshtetter's trip.

Time passed, and I worked as a counselor with delinquents, moved to Israel, studied at a women's seminary, and became a tour guide, which involved nonstop public speaking. I often thought back warmly to that trip and silently thanked Mrs. Hoechshtetter.

Some years later, on a visit to my family in Pittsburgh, I was in quite a gloomy state after a potential marriage prospect fell through. I attempted to be cheerful, but I was miserable.

My sister-in-law told me that every Friday the Jewish high school students would go to a hospital, receive a list of the room numbers of all the Jewish patients, and visit them with wishes for a good Shabbos. Would I like to join them?

On the inside, I said, "Really not!" But I did not want to appear to be shirking the mitzvah of visiting the sick, so I reluctantly agreed.

Next thing I knew, a group of us were climbing out of my sister-in-law's station wagon and walking into the lobby of Montefiore Hospital. I was given a list of Jewish patients on the sixth floor, and we arranged to meet again in the lobby in an hour.

This was truly not my cup of tea — walking into the hospital room of a very sick stranger and striking up a conversation. I uneasily did my best, visiting about six patients, until I saw the clock was nearing the appointed time to quit. There was one Jew in one room left. I stood, hesitating. "Oh, go ahead into the last room," I decided at the last moment.

Full Circle

There on the bed, with her eyes closed, was a pale woman who had lost her hair to chemotherapy. Sitting across the room, on a chair in the corner, was a stylish young woman. I said to her, "Hello. My name is Tova Saul. I came to wish patients a good Shabbos."

She sprang to her feet, crossed the room, and exclaimed, "Oh! That's so nice!" She extended her hand and said, "I'm Wendy Hoechshtetter."

In an instant, I recognized the woman on the bed. After all the years. "Wendy...it's me...Tova Saul, who went with you to Assateague Island. Remember?"

She cried out, "Oh! Mummy will be so glad to see you! The nurses don't think she understands anything anymore, but I think she does!"

She led me close to the bedside and gently woke her mother who was too weak to speak. She placed her mother's hand in my two hands, and said, "Mummy! This is Tova Saul! Remember her from when we went to Assateague Island?"

Mrs. Hoechshtetter's eyes opened wide as she stared at me in silent, amazed recognition.

I slowly and clearly said to her, "Mrs. Hoechshtetter, I always wanted to thank you for taking me to Assateague Island. It was a turning point in my life. I was so shy and miserable in high school. And that trip really changed me."

She was in rapt attention, and a tear rolled down her cheek.

"Mrs. Hoechshtetter, because of you, I learned to enjoy being with people. Thank you so much."

I went back in a few days to see her again, but the nurses told me that she had passed away. I was so grateful to God for putting Mrs. Hoechshtetter in my life when I needed her most. And grateful that I could tell her how much it really meant to me.

RABBI YAAKOV SALOMON

"Did You See Darya in the Stairwell?"

"God, hold our heroes in the palm of your hand."
(scribbled on the Ground Zero VIP viewing stand)

T his is not a story about September 11.
It was supposed to be, but it just didn't turn out that way. Allow me to explain.

My desire...need...urge...wish...to visit Ground Zero was born early — in late September 2001, I think. Like many others, I knew I just had to go there, but I wasn't sure why. Access to the concrete graveyard was, of course, severely restricted at that time, but maybe that was part of the peculiar allure that gripped me over three months ago.

"I'll go soon," I reassured myself.

October came. Sukkot, weddings, deadlines, daily nightmares

RABBI YAAKOV SALOMON is creative director of the Aish HaTorah Research and Development Department (North America) and a senior lecturer for their Discovery Seminars program. He is also a psychotherapist in private practice in Brooklyn, New York, and an author and editor for ArtScroll/Mesorah Publishing. He is tolerated at home by his wife, eight children, and three adorable grandchildren.

in Israel, kids' homework, seminars, war, conferences... October went.

Friends went. They reported back to me.

"The rubble itself must be ten stories high."

"I couldn't see much, but it didn't matter. The stench was enough."

"We all just stared in silence. There must have been hundreds of us."

I heard their descriptions. They were punctuated by pain, enveloped in emotion, and searing with uncertainty. But somehow...the message didn't sink in.

> *"In memory of those who gave the ultimate sacrifice."*
> *(scribbled on the Ground Zero VIP viewing stand)*

November arrived. Time to begin "the research." How do you get there? When's the best time to go? Who should I go with? Where did I put my old shoes? Do I have any "connections" that can get me up close?

Where does one park? What is my real purpose in going? Is it wrong to take a camera? Binoculars? Are my children ready for this? Can the new mayor ever fill Rudy's shoes?

The fine line between "research" and "rumination" was fading fast. So was November.

In therapy, they call it "resistance." You think you want to change, but the fear is too great. Could I be "resisting" the very urge I wanted so much to satisfy? Could I be avoiding the startling visual and visceral stimuli that might generate genuine life changes? Impossible. Seeing the carnage that can penetrate the deepest recesses of the soul is not only important; it's something I really want to do. I just need to go when the timing is right.

> *"Did you see Darya in the stairwell?"*
> *(scribbled on the Ground Zero VIP viewing stand,*
> *next to Darya's picture)*

Along comes December. The Taliban is tumbling. Anthrax is slipping to page 23. Global warming meets New York City. The

Dow rebounds. And the 24-hour Ground Zero work teams forge ahead. The buried pockets of endless smoke are no more. Wood planks of various sizes are shaped into official spectator viewing sites. The final standing charred remnants of the North Tower are dismantled and reunited with its crushed beams and mortar. Ten stories of rubble are dumpstered, dissected, and carted away. Some chunks are sold as scrap metal; other chunks are saved as museum relics. The crew is already months ahead of schedule.

Predictably, I intensify my plans for the inevitable visit.

The day arrives. The calendar reads January 4, 2002. It is 115 days after that unforgettable Tuesday morning — about 80 days later than I should have gone. The sun is brilliant...again. I find my old shoes, but I no longer need them. Even with the police escort that I was able to arrange, I get no closer than the VIP viewing stand. It's like being in Row W of the bleachers at Wrigley Field.

But on this day, there were no players on the field. The game, you see, was long over.

Oh, sure, there was plenty of work going on. Cranes in place, trucks shuttling back and forth, a security guy fumbling with a stubborn, wind-blown American flag, etc. And images of the specter of what took place, nearly four months ago, did dance through my mind as I leaned over the makeshift railing. But the game was clearly over. No striking evidence, no real remnants of the horror, no smoke...no tears.

I felt embarrassed. I looked down at the stupid, old shoes I had donned for the occasion and just shook my head.

"Steven I miss you so.
Please help me to be strong for our Emily."
(scribbled on the Ground Zero VIP viewing stand)

I stood there for about 30 minutes. I had reserved two hours for the visit and hoped it would be sufficient. My son, Naftali, 25, stood beside me and feigned emotion. Neither of us spoke. But our thoughts were the same: "We missed the boat."

I thought back to the beautiful lesson attributed to the Baal

Shem Tov, 18th-century sage and founder of the chassidic movement. Small children are the paragons of purity on this world, he said. We grow up and forget what it is like to be a child, unencumbered by conflict, shame, and pride. But observing the daily activity of any healthy child can afford us some wonderful reminders of what life should be like. Three important lessons emerge:

1) Kids are relentless in their demands. So when you really want something, cry for it.

2) A child's get-up-and-go attitude prevents boredom from seeping in. So approach every situation with vitality and freshness.

3) Kids want everything now. Their inability to put things off for later can be frustrating to parents, but it is often a blessing in disguise and a powerful message to us. Never...ever...delay.

Lesson three haunted me as I took one final gaze at my lost opportunity. I so much wanted to see something that I could take home with me. A vision, a message of inspiration or consolation, a memory that would impact me forever, a tidbit of morbidity that could remind me to treasure every precious moment of life.

But it was too late for that.

I pulled my scarf a little tighter around my neck. A slight wind blew, though the temperature was a few degrees above normal for early January. But it felt a lot colder than it really was and I knew it was time to leave. I turned to Naftali. "I'm glad we came," he said with ambivalence. We both grinned a little, and he shrugged his shoulders.

My old shoes led me back to the steps. I looked back at the scrawling on the viewing stand as I left, desperately seeking some parting message of inspiration or consolation. The handwriting was painfully young.

"Dear Daddy, I miss you. I love you."

This was supposed to be a story about September 11. I was hoping to learn something from the visit. Oddly enough, I think I did.

ANDREA KAHN

Cosmo Girl

S even years ago, had I encountered the woman I am today, I would have pitied her: long sleeves and an ankle-length skirt in the middle of summer; no driving, writing, talking on the phone, or cooking from sundown Friday until sundown Saturday; recently married to a man she'd never touched — not so much as a peck on the cheek — until after the wedding. I'd have cringed and dismissed this woman as a Repressed Religious Nut. Now my pity — or at least a patient smile — is for that self-certain Southern California girl I was at 25.

I grew up in Tucson, the older of two daughters, in a typically upper-middle-class, well-educated, liberal Jewish family. My dad is a physician, my mother active in the local Jewish community. My religious and ethnic identification consisted of fundraising for Jewish causes, Israeli dancing, and Sunday brunch: bagels and lox.

As a gawky 13-year-old, I had a bat mitzvah, along with the obligatory party at a posh country club. If God was there, I didn't

ANDREA KAHN is a freelance writer whose work appears regularly in the *New York Times* and other publications. She lives in the New York area with her family.

notice. The most religious person I knew was my high school English teacher, a Southern Baptist for whom I wrote polemical essays questioning all religious beliefs. Through my research and experience (which consisted mostly of listening to Bob Dylan and Pink Floyd, skimming the *Marx-Engels Reader*, and having deep, earnest discussions with friends), I concluded that religion was, at best, irrelevant in an enlightened, late 20th-century world. At 16, I joined the group American Atheists.

But generally, I did what teenagers do. I spent the scorching Arizona summers watching soap operas and lying by the pool at my friend Annie's house, comparing tan lines. We crossed the border into Mexico to buy tequila, sneaked into dance clubs with fake IDs, philosophized about life and boys, felt immortal.

I continued my liberal pursuits in college in Philadelphia, and after graduation, I drove my Honda with its "I'm Pro-Choice — And I Vote!" bumper sticker to California. I took advantage of all Los Angeles had to offer: I ate sushi and gelati, played beach volleyball, studied Kabbalah, and once went to a *"Nam-myoho-renge-kyo"* chanting session, where a skinny woman with bleached blond hair swore that the incantation had secured her latest role, as Victim in a new slasher film.

At the time, I was living in a Beverly Hills basement with a friend, working for the National Organization for Women, helping organize pro-choice rallies. I also did stints as aerobics instructor, waitress, cashier, SAT tutor. Finally, I entered USC as a graduate student in journalism. In the next few years I wrote for the *Los Angeles Times* about miniskirts, paisley, and the plight of L.A.'s lovelorn. Then I worked for *Teen* magazine, penning endless variations of "how to get/dump your guy" stories and answering hapless teenage girls' letters in *Teen*'s "Dear Juli" column. While I loved my spacious office with its view of the city, I also found the job mind-numbing and depressing. How many ways, I wondered, could I teach a girl to flirt?

I moved to a "Beverly Hills-adjacent" apartment, complete with ceiling fans and high arches. There I was — 25 years old, finally having achieved what should "do it": a promising career, friends, things. Yet I felt as though something was profoundly lacking — as if I were a Ferrari engine stuffed into a VW Bug.

Though I was at times excited, even ecstatic, I rarely remember being content or truly joyful. Though I believed in spirituality, religion was the "opiate of the masses," a crutch for emotional and intellectual weaklings and conservative Republicans. I favored Tarot card and palm readers and a particular psychic who told me I was Napoleon in a past life.

Then one night, a friend and I dropped in on an Orthodox Jewish gathering near my apartment — not so much to find enlightenment as to meet guys. I don't recall what, exactly, but something the rabbi said resonated. I decided to take a class. I certainly had no intention of becoming — ick! — religious. I just wanted to learn more about Judaism's philosophy and mysticism. As for those archaic laws? How dare anyone tell me I'm restricted from certain activities because I'm a woman or that I have to dress a certain way to protect my dignity.

I'm a passionate person. During the past seven years, however, I've decided that it may be easier to be passionate about the wrong things than the right ones. I thought I was open-minded, thoughtful, yet I really just believed what every other liberal, educated, cultured person I knew believed. I was tolerant of everything except "intolerance." My only absolute was that there are no absolutes.

Yet, as much as I fought and rebelled, I was drawn to the Orthodox world. I recognized something profound there — the values, the consciousness, the sensitivity to others. I examined my worldview and myself in a different way. I began to see that in a society in which individuality, self-determination, and freedom of choice are the highest values, I had, in fact, been limited by pressures I didn't even recognize. I had been conforming to what's considered "normal," its definition changing every few years. Now, for the first time, I understood what I had always felt, that I had an essence, a soul. I glimpsed a higher meaning to life and the infinitely deep layers of existence leading to the Ultimate Existence: insight into which a 25-year-old — even one with a personal trainer and her own advice column — might not be privy.

To the shock of my family, which was half-sure I'd been sucked in by a cult, I quit my job, sublet my beautiful apartment, and traveled to Israel to continue my studies. The Torah and its volumes of commentary address every aspect of the human condition. It proscribes, prescribes, and describes in amazing depth and detail. And it infuses people with the bigness of character and soul I had always admired but rarely experienced.

I spent many months grappling with the "female" question. So much of what I saw in the religious way of life seemed at odds with what I thought I knew. But at one point I had to ask myself: What have I been told by my schooling and my society, and what do I really see in the world? What is my experience? My answer: Men and women are significantly, dramatically different, emotionally and physically (and now, I realize, spiritually). Judaism addresses these differences. I looked — really looked — at the religious women around me. I had never met stronger, more emotionally and spiritually refined, capable, loving, non-neurotic women. Or more sensitive, respectful, devoted men. Or more happy, physically intact, cared-for children. I wanted that.

Everywhere, I see people driven by external achievement; I see the pain, the struggles, the Prozac nation. Becoming observant does not make a weak person strong. It is not a quick fix for a lifetime of emotional damage. But the Torah's guidelines provide the boundaries and tools for inner healing and transformation. Now, being "religious" frames everything I do, say, and strive for. I knew that the man I would marry must share the same priorities and values.

My husband and I met in New York, through a mutual teacher who knew us well. I'd spent plenty of time engaged in the rites of Los Angeles-style dating. This was a whole different ritual. In venturing into this *shidduch* — which, loosely translated, means "date" — we had agreed to an express purpose. We were to decide if we were a match — and with far less dilly-dallying than in most modern courtships.

Aaron and I spent hours together eating Chinese food, playing miniature golf and pinball, ice-skating, boating in Central Park. I came to respect his integrity, his strength, and his constant striving to do and be better. (And he's cute!) Four months after we met, we began a ten-week engagement. (My mother, who had spent a year planning my sister's nuptials, was aghast.) We never touched, but got to know each other, unclouded by the bond of physical intimacy, which so often superglues the wrong people together.

People look at Orthodox women as repressed. But I often think about a truer definition of repression. When I see women in skimpy clothing, intimately involved with men they barely know, I think: "Wake up, girlfriend! You think men are seeing your soul? Thinking about your needs? About who you are? Your body has become your self." The real feminine mystique consists of a woman's private side, the richness of her inner world.

I had been living the Cosmo fantasy. Now I feel as if I've awakened from a long, sweaty dream. Once I aspired to make it as a writer, and perhaps get married and have a kid or two along the way. Today, although I still work as a freelance writer, it is not my identity. I live in a religious community outside Manhattan, full of the type of people I used to look at with pity, even contempt. My goal is to become like these women: sensitive, strong, fantastic wives and mothers — not, as I once thought, because they had been subjugated for centuries and didn't know better or because they were lacking self-esteem, but because they recognize that the most important thing a person can do is to develop character by giving, building, and supporting another.

A Jewish wedding revolves around making the bride and groom happy. After the ceremony, but before the dancing — what exuberant, unabashed dancing! — Aaron and I went to a separate room to spend a few private moments. There, he held my hand for the first time. That small gesture had a richness and intimacy I could never have imagined.

HEROES

SARA YOHEVED RIGLER

Of Angels and Poinsettias: A Jewish Story

My father did not believe in angels. He could not be bothered with spiritual notions or metaphysical concepts. But when he died, and I stood beside his sheet-covered body in the mortuary's refrigerated room, I was overwhelmed by the sense that legions of angels were surrounding my father and escorting his soul to the next world. And I, his ardently spiritual daughter, stood there envying his place in the World to Come.

According to Judaism, angels can be created by human beings. Every good thought, word, and deed gives birth to a positive force in the universe, which is called an angel. These angels are eternal. They hover around us throughout life and accompany us to our reward after death. Conversely, every evil thought, word, and deed creates a bad angel, or demon. They also hover over us until, in the heavenly court, they become our accusers.

I could recognize the faces of many of the angels that filled

---

Written for the *aliyat neshama* of my father, Yisrael ben Yosef Yehuda, on the occasion of his 11th *yahrtzeit*. (See biography of SARA YOHEVED RIGLER, page 17.)

that cold, white-tiled room in Bershler's Funeral Parlor. One contingent was born on those rainy mornings when my father, driving to work, would pull over to the bus stops along the way and offer a ride to anyone going to Camden, New Jersey.

And over there was the angel of the black eye, which my father got when he accosted a man he caught shoplifting in his drugstore. A policeman who happened into the drugstore at that moment arrested the man, but my father refused to press charges. Instead, he offered his assailant a job in the store, so that he could earn money to pay for the items he had tried to steal.

I recognized another angel, born at the end of a cold winter day when I was catching a ride home from the drugstore with my father. He daily delivered prescriptions to the homes of people who were too sick to come in for them. I was in a hurry to get home that day, but my father assured me he had only one delivery to make. He drove up to a dilapidated house in the ghetto which Camden had become and disappeared into the house. By the time he emerged 15 minutes later, I was rabid.

"What took you so long?" I scolded him.

My father, who never explained himself, but who did not want to listen to my harangue, answered simply, "The house was ice cold. No wonder the woman is sick. I tried calling the coal company to order her a load of coal, but their line was busy until a minute ago."

World without Strangers

Hovering close to my father's body were the poinsettia angels. Christmas was a rare day off for my father, since the drugstore was open six days a week, and Sunday he invariably went in for a few hours to finish work from the previous week. But instead of relaxing on Christmas, when he, as a Jew, had nothing to do, my father would fill up the back of his station wagon with gift poinsettias. Most of these poinsettias he delivered to the poor black and Puerto Rican women who lived in the neighborhood of his store.

When my brother Joe was a teenager, he usually did the

footwork of taking the poinsettias into the houses. Many of the women, without husbands and with a brood of children to tend to, told Joe that this poinsettia was the only thing of beauty they received all year long.

Among the regular poinsettia recipients was a woman suffering from multiple sclerosis (M.S.) who lived in a nursing home. Every year Joe would bring the poinsettia into her room, place it on the table, and mumble, "Merry Christmas," while the paralyzed woman would follow him with her eyes, unable to even nod a thank you. Finally one year, Joe asked the nurses who this woman was. They told him that she had been a wealthy daughter of a fine family, engaged to be married, when she contracted M.S. Her fiance broke the engagement, her money was used up in doctor and care bills, and eventually her family dropped all contact. In the course of a year, the nurses told Joe, the only card, letter, or gift this woman received was this poinsettia from my father.

After Joe went away to college, my father did all the poinsettia deliveries by himself. Overweight, with varicose veins from standing in the drugstore since 1925, and stricken with the arthritis which made it increasingly painful for him to move his legs, my father delivered these poinsettias until he retired from the drugstore at age 75.

One corner of the mortuary room was filled with library angels. After my father retired, he volunteered at the local library to deliver books to shut-ins. Leaning on his cane and limping from arthritis, he often had to climb flights of stairs to reach the desolate apartments of people, usually younger and sometimes less incapacitated than he, who had run out of reasons to get out of bed.

My father involved himself with the plight of each one. Did this man suffer from aching back pains? Then and there, without an appointment, my father took him to his own orthopedic doctor. Had this woman lost all sense that she counted for anything? My father arranged to pick her up on Election Day to take her to the polls, convincing her of the importance of her vote.

My father lived in a world without strangers. He could not

stand in a supermarket line nor sit at a restaurant table without striking up a conversation with the person next to him. I was always terribly embarrassed by his utter disregard for personal space. Perhaps the young Irishman at the adjoining table would rather converse with his family than with this bald-headed Jew with whom he had nothing in common.

Invariably, however, my father found a point of connection. Either the Irishman had an uncle who was a pharmacist, or had an aunt who had graduated Camden High with my Aunt Mamie in 1929, or he used as his children's pediatrician Dr. Hanson, my father's old friend, or he had once summered in the same Poconos resort to which my father once took us. By the time the waitress brought our check or we reached the cashier in the supermarket line, the erstwhile strangers were always smiling as warmly as if they had found a long-lost uncle. Didn't my father know that in the latter half of the 20th century, alienation was the pervasive mindset of society?

Perceived as the Enemy?

Although my father lived all of his 86 years in that century, he was never a 20th-century man. When I was a psychology major at Brandeis University, arguing with him once about some sociological issue, he stunned me by announcing that he did not believe in sociology or psychology. I was flabbergasted. Was sociology some nebulous religious system that one could choose to believe or not believe?

In the late '60s, fired up by my leftist political convictions, I inveighed against the oppression of the lower classes, citing statistics of starvation in affluent America. My father retorted angrily, "Ridiculous! If someone in Camden is hungry, all they need to do is come to me or to the minister in the church on Stevens Street."

That there could be societal problems that could not be solved by a kind and generous neighbor was beyond my father's comprehension. Now, more than 30 years later, I wonder whether he wasn't right.

At Brandeis, I belonged to the radical leftist Students for a Democratic Society. I had taken my stand with minorities and oppressed Third World peasants against the bourgeoisie conservative establishment of America. Thus, I was mystified, on one of the occasional times I entered my father's drugstore during my college years, to see a black teenage girl whispering to my father that she wanted to see him privately.

When I later asked him what she had wanted, he answered matter-of-factly (for it was apparently a routine occurrence) that she thought she had venereal disease and was asking him what to do. Why should a black teenager, in the age of the Black Panthers, be confiding in this middle-class, white, Republican, Jewish pharmacist? If I perceived him as the enemy, why didn't she?

Another time, I came into the store with him one summer morning. Five or six matronly black women, who were sitting at the soda fountain, greeted my father with cat-calls and complaints: "We ain't talkin' to you no more, Mista Levinsky."

"You's in trouble in our book, Doc."

I wondered how my father's characteristic gruffness or fiery temper had hurt or insulted these women. He ignored them, and went directly back to the prescription counter. I, however, was concerned with their plight. I approached and asked them what my father had done to them.

One of them replied, "Yesterday afternoon he done told the ice cream man to give popsicles to all the kids on our block 'n he would pay for 'em. Us mamas had to spend all afternoon pickin' up popsicle wrappers. No, we ain't talkin' to him no more." And they all roared with laughter.

When, in the early '70s, race riots wracked America's cities, Camden's business district was also ravaged. Starting at one end of Broadway, the main street, rioters burned or looted virtually every store. They set fire to the jewelry store next to my father's drugstore, razing it to the ground. Then it was the drugstore's turn. According to an eyewitness, one of the rioters shouted, "Don't touch that store. He's our friend." The angry mob bypassed my father's store, going on to break the windows and pillage the shoe store next door. A chilling tribute to "Doc," as they called my father: When the smoke cleared the next day, his was the only store on Broadway that had emerged completely unscathed.

One-Inch Notebook

My father was not a rich man, but he gave and lent money as if he had it. During the Six Day War, when the American Jewish community rallied to Israel's emergency need, my father, with two children in expensive private colleges, found he had no money to give to Israel. So he went to the bank and borrowed $4,000, which he donated to the Israel Emergency Fund. Later, when the local Jewish community was collecting money for a geriatric home, my father took out a second mortgage on his house in order to have a proper sum to contribute.

My father regularly lent money to any of the drugstore customers who asked him. Most of these loans were never repaid. When we were sitting *shiva* for my father, Carl, the Italian pharmacist who had bought the drugstore from him, told us how, when my father was transferring the store over to him, they came upon a one-inch-thick notebook, filled with entries. Carl asked what it was. My father replied that this was his record of outstanding loans. Carl asked how much it was worth. Tossing the book into the wastebasket, my father shrugged, "It's priceless."

Born to my grandmother just a year after his parents immigrated from Odessa in 1902, my father was barely 17 years younger than his mother. I remember seeing him in his 60s, a big, six-foot-tall man, his thinning hair completely gray, waiting on his 80-year-old mother with filial solicitude. Many times I watched in awe as my father mutely accepted my grandmother's petulant scoldings. My father paid for his mother's two-bedroom apartment plus full-time help. When he finished his ten- or 12-hour workdays in the drugstore, almost daily he went to check on his mother and made sure she had everything she needed. My mother used to wait to serve our dinner until Dad came home after 7 P.M.

When Carl bought the drugstore, his lawyer and my father's lawyer drew up a purchase agreement. After it was signed, as Carl and his lawyer walked to his car, the lawyer said to Carl, "You just wasted your money."

Carl gulped. The lawyer continued, "With that man, a handshake would have been sufficient."

The day after my father died, his rabbi came to talk to our family in preparation for the funeral. Of course, he knew my father well, for Irving (Israel) Levinsky had been a pillar of the synagogue and had accompanied my mother to Shabbat services every week. Nevertheless, the rabbi asked the various family members gathered in the living room if there was anything special we wanted him to include in the eulogy.

An amazing scene of revelation unfolded. As each family member recounted tales of my father's acts of kindness that he or she had personally witnessed, the rest of us learned of them for the first time. My father never talked about anything he did, not even to my mother. A gruff man with a short temper and a big voice, his shortcomings were as obvious as his merits were hidden. We knew that he was generous and that he had helped many people, but not even those of us closest to him knew the extent of the money he had loaned, the jobs he had found, the individuals he had rescued.

Road to Heaven

My father did not believe in life after death, nor in the World to Come. He expected no rewards for giving people rides in the rain or for finding jobs for the sons of his ghetto clientele. How amazed, then, he must have been to find himself ascending to the Next World, escorted by legions of familiar angels. Standing meditating over his body in that chilly mortuary room, I found myself saying, "Surprise, Dad!"

But there was also a revelation for me in that angel-thronged room. I saw that deeds are what primarily count. Although I had been practicing Torah for five years, and I knew that Judaism is a religion less of faith than of action, of performing concrete mitzvot, I preferred to live in the ethereal realm of the mind and the spirit. Standing beside my father's body, gazing at his luminous face, I was shocked to realize who he had become by virtue of his deeds alone.

My father's road to Heaven was paved with poinsettias and popsicle wrappers. And if there was a gap created by the faith he did not hold, or the mitzvot he never learned to do, I saw that it was spanned like an immense bridge by that book of loans he had tossed away.

I, who had spent my 42 years wrestling with profound concepts and lofty aspirations, had nothing in my entourage as significant as my father's coal order for the sick lady. So I could feel my father winking at me, his religious daughter, from his honored place in the Next World, saying, "Surprise!"

RICHARD RABKIN

My Zadie

T he most religious person I knew growing up was my *zadie*. He wasn't really religious in the sense that he kept the Sabbath or was particularly mindful about the kosher dietary laws, but my whole family could feel that he, and my *bubbie*, were closest to "the tradition."

For this reason, when I became religious about four years ago, I thought that my *bubbie* and *zadie* would be the most understanding of anyone. But when I went to visit them in their senior citizens' home in Montreal for the weekend, I was in for a surprise.

No sooner did I put my bags down in their room than I heard Bubbie say, "Nu, Richard. Your mother tells us that you are religious now," in her familiar Bubbie not-really-a-question-but-not-quite-a-statement tone.

Zadie looked at me. I smiled expectantly, sort of hoping he would leap up from the plastic-covered couch and start dancing

---

RICHARD RABKIN received an undergraduate degree in religious studies from the University of Western Ontario, and a law degree from the University of British Columbia. He presently lives in Toronto and dreams of coming back to Israel where he spent time learning during 2001–2002.

the hora around me. Instead he said, "Leave him alone, Adelle. At least he's not in a cult. You know a lot of people have grandchildren in cults. The woman down the hall, her granddaughter shaved her head and became a Hare Krishna. And doesn't Abe Lerner's grandson practice voodoo magic or something?"

"No, Willie, that was a program you saw on TV," my *bubbie* answered.

"Anyway, at least you're not in a cult," Zadie said under his breath, while reclining back in his seat.

I was a little confused. This wasn't quite the reaction I expected, but I knew they were just expressing their concern for me. At least that is what I told myself.

"Too Good" for the Elevator

After I accompanied my grandparents to the Friday evening services, we went to the dining hall for dinner. Bubbie introduced me to all her friends, and I was an instant celebrity. As soon as we were finished eating, we had to make room for the other residents who had not yet eaten, so we left to go back upstairs.

This presented a problem. They lived on the 10th floor, and my grandparents were going to take the elevator. I wasn't prepared to go along, since it is prohibited to use electricity on Shabbat.

I asked the woman at the front desk if I could take the stairs. She wasn't even sure if there were any stairs, because she had never heard of anyone using them. I was trying to do this quietly, but my inquiries were overheard by a group of women seniors who were sitting by the elevator.

"Why don't you just take the elevator," asked one of the ladies.

I tried to be as diplomatic as possible. "Well, I observe Shabbat and would prefer not to ride the elevator."

"Aw, come on," she said in her you-can't-fool-me tone. "It would kill you to take the elevator?"

"I would actually rather walk up the stairs. Do you know where they are?" I asked, trying to get out of this situation. But I saw more people gathering around me.

"Miriam, this young man wants to know where the stairs are

because he thinks he's too good for the elevator," one of the women belted in a voice reminiscent of Estelle Costanza.

"So the elevator is good enough for the rabbi but it's not good enough for you?" another woman chimed in.

"He doesn't want to ride the elevator. Let him take the stairs," Zadie said in my defense, joining in on what was about to turn into a senior citizen's brawl.

"What are you, some kind of fanatic or something?" one of the ladies asked me in all seriousness.

"I am not a fanatic..." I tried to explain, but got cut off.

"Oh, he's a fanatic all right," the man from the back agreed.

"He's not a fanatic," another man said, apparently coming to my rescue. "He's a maniac!"

Just when I thought things couldn't get any worse, and my face couldn't get any redder, one of the maintenance men came into the lobby and said, "Okay, where's the crazy man who won't ride the elevator?"

The entire lobby of seniors extended their arms toward me like it was aerobics hour.

"Follow me, son. The stairs are this way," he said as though he had done this before. I walked away from the battleground with my head down, slightly embarrassed at the scene that I had managed to make. But I caught my *zadie* giving me a little wink. I think he was impressed with the fact that I held firm in my commitment despite the commotion. Or perhaps he was just impressed that I had the energy to walk up ten flights of stairs.

Praying with Zadie

The next morning, with the elevator episode squarely behind me, I went downstairs with my *zadie* to the synagogue in the seniors' home. Praying together with him not only gave him a lot of *nachas* (pride), but it did the same for me. He introduced me to all his friends, announcing with a smile, "This is my grandson."

I responded with an even brighter smile and said, "This is my grandfather."

That weekend was the last time I saw my *zadie*. He passed away about a year later. However, I have realized how lucky I was to spend that Shabbat with him. Sitting next to him and praying with him in the synagogue made me realize how similar we really were.

Before that weekend, there were times when I had trouble relating to Zadie. He was born in Poland, English was not his native language, and there was a wide generation gap between us. But as we shared our Judaism together, I realized how much we actually had in common.

The fact that we were born in different countries or that we were generations apart was practically meaningless. What was more important was that we had 3,300 years of common history and tradition behind us.

When the rabbi gave the eulogy at his funeral, I realized how proud my *zadie* really was of me, and how much our Shabbat experience had meant to him. Apparently, he would often brag to people in the seniors' home, "My grandson Richard became religious."

In his old age, perhaps my *zadie* realized that even though he wouldn't be around forever, Judaism would be.

From that time on, I became more aware that by observing precepts in the Torah, I was not only fulfilling a Divine command, but I was connecting myself to my *zadie*, and all my other ancestors before him who also practiced Judaism. It comforts me to know that every time I go to synagogue to pray on Shabbat, my *zadie* is somehow right there, davening beside me. I hope it comforts him, too.

DANA SCHWARTZ

To Life

I was born in 1935 in Lvov, Poland, an only child. A lot of what happened with my life, and who I became, was shaped by my first ten years.

Both of my parents worked, so I spent a lot of time with the nanny. I hated waiting for my mother to come home. One day my nanny took me to the park, and as she was busy talking, I went over to the forbidden path and picked a daisy. As I picked it I heard a tremendous boom. I was shocked and terrified. A man ran by with a white dog and shouted, "Go home. The war has started."

The wonderful thing about the war was that the nanny was let go, since my parents no longer worked. My father would let me sleep in my clothes and gather me up in the middle of the night when there was an air raid siren. We would all run down to the big cellar that was the apartment's laundry room.

After awhile, my father said, "We're getting out of here." He

DANA SCHWARTZ is a child survivor of the Holocaust. A licensed psychotherapist, she speaks at schools and museums about her wartime experience. She has also interviewed other survivors, most of whom were children during the war, for Steven Spielberg's Shoah Foundation. Along with her husband, an internist in private practice, she founded the Concern Foundation, which specializes in cancer research in Israel.

hired a car and driver to take us to Romania, which was still free.

On the way we ran out of gas, so we hired a horse and buggy and continued. We crossed a big river and it was very scary. Finally we stood at the bottom of a hill, seeing the border of Romania halfway up.

At that point, my mother turned to my father and said, "But honey, what about our Persian rugs and our silver and our paintings? We can't just walk away from it all!"

My father began pacing back and forth thinking. Finally he said, "This is the 20th century. It's the Western world. We're educated. I'm a lawyer. I have plenty of pull. What could happen?"

He turned to my mother and said, "You're right. Let's go back." So we turned around and went back.

We were so close. Of the 182,000 Jews in my hometown, only 184 survived.

Smuggled Out

We went back to Lvov and the Russians came. They took my father into the army, but he escaped and returned to us. Then the Germans came. They gave us half an hour to pack a bag and leave. I recall the silence as we walked out of there — my parents walking tall with me between them.

We walked into the ghetto. We lived with my grandmother, my uncle, and a woman whose husband in the good days had been a senator. He was dead and she had nowhere else to go. We were there for about a year. It was a horrible, scary, cold year with a lot of hiding from actions, filled with fear and hunger. And people who somehow kept disappearing.

Eventually my father was able to get non-Jewish papers for my mother and I, and we were smuggled out. We met my father at the gate to say goodbye and I wanted to hug him, but I was not allowed to because then the German soldier would be suspicious. My mother warned me at all costs to keep my arms down. I remember how my arms hurt from holding them down when I wanted to reach for my father.

We went to a small village where my father had paid a farmer to look after us. He was to pretend that we were his cousin's wife and daughter and although he was obligated to look after us, he couldn't stand us. That allowed him to keep his distance.

When we arrived, he gave us a big bed to sleep in. I can visualize it to this day. We slept and slept. When we awoke, it was sunny and light and peaceful...and the birds were singing.

This farmer was the only one who knew we were Jewish. Eventually he found us a place to stay with another farmer and we were put in a barn. There were partitions for cows, horses, and sheep — and we had one partition. From our hiding place we watched the remaining Jews in the town being taken away.

On the Run

There was a young Jewish woman upstairs in the building next door. She was a dentist, very pretty, with a broken leg. A German soldier came and she pleaded with him, "My leg's not set yet and I'm the only dentist in town, maybe you'll need me." He said, "That's a very good idea, but my orders are to take you downstairs." Then another German came and when she repeated her story, he shot her over and over and over again.

Six months after all the Jews had been cleared out, a man came with his son in his arms, begging the farmer to help him. "We've been in the forest for months, and everything was okay until my son got gangrene. I can't cut his foot off. Please will you help me get a doctor?" The farmer said "sure," and got the Nazis instead. His reward was two kilos of sugar.

My mother and I stayed with that farmer for a few months, and then with other farmers and in other places in the village and the forest.

Finally the war ended. We went back to Lvov and found out that my father and everyone else we knew and loved had been killed. We were homeless, with two raw eggs between us. We were at the end of our rope. It was horrible. There was nobody left to beg from.

Many stories later, we found ourselves deep in the USSR. I remember a drunk Russian soldier was waving a revolver and trying to rape my mother. She screamed and I was the only one who could save her. I jumped on the soldier's back like a monkey and kicked and scratched him. I yelled to my mother, "Run, run, run!" She ran while I kept kicking and scratching until I knocked him down. By the time he found his equilibrium we were both gone.

That was a defining moment. My mother said to me, "I'm going to take you away from all this. I'm going to take you to a country where you can be a Jew and be respected for who you are, and where you are free to study and learn Hebrew."

Safer Future

We escaped from the USSR back to Poland. We were dirt poor and had many more adventures. I went to school for a while and there was a boy in my class who refused to stand up and pray when everyone else did. He said he was a proud Jew and his home was Palestine. I was astonished because I thought of Jews as terrified, haunted and ashamed, not worthy of life, to be destroyed. This young boy gave me a different way of looking at things.

A few years later I was in Sweden in a Jewish community building. Everyone was listening to the man on the radio yelling out names of countries and answering "yes" or "no." The UN was voting to partition Palestine. The next thing I knew, everyone was dancing and singing "Hatikva." Tears streamed down their faces and I knew that I had lived to see the day my forefathers had only dreamed about.

In a way, my life has come full circle this past year with all the terrible violence in Israel and America. All these years I have been optimistic that it could never happen again.

Recent events make me very anxious. It's a terrible crisis of belief in the goodness of man. I think those who lived through the horror are more ready to believe that horror exists. We know the unthinkable can happen.

Yes, there is evil in the world, but there is also great kindness and goodness. I dare say that I have been spending my life telling stories that touch people. I need them to know about the people who have died. I want to keep the stories of those I love alive. For them. But mostly so that Jews will be safer in the future, so people will understand who the Jewish people are, and will want to save Jews if need be.

In many ways, I've been very lucky. I've had an amazing life. I have a wonderful husband and three terrific sons. I'm so fortunate to have survived, and I feel it's incumbent on me to do whatever I can for my people.

People ask me what is the key to success. I think you need the courage to walk between the raindrops.

Postscript: On December 11, 2001, U.S. President George W. Bush hosted the first-ever Chanukah party in the residential part of the White House complex. The evening was marked by the lighting of a 130-year-old silver menorah from Lvov, the Polish town that Dana Schwartz fled from at age ten. President Bush said: "The Jews of Lvov fell victim to the horror of the Nazi Holocaust, but their great menorah survived. And as God promised Abraham, the people of Israel still live."

SARA YOHEVED RIGLER

Holywoman

I was in Israel, hot on the trail of a hidden holywoman.

I had only an address and a name — Rebbetzin Devorah Cohen. Her husband, Rabbi Emanuel Cohen, was considered by Israel's greatest rabbis to be one of the 36 hidden *tzaddikim* in whose merit the whole world exists. "Rebbetzin Devorah is as great as he is," my source had told me.

As the bus pulled out of Jerusalem's central bus station, I settled in for a long ride, grateful for the time to think. I had been in Israel for barely two months, studying about my Jewish background. Having spent the last 15 years living in an Indian ashram, I had many unresolved issues with Judaism.

My major obstacle, which I called "Issue Number One," was accepting the Jewish emphasis on having children.

For 15 years I had invested myself in a celibate path, having been taught by my guru that sexual relationships dissipated spiritual energy and that children were little noisemakers who made it impossible to meditate. I believed that children and

---

All names and places in this article have been changed in order to protect the holywoman's anonymity, a condition for her allowing me to write about her. (See biography of SARA YOHEVED RIGLER, page 17.)

spiritual practices were mutually exclusive, and that if I pursued the path of Judaism, all my spirituality would end up in the diaper pail.

"Issue Number Two" was my sense of spiritual alienation from most other Jews I met in Israel. Although I was convinced that Torah was true, I felt that it applied to "them," but not to me. I was a unique exception.

The Holocaust and After

When I finally alighted at Rebbetzin Devorah's ramshackle rural community, I made my way to the home of Nomi, who had arranged the meeting.

She filled me in on Rebbetzin Devorah's life. Born in Hungary, she had been taken to Auschwitz at the age of 20. Her parents and sisters were killed in the gas chambers the first night. But the young Devorah was kept alive to be experimented upon by the notorious "angel of death," Dr. Mengele.

Right after the war, she made her way to Palestine, where she married Emanuel Cohen, also a survivor. The couple never had any children, although they raised many unwanted children who were left on their doorstep, including one Down syndrome boy who, 30 years later, was still living with them. They lived in abject poverty, eking out a meager income by raising poultry.

"Through it all," Nomi concluded, shaking her head in wonder, "Rebbetzin Devorah is always smiling. I see her almost every day, and she is never without a smile. I still can't figure out what she has to smile about."

First Meeting

On Shabbat morning, I attended services at the community's simple synagogue. Suddenly the door swung open, and a woman walked toward me, smiling broadly, her arms outstretched. She greeted me with a bear hug, like a long-lost daughter. I knew immediately this was Rebbetzin Devorah.

As I stared at her, she took the new prayer book from my hand. She leafed through it until she found "Ethics of Our Fathers," aphorisms by the sages of two millennia ago. Handing the prayer book back to me, she pointed to a passage, and asked, "Have you ever seen this one?"

As I read the words she was pointing to, I broke out in goose bumps. Here was a rejoinder to my Issue Number One: "Rabbi Shimon ben Yehudah says...Beauty, strength, wealth, honor, wisdom...and children — these befit the righteous and befit the world..."

While I stood there dumbfounded, she took my prayer book again and turned a few pages. Handing it back to me, she pointed to another passage and asked, "And have you ever read this one?"

Staring at me were the words: "Hillel said — Do not separate yourself from the community." Issue Number Two in stark rebuttal.

I looked up in consternation. The holywoman laughed, then turned and left.

Through the Looking Glass

Later that afternoon, I followed Nomi's directions to Rebbetzin Devorah's home, which looked like a shack from some chassidic story. I came upon Rebbetzin Devorah as she was setting out a dish of food for the stray cats. She greeted me with a beaming smile and invited me in. Soon we were engrossed in conversation. We spoke Hebrew, a language I barely knew, yet somehow I understood everything she said.

She asked about my background. I told her about the ashram. Then I asked about her experiences in the Holocaust, a subject which had always absorbed me. She described how, on that first night in Auschwitz, a veteran inmate pointed to the smoke issuing out of the chimney of the crematorium and told her, "That's your parents."

Nevertheless, she asserted, "Auschwitz was not a bad place."

What?! I must have misunderstood, and asked her to repeat herself.

"Auschwitz was not a bad place," she repeated clearly. "There was a group of religious Hungarian girls. We stuck together. All the mitzvot we could do, we did. For example, one girl kept track of the days, so we knew when it was Shabbat, and we avoided doing forbidden work whenever possible. On Passover, we didn't have any matzah or wine, of course. But one of the girls had memorized the Haggadah. She would recite a line, and we would all repeat after her. In this way, we were able to fulfill the mitzvah of recounting the Exodus."

The holywoman fixed me with her pale blue eyes. "A bad place is a place where Jews can do mitzvot, but don't do them. For you, the ashram was a bad place."

She had just turned my whole reality upside down. A bad place had nothing to do with bad things happening to you. No matter that the Nazis had murdered her whole family. No matter that Dr. Mengele had experimented on her and probably sterilized her. All that really matters is what issues from you. No wonder she was always smiling, despite her barrenness, despite her poverty, despite the grueling hardship of her daily life. She was performing mitzvot. She was bonding with God. She was projecting her own light even in the darkness of hell.

I had met many holy masters in India. I had sat at the feet of great swamis and had bowed before Anandamaya-ma, the woman considered by millions to be the incarnation of the "divine mother." But sitting in that bare room with its tin roof, eating cucumbers and farmer's cheese across a rickety table from Rebbetzin Devorah, I felt like I had just emerged from a whole lifetime spent through the looking glass. I had been seeing everything in reverse. Now I was at the top of the rabbit hole, awakened from the dream, squinting my eyes at the brightness of a world of total spiritual clarity.

I looked long and hard at Rebbetzin Devorah. She gazed back at me, and laughed.

TOVA LEBOVITS

Smuggling out of Hell

I am the child of Holocaust survivors. I belong to a generation that will always be overshadowed by the calamity of our parents. I belong to a generation of kinless childhoods, where we grew up without grandparents, uncles, aunts, cousins. Our numerous relatives had perished, yet their silent presence loomed in the background. I belong to a generation that has to face the horrors of the past, and bridge that past to an uncertain future.

I cannot explain Hitler nor can I make what happened go away. But I can remember and I must pass that memory on. I must remember the Nazis, their great evil, and their threat to my existence, my people, and humankind.

My father, Shammai Davidovics, taught me to fight for life. He could not speak about what happened to him during the war, nor of his family who perished. He kept a lifelong self-imposed silence, which I painfully learned to accept despite my need to know.

Over the years, survivors and people he had saved would find us, and then I would hear their tales. It is only before his death that

TOVA LEBOVITS was born in Israel, grew up in the States, and now lives in Jerusalem. She studied communications and journalism at Hebrew University in Jerusalem.

my father broke his silence and substantiated the stories my brothers and I had collected. And it was only then that he answered, painfully, some of our most painful questions.

Underground Forgery Ring

My father was born in 1912 to a chassidic family in Danilev, a small Czechoslovakian town in the Carpathian Mountains. My grandma Gitle, after whom I am named (git=good=Tova), was said to be a cheerfully energetic thin wist of a woman. She managed to bring 14 babies into this world, of whom 12 reached adulthood — eight sons and four daughters, with my father somewhere in the middle.

Like those around him, my father went to cheder (Torah school), spoke Yiddish, and led a religious life. Yet his curiosity and adventurous nature led him to seek knowledge in the big world outside the shtetl (village). He studied Hebrew and other secular subjects. At age 16, he was accepted to a German gymnasium (high school) in Berne, while he continued his Torah studies on the side. From there he joined the Czechoslovakian army, and later was one of the few Jews accepted to the University of Budapest.

By the end of 1943, when the German army invaded Hungary, he was fluent in 12 languages, had completed his Ph.D. in sociology, and had received ordination from the Rabbinical Academy in Budapest.

At first, the Germans deported only those Jews who did not have Hungarian or Czech citizenship papers. Unfortunately, most Jews, though having lived in their small villages for centuries, did not have such papers. My father and several of his friends organized an underground forgery ring, where they began producing forged citizenship papers and other necessary documents. They were financially backed by wealthy Jews, and worked with Raul Wallenberg, providing him with needed documentation.

Master of Disguises

At this time my father also became a master of disguises, taking on various identities when necessary for his mission. Fortunately he looked Aryan, spoke fluent German, and unlike some who could not see the writing on the wall, he believed that these times required desperate measures.

His exploits were described to us by several survivors of my father's hometown of Danilev, and were later corroborated by my father.

In those critical days of the German invasion, my father collected all the names of the Jews of Danilev without citizenship papers and worked as fast as possible to forge those papers, several hundred in all. He knew that time was of the essence. The German army was now deporting Jews of nearby regions and would get to his hometown and family within weeks.

With papers in hand, he set out to Danilev in great haste. As he neared the region, he heard that the Germans had worked much faster than anticipated. He arrived at his hometown too late. The entire population, including his family, had been herded onto cattle cars and the trains were about to depart. My father saw the German soldiers guarding the trains and taunting his people. He could only do one thing...

> On the scene arrives an impeccably dressed high-ranking German official. He walks with a quick gait and haughty self-confidence. And he is furious. He approaches one of the guards, who immediately salutes him. In harsh tones, he demands to see the officer in charge, and sends the guards scuffling off to obey his orders.
>
> A perplexed and harried officer quickly appears, and receives a humiliating scolding. "Do you realize you have blatantly disobeyed and violated military orders?" yells the arrogant stranger as he slams a stack of papers in front of the officer.

This stranger was my father. The Jews who recognized him could not believe their eyes. On that day, through sheer chutzpah, he succeeded in reversing the decree. The Jews of Danilev were released from the cattle cars and returned to their homes (what was left after the looting, that is). They were now all legal citizens.

Where Can We Run?

Theirs was not a happy ending, however. The Jews were safe in Danilev for just one more year. During that time, on his occasional visits, my father tried desperately but in vain to convince his family and townsfolk to flee. He succeeded with but a handful of people, mostly teenagers. The others simply did not believe him. The things he said "will" happen, they argued "could not" happen. And besides, "Where can we run to?"

He offered to get them forged gentile papers and help them escape to the forest, providing them with peasants' clothes. But to them, such acts seemed too desperate. They felt they stood a better chance of surviving at home than in the forest.

My father remembers begging his favorite brother Hillel to come with him. But when Hillel heard it would entail hiding his Jewish identity, he could not.

Almost a year later, the Jews of Danilev were again herded together, and this time they were deported and murdered. My father arrived several days too late and was only able to reach one sister in time. Until his dying day, my father felt responsible for his family's death. He believed he should have been able to get through to them and somehow save them.

24-Hour Diplomat

When the Nazis occupied Budapest, they made an agreement with the Hungarian authorities: the Hungarians would recruit a special police force — called the Kishket — that would be in charge of buildings to which the Germans gave political immunity, such as the Austrian Embassy.

My father and several of his Jewish friends joined this force (as gentiles, of course, since Jews were not allowed). This way, they created an underground that could gather information about enemy activities. (Years ago, the Yad Vashem Holocaust Museum displayed a life-size portrait of my father in his Hungarian Kishket uniform, as an example of Jewish underground activity.)

By then, Jewish citizenship papers were no longer good

enough. My father obtained gentile papers for my mother and her entire family, and later when that became too dangerous, he hid them in an attic. He brought them food and provisions throughout the remainder of the war.

One day my mother came running tearfully to my father. Her mother and her uncle had become careless and gone out of hiding for a bit. They had been caught by German soldiers and taken to a concentration camp. My father must help!

My father found out exactly where they were detained, and with the help of his friends, organized an escape. He found out that the Austrian counsel in Hungary was leaving the capital for a few days. And so my father assumed the identity of the Austrian counsel for 24 hours. He had friends in a Kishket police car wait outside the camp for him.

The "Austrian counsel" entered the concentration camp. He approached the officer in charge and introduced himself with perfect Austrian German. The counsel was also in charge of the Swiss in Budapest, so my father said it had come to his attention that through some terrible error, two Swiss citizens had been wrongfully deported and were now detained in this very camp. He held their papers in his hand.

The officer in charge said this was impossible, but my father insisted. He had personally promised their relatives he would attend to the matter.

So together they went from floor to floor, announcing the names of these citizens. And so they found my grandmother and her brother. They took them out, into the waiting police car, and sped away, back into hiding.

My father sadly recalled as he walked through the camp how many Jews begged and pleaded with him: "We too are Swiss citizens. We too are Austrian citizens. Help us." But he could do nothing for those unfortunate people, and would never forget them.

Traveling Priest

One time in Israel, my father was on a public bus. The driver took one look at him, gave a shout, jumped up, and hugged him hard. He began weeping and crying my father's name, "Shammai, Shammai." He refused to take payment, sat my father in the front seat, and as he drove he told his tale out loud to the astonished passengers.

My father — disguised as a priest — would travel from village to village for weeks at a time, even entering concentration camps to rescue fellow Jews.

How did this disguise come about? While attending university, my father was required to attend Christian prayers and theology classes. He learned his lessons well and also became fluent in Latin. This oddity later saved his life many times, and helped save others. God works in mysterious ways.

My father used his black graduation robe from rabbinical seminary as his priestly garb. He became a traveling priest, carrying a special pouch with various relics and talisman. He knew how to perform the various rituals. He always had two "altar boys" to assist him, and he would pick them up here and there, wherever he found lost Jewish children. He would dress them in gentile clothes and teach them their prayers and duties, and they would travel together until he found a way to smuggle them out of the country.

This particular bus driver was one of those he'd smuggled out of hell to Israel.

Left for Dead

One day, while my father was living with me in Jerusalem, someone called and asked if Dr. Davidovics was there. When I replied, "Yes," he insisted on coming over with his wife and son. They had just flown in from Hungary and when they entered our home, the man ran excitedly to my ailing father, got on his knees, and kissed his hands.

My father's eyes became red, as they do when he cries tearlessly — the closest he ever got to crying. Years earlier, my father had found this orphaned boy, neglected and frightened on the street. He took him in, washed him, fed him, dressed him, and got him new gentile identity papers. Then he took him to a Christian orphanage where he was cared for by nuns. My father told him: "Do as you are told, but never forget who you are. One day you will again live as a Jew."

And so it was.

Ironically, this same priestly disguise almost cost my father his life. On one of his many trips to the concentration camps, as he forced himself to walk quickly past the human skeletons that were his people, he was seen by a neighbor from Danilev. The man was so overcome with joy that he yelled out, "Shammai! Shammai!"

My father tried desperately to signal him to stop, but it was too late.

Seeing they had been fooled, the Nazi guards turned on my father. He was tortured and beaten and finally left for dead. His body was thrown onto a pile of other bodies, but through some miracle he managed to crawl away from that hell and live. He had marks all over his legs for the rest of his life, and sometimes he would get headaches where they had beaten him. But he never complained.

The smell of burning human flesh came back to haunt him, and he lived with these horrors for the rest of his life. Yet my father had done all he could to reverse the evil. His message echoes in my ears today: Do whatever it takes to help make a difference — even if the results don't always reflect that effort. For not everything is in our hands.

SARA YOHEVED RIGLER

Heroes: A True Story

Anne was an abused child. When she grew up, she did what many abused kids inexplicably do: She married a man who turned out to be an abuser. When she realized the scope of the damage her husband was inflicting, Anne took their three children and fled.

Life has not been easy for Anne. Although she is a college graduate, she cannot use her diploma since she is in hiding under an assumed name. She supports her children by cleaning houses and taking in ironing.

Money is scarce. Half her meager monthly income goes to pay psychotherapists for her children. The kids, especially the boys, are aggressive, belligerent, and rebellious. They feel they got a raw deal in life. Since their father is not around, they blame their mother. It doesn't help that she has no money to buy them the things that other kids have, not even treats. The oldest, 14-year-old Nate, was caught stealing candy at the local supermarket.

A strong, strapping boy, Nate often gets into fights with the neighborhood kids and with his younger siblings. Verbal sparring matches between Nate and his 12-year-old brother Donny sound

---

See biography of SARA YOHEVED RIGLER, page 17.

like a dialogue out of *Who's Afraid of Virginia Woolf?*

Like many people who were abused by their fathers, Anne has a hard time forging a relationship with God. Since moving to a Jewish neighborhood and living among religious people whose lifestyle she admires, Anne has set new goals for her family. They now keep Shabbat and kashrut, and the children go to religious schools. As much as she appreciates the beauty of Judaism, however, Anne has a host of gripes against God.

"I don't blame Him for the marriage," she says. "I went into that with my eyes open. But why did God have to give me such monsters for parents? And why, even now, does He have to make my life so difficult?"

Anne suffers from a battery of minor health problems. Frequently, she must choose between buying a new pair of shoes for one of the kids or paying the electric bill. The telephone company recently disconnected her phone. "It's easier to live without a phone than without electricity," she explains to me. "My kids are afraid of the dark."

Last Friday, Anne called me. (Someone lent her money to pay her phone bill.) "I'm about to have a nervous breakdown," she told me grimly. "On top of everything else, my iron broke. How does God expect me to earn money without an iron? And I can't afford a new one."

On Saturday night, after Shabbat, I phoned Anne with the good news that a neighbor of mine had an extra iron that she was willing to give her. Anne informed me that over Shabbat the plumbing in the upstairs bathroom had broken down. She had no money to call a plumber.

"I just wish God would lighten up on me," Anne sighed.

I didn't know what to say. She certainly does have a difficult life, I thought. I tried desperately to summon up a spiritual perspective which would lift her out of her depression.

"God does give you a lot of challenges," I said finally. "But who knows? Even all the stuff you suffer — the broken iron, the broken plumbing — maybe it's God's mercy, instead of giving you something worse like..."

Here I faltered. What could be worse than all the hardships she has endured?

Nothing Changes; Everything Changes

The next morning, Sunday, Nate needed to go to the nearest big city. He stood at the entrance of their small town in order to hitch a ride. A white Mitsubishi with three women he knew stopped to pick him up. Nate got in the car and asked them where in the city they were headed.

When they told him, Nate had second thoughts. He didn't really have money for bus fare in the city. Maybe he should wait for a different ride which would take him closer to his destination. On the other hand, maybe not. For a split second, he vacillated. Then Nate thanked the three women and got out of the car.

Five minutes later, the father of one of Nate's friends picked him up. They had traveled no more than a few minutes down the highway when the traffic stopped dead. Nate got out of the car to see what the trouble was.

He saw the road splattered with blood. Then he saw a hand lying on the road. Then a foot. Horrified, his eyes moved to the two vehicles which had collided: a bus and the white Mitsubishi, now crushed like a discarded tin can.

All three women were dead.

As soon as Nate reached the city, he called his mother. His voice was shaking. "I was in the car," he repeated over and over again. "Five minutes before the accident, I was in the car. I'm not even sure why I got out." Anne could not remember the last time she heard Nate crying.

When Anne called me a few hours later, she was still trembling so hard I felt like the telephone wires were shaking. "Do you realize how close he came to being killed?" she asked me, trying desperately to convey how her son had been miraculously plucked out of the doomed vehicle just in the nick of time.

She had one pressing question for me: "How do I thank God?"

Nothing had changed. Anne still had no money, no good job prospects, poor health, broken plumbing, and three scarred kids.

But suddenly, in the split second that it takes two vehicles to collide on the highway, everything had changed. Her eldest son was alive.

She felt like a woman blessed beyond words.

Giving Back to God

The accident was Sunday. On Monday evening, while Anne was washing dishes in the kitchen, her eight-year-old daughter came running in. "Mom, there's a flood."

Anne rushed upstairs to see two inches of water covering the entire upstairs floor, gushing out from under the bathroom door where Donny had gone to take a bath. All she could think of was the electronic game always sitting, plugged in, on the floor of her sons' bedroom. Yelling to her daughter to stay downstairs, she ran to the bedroom. Water covered the floor except for the corner where the game lay.

Next she ran to the bathroom. Flinging open the door, she saw Donny floating face down in the tub. Her heart stopped. She grabbed his body and yanked him out of the tub. Donny burst into laughter. He had been playing dead. He had not noticed the bathtub overflowing.

Anne took a deep breath and surveyed the damage. They were in the process of moving to a smaller apartment; packed suitcases and boxes lay all over the floor of the hallway and bedrooms. Now everything was soaked. She would have to unpack, hang up every item of clothing, every sheet and blanket, and throw away what could not be salvaged.

She returned to the bathroom and motioned Donny to come to her. Donny knew that look on his mother's face, that look of tension, of being so overwhelmed that she lost control. People often parent the way they were parented. Donny put his hand over his face and flinched.

Then something miraculous happened. More miraculous than Nate getting out of the car. More miraculous than the water not reaching the electronic game. Instead of slapping her son, Anne cradled his face in her two hands and said, "I'm really upset about all the work you caused me, and all the ruined stuff. But you're my child, and I love you no matter what you do." And she bent down and kissed his forehead.

All she could think was: "Thank God my children are alive."

Momentous Actions

That very same night, Nate was rehearsing for a school play. During the break, one of the teachers gave Nate money to go to the pizza parlor and buy pizza for all the performers.

Nate was chosen to go because he had a spiffy new bike. His aunt had sent him 250 dollars for a super-duper bike, a bar mitzvah present that was a year late, because it had taken her that long to save the money. Nate had purchased the bike, the only truly wonderful object he owned, two weeks before. Because there was no money left over to buy a lock, Nate never left the bike unattended.

That Monday night, Nate took the bike into the pizza parlor with him. A gang of kids, a year younger than Nate, was hanging out there. Nate knew them. A couple months before he had helped these same kids drag a load of wood up a hill. He had seen them struggling, and because he was bigger, he had helped them.

When Nate turned to order the pizzas, the kids grabbed his bike, took it outside, and slammed it against a wall so hard they demolished the bike. Nate came running outside after them to find his precious bike a mangled carcass.

Nate's first thought was: "How could they do this to me? I helped them!"

His second thought was: "I want to kill them."

His third thought was: "I promised my mother I won't fight or swear anymore."

His fourth thought was: "Violence doesn't help. Even if I cream them, it won't bring my bike back."

Then Nate did something so momentous that its effect will be felt for generations: Nate refrained from beating up the boys who had destroyed his bike. In so overcoming his past and his tendency toward violence, Nate picked up a machete made of his aspiration to become a better person and, with one mighty blow, severed a chain of violence which stretched back generations.

The Talmud says: "Who is a hero? He who overcomes his own self."

Nate left the pizza parlor dragging the remains of his new bike. If I were a filmmaker, I would shoot the scene in slow motion, like the climax of *Chariots of Fire*, when the Olympic runner breaks through the finish line. I would play a score of triumphant music in the background, with lots of trumpets. I would have fireworks going off in the night sky above Nate and his mangled bike.

And that's probably how it looked in the higher worlds. But in this physical world, there was simply a tearful boy dragging home the mangled mess that had once been his most prized possession.

That day, when Anne foreswore violence and kissed her child in the soaking bathtub...and when Nate kept his cool with the bike...the world changed. Anne and Nate had conquered their own selves, their own demons. They are the true heroes of our time.

SARAH SHAPIRO

A Handicapped Look at Disability

I was on 72nd Street, peering into the window of what had once been a kosher restaurant, when a stranger in a motorized wheelchair pulled up alongside and greeted me. "Hello? Can I help you?"

A woman was smiling up at me, and I recalled having vaguely noticed a hatted lady in a wheelchair coming toward me on the sidewalk. Later on it would come back to me: how instinctively I had averted my eyes from Miriam. After all, aren't we taught from an early age not to stare at cripples? Isn't it embarrassing to face somebody like that, whose misfortunes are that much greater than your own?

I didn't know, then, how this woman was going to turn my notion of misfortune inside out; I didn't know that if insights

SARAH SHAPIRO lives with her family in Jerusalem. She is the author of *Growing With My Children: A Jewish Mother's Diary* (Targum Press); *Don't You Know It's a Perfect World? and other essays* (Targum/Feldheim); and *A Gift Passed Along: A Woman Looks at the World Around Her* (ArtScroll). She is the editor of the series of anthologies of Jewish women's writing entitled *Our Lives* (Targum), and *Of Home and Heart* (ArtScroll).

acquired suddenly would only stay put, I could have rid myself in one evening of misconceptions that have crippled me over a lifetime.

I answered Miriam's question, saying that I was looking for the restaurant Famous Dairy. She told me it had gone out of business years ago, and then added, "Do you have a place for dinner tonight?" I explained that I was visiting Manhattan by myself. It was late Friday afternoon, and Shabbat would start in a few hours.

"We live right around the corner," she said. "Come to us!"

A Shabbat to Remember

That night, upon entering what seemed at first sight a small, cramped apartment, I wondered how Miriam and her family could live with so many papers and books stacked all around.

Later on I would learn that the muscle-function of Miriam's hands, arms, and lungs had been so drastically diminished by polio at the age of three that she can't afford to spend her limited physical strength and energy on unnecessary, demanding activities such as putting away what she'll soon need to take out again. She's a writer, and her husband, Daniel, has been blind from birth. The house is organized mostly for purposes of access.

As Miriam prepared the Shabbat candles, our conversation turned to what we'd each been doing that afternoon. Suffice it to say that my own afternoon is long forgotten. Hers, however, I do recall.

Forgoing the expense of a taxi for a trip downtown to do an errand, Miriam had opted to go by bus. For some unknown reason, however, the bus driver had to pull over in the middle of his route, whereupon he announced that another driver would arrive shortly to take his place. Those passengers who so desired could get transfers and disembark.

The bus emptied out. Miriam — for whom a brief wait was preferable to the trouble of getting off and on again in her wheelchair — asked if she could stay and await the second driver.

A few minutes turned into 30. She was alone on board. The doors were closed on that hot September day. The mechanism on the door for lowering wheelchairs to the street had to await the second driver's arrival.

I wanted to ask how she had endured the frustration, the exasperation, the stifling air, the imprisonment. I wanted to ask if she'd had anything to read. But I couldn't ask — I was still pretending to be blind, and sought to conceal my astonishment, as well as some other emotion, like dread or fear, that I still can't identify.

If she had seethed at the unfairness, the inconvenience, the boredom, and the waste of her precious time, if she'd felt maddeningly trapped, if she'd gotten desperate at her helplessness, and infuriated by people's negligence, she didn't say.

She had endured the wait, apparently, without banging on the windows and shattering them, without screaming for help, without going out of her mind.

Ninety minutes later, the second driver arrived and the bus continued on.

Making It Despite the Odds

It emerged in conversation that Daniel directs a municipal program that teaches disabled people how to use public transportation, and that Miriam's articles are published with some regularity in women's magazines such as *McCall's* and *Family Circle*.

Ten years earlier, doctors had told them that due to problems unrelated to either of their disabilities, having children would be impossible. Some of the doctors had advised that, in any case, child-raising would have been out of the question for them.

A woman who can only stand, precariously balanced, for a few minutes at a time — such a woman, they informed her, can't responsibly consider bringing children into the world. A woman who has to spend a fair amount of time lying down, to regularly recoup her strength, and whose atrophied hands and arms can't handle the usual maternal duties — such a woman would be unwise to insist on motherhood.

Daniel and Miriam have two children, a boy age five and a girl, seven. These children's demeanor quickly aroused some self-doubts about my own mothering.

I found myself summoning up the image of my own children at that age, trying to remember if they had been equally happy and uninhibited. These two definitely seemed more whimsical and more grounded than most, yet at the same time, perceptive and responsible beyond their years. I leaned over to murmur a comment to that effect to Miriam.

"That's a stereotyped image people have of the children of handicapped people," Miriam replied gently. "People think that the children of disabled people are in some ways deprived of their childhoods," she said, "by having to be helpful more than is considered normal."

I was embarrassed. Here I'd thought she'd be flattered, and instead, I'd come out with a familiar cliché. Suddenly I got my first inkling, without being able to yet articulate it, of a strange dichotomy in my reaction to all this. On one hand, there was my horror at these severe disabilities, and some odd need to ignore them. On the other, a tendency to perceive their difficulty as something enviably meaningful.

Unusually Well-Adjusted Children

We didn't know each other yet, so I was reluctant to press the point. But I did inquire how she could deny that her children were unusually mature for their age, and yet obviously not deprived of childhood, either. "Isn't it so," I asked, "that when you want them to understand something, or obey you, you have to converse with them instead of just forcing them to comply? Maybe that's the difference, that on account of that, they're more developed intellectually and emotionally?"

"True," she conceded. "I can't go across the room, grab them, and march them off to the bedroom. I have to rely on words."

Her husband spoke to the children attentively in a low, measured voice, as well, and the pleasure he was taking in them was palpable, even when he was issuing reprimands. He seemed constantly buoyed by amusement at their antics, astute remarks, and irrepressible liveliness.

A thought kept eating away at me: I consider myself a loving parent, and know that my children would agree. But was my appreciation for the sheer fact of their existence as palpable as the parental affection bestowed upon these two?

Precisely on account of his limitations, Daniel has to tune in completely to everything they say with the most focused manner of alertness. Whereas so much of the time, the world draws me away.

I suspect now that had I expressed a comment such as this, Daniel might have retorted wryly that like most of us, he's just on his best parental behavior when guests are around.

As the hours went by that Friday night, it became apparent that Miriam and Daniel, functioning together, approximated — as far as practical needs are concerned — two sighted, mobile parents. Nonetheless, to my mind, their parenting was greater than the sum of its parts.

Taking Nothing for Granted

What do those children learn by having a mother and father for whom each trivial deed is a challenge, minute by minute, parents who are compelled to negotiate all of life's mundane demands less with physical agility than with ingenuity and willpower, parents who can't easily afford the luxury of losing patience over life's stumbling blocks?

Equipped as I am, thank God, with a normal body that takes me unthinkingly and quickly here, there, and everywhere, that has me running in and out of the kitchen 20 times during any meal — how often is my attention undivided?

As for their marriage, I imagined that Daniel's never having seen his wife only enhanced his consciousness of the nuances of meaning contained in her voice.

Wouldn't any woman like that kind of attention paid to her words?

I was getting jealous, jealous of these people who I had initially assumed were lacking so much. They were lacking, it couldn't be denied, much that Western culture regards as essential to happiness. But two things they had cultivated in abundance —

love, and the belief that all events have their source in God.

Months later, I would tell Miriam that this is what I'd been thinking about that first night of our acquaintance. She smiled indulgently, saying that they and their children experience the clashes and conflicts of any family.

"All right," I replied. "If you insist."

An Extraordinary Environment of Love

But to my mind, there was no denying the extraordinary environment of love prevailing in their home, one that must have arisen and grown out of the family members' ultra-high level of mutual sensitivity.

Miriam would say that such idealization of their lives is the flip side of pity. Either perspective is condescending. Daniel would say that I'm viewing their disabilities as some sort of poetic metaphor. He would much prefer they be viewed as people whose disabilities are in no way their primary characteristics.

And I would say that on account of fear, and the embarrassed awkwardness about not knowing how to react, and out of a guilty sense of privilege about being sighted and mobile, most people are bound to perceive Miriam and Daniel first and foremost, at least at the outset, through the lens of disability.

By the Shabbat candlelight around their table, as the children listened to their parents' harmonizing voices so keenly and subtly attuned one to the other, it seemed to me indisputable that that boy and girl could not help but absorb two truths I would most wish my own children to carry out of childhood:

1) that love can transcend physical limitations, and

2) that to the extent we identify with our eternal and intangible selves — our Divine images — to that extent are we human, and truly living our lives.

A few years ago I read an article about a writer, now deceased, who had lost the use of both legs in an accident; he had stopped to help a stranded motorist and had gotten hit by a passing car. In the article, this line was quoted: "Quads [quadriplegics] want to be paras [paraplegics.] Paras want to be normals. And normals want to be Jane Fonda."

How thorough is our faith in bodily wholeness! How desperately we channel the human soul's natural drive to develop, to reach greatness, into the quest for physical perfection!

Miriam, from age three, had no choice but to develop a self-image based on something other than her external self, derived from something other than the imagined reflections of her face in other people's eyes. In her and her husband's home, where the physical level of existence could so easily exert a tyrannical grip over their lives, there's no better alternative than to rise above it.

A Spiritual Triumph over the Physical

Months later, I finally dared to share with Miriam some of my real questions. It was the first time I've ever been able to ask anyone what it's like to be severely disabled.

"Maybe you've had to extinguish so much of your egotistical self," I suggested tentatively, "in order to get along in the world — that's why your singing voice is so beautiful." I paused, scared that once again she'd think I wasn't seeing her realistically.

"Don't think," she said, "that my spirit always triumphs over the physical."

"But always having to depend on people for help," I continued, afraid of saying something ridiculous, "and the constant insult of having people look at you as some sort of separate species of human being...having to endure that humiliation..." I could sense her waiting indulgently. "So what remains of your personality is sort of like purified water."

She took this in for a moment. "Purified water?" There was a pause. "Sarah, please, I'm not an angel. I'm as egotistical as anyone."

I felt curiously relieved. Maybe she wasn't so different from me, after all.

And yet...

Miriam doesn't hear her own voice as she sings at their table in the flickering candlelight. In an apartment that at first had seemed small and cramped, she herself is neither.

Together these two have built a basically joyous existence for themselves, even though for Miriam taking a breath is hard and sitting up is hard, as is standing, talking on the phone, getting into the elevator, and in and out of bed. And brushing her teeth, and picking up a fork. And typing on her computer, and getting to the synagogue on Shabbat morning. And even though for Daniel, the world is sheathed in what the rest of us can only imagine as darkness.

Sometimes nowadays, when I'm in the midst of one of my own life's various difficulties, I try to think of Miriam and Daniel. Is the hardship I'm experiencing overwhelming? This is my chance to acquire some of the nobility and dignity they developed.

What We Lack Builds Us

My husband once told me that one of the daily blessings recited in the morning prayers, "Blessed are You Who has provided me with all my needs," can be interpreted as follows: Thank you for providing me with all that I need — in other words, with all that I lack. For it's through dealing with what I don't have that I'm compelled to become the person I'm meant to be.

May we appreciate, and put to use, whatever pains are sent our way, and thereby give our atrophied spiritual limbs their necessary exercise.

Would I ever trade places with Miriam? Never, not willingly. I'd choose a normally functioning body over enlightenment any day.

But at least let me accept one of this world's basic truths: Life comes with hardships. None of us is exempt, and it's the limitations that can make us fly.

DR. RICK HODES
Introduction by Gail Schiller

On the Brink in Ethiopia

As rebel armies surrounded Addis Ababa in 1991, more than 14,000 Ethiopian Jews were rescued and flown to Israel. Dr. Rick Hodes was there in Addis Ababa to pull Jews out of the hospitals and treat those who were ill, so that they too could be part of the largest civilian airlift in history.

When 1 million Rwandan refugees fled to neighboring Zaire, Tanzania, and Burundi to escape genocide and a vicious civil war between Hutu and Tutsi tribes in the mid-'90s, Rick Hodes was there to help save hundreds, if not thousands, of refugees dying from a cholera epidemic.

And when the Serbian government carried out a systematic campaign of murder, persecution, and mass deportation of Kosovo's ethnic Albanian population in 1999, Rick Hodes was

DR. RICK HODES, originally from New York, has lived the past ten years in Addis Ababa, where he is responsible for the health care of thousands of Ethiopians.

GAIL SCHILLER is a free-lance writer and mother of five living in Los Angeles. She worked as a correspondent and editor for Reuters News Agency in its Jerusalem, New York, and Los Angeles bureaus for ten years. She has also written for *People Magazine* and *Newsday*.

there yet again to treat thousands of people who had fled to Albania seeking refuge.

A 40-something doctor from Long Island, New York, Hodes is very far from home and the luxurious lifestyle he could have chosen as a U.S. doctor trained at the prestigious Johns Hopkins University hospitals in Baltimore.

Since 1990, Hodes, an observant Jew, has lived and worked in Ethiopia on behalf of the American Jewish Joint Distribution Committee (JDC), the overseas arm of the Jewish Federations, where he is in charge of providing health care for all Jews seeking to immigrate to Israel. He also works as a volunteer doctor at an Addis Ababa clinic that treats the country's sickest and most destitute patients.

Hodes' life, both professional and personal, seem to be based on one overriding principle: using whatever resources he has — his medical training, his own money, his modest Ethiopian home, his free time, even his own blood — to help those in need.

That principle came into play in 1990 when Hodes read about the medical problems of the Ethiopian Jews who were stuck in Addis Ababa. Hodes had taught medicine at Addis Ababa University from 1985 to 1988 as a Fulbright Fellow, and thought he might be able to help since he spoke Amharic and knew many of the doctors in Ethiopia.

He was initially hired for six weeks to oversee the medical care of 25,000 Jews who were migrating en masse to Addis Ababa from the Ethiopian city of Gondar. But over a decade later, Hodes is still living and working in Ethiopia where he has supervised treatment of tens of thousands of people.

Hodes is known in Ethiopia as Museh, Amharic for his Hebrew name Moshe. He lives in a three-bedroom stone cottage in Addis Ababa that usually has no gas for cooking and at times has no electricity or running water. He keeps jerry cans of water on hand so he can brush his teeth, and usually swims one to two kilometers a day at a local pool in lieu of a shower.

The only observant white Jew in Ethiopia, Hodes first became interested in Judaism while teaching at Addis Ababa University in the mid 1980s when he heard weekly discussions on the BBC about the Torah portion of the week.

On Shabbat, Hodes has guests over for a dinner of Ethiopian vegetarian food. Because they have no kosher wine, Hodes boils raisins to make raisin juice for kiddush and says the *Hamotzi* blessing over the local barley bread. Among his regular guests are a Jewish demographer from Washington D.C. and his Ethiopian daughter, a graduate student who lives in a dirt-floor hovel nearby, and a Jewish Rastafarian who believes that former Ethiopian emperor Haile Selassie is the Messiah (but who is happy to join Hodes' family for Shabbat dinner). Frequently, observant travelers to Ethiopia contact Hodes and join him for Shabbat as well.

On top of it all, Hodes has also adopted eight indigent Ethiopian children as his own, and provides for their every need.

In His Own Words

For several weeks now, I've spent most of my evenings surrounded by dying kids. I work in Addis Ababa, at Black Lion Hospital, a model of modern Ethiopian medicine.

When a new doctor from America came to visit, we drove out to see the hospital. As we drove by, we saw beggars at the roadside sitting quietly with extended hands. Some had leprosy and were missing fingers, some were mothers with babies at their breasts, some were ex-soldiers who had lost a limb or two.

"Most Ethiopians are poor, and walk great distances," I explained. "My gardener walks an hour from his home to mine to save the 12 cents taxi fare. Peasants walk to bring produce to market, followed by two or three donkeys. Women trek along, carrying huge loads of eucalyptus branches on their backs for firewood. Wealthier people also walk, but they carry umbrellas to protect themselves from the sun."

After a half-mile, we turned into the hospital compound. The hospital is an eight-story, 600-bed edifice, which includes the Addis Ababa University Medical and Nursing Schools, and the National Medical Library.

When we walked in, I saw Mesfin, a former student of mine who is now a resident in pediatrics. "Mesfin, how's your night going?" I asked.

"Okay," he replied. "Two admissions, and many sick kids to consult on. We have no empty beds, so we put them in this tiny room off the emergency room." He walked down the hall, which served as the waiting room, and opened a door to what could have been a large, unventilated, walk-in closet. It held eight children, each with a parent.

"Here we have two pneumonias, two meningitis, I think this one has TB," Mesfin said, pointing to a five-year-old boy coughing, "and the other two have diarrhea. I don't know about this one," he said, pointing to a six-year-old girl.

There was clearly camaraderie among the parents in the room, who chatted informally with each other, sharing their food and miseries. "How long have you been here?" I asked the mother of a boy with meningitis. "*Amist kan*, five days," she said without any sign of frustration.

Pediatric Emergency Room

We headed to the main pediatric emergency room, about the size of my living room, perhaps 25 by 30 feet. There were 20 to 30 sick babies and children lying on wooden benches. Ethiopians fear blowing winds, so windows are always closed. Pneumonia and tuberculosis are common here, and the stagnant air makes the hospital a breeding-ground for disease.

I thought that after nearly a decade as a doctor in Africa I had seen "everything," but now I saw a four-year-old girl whose eyeballs had literally popped out of her head. They were extruding from what appeared to be underlying masses, grossly infected and filled with pus. I asked the duty doctor what was going on. "She is a young Gurageh girl who came in from the countryside with retinoblastoma," he said. I had seen this rare eye tumor as a medical student in India, but never so far advanced. Her father wore a Moslem head covering and sat on a chair, holding her hand and praying quietly. Her mother dozed on the floor.

We briefly looked at the other patients: dehydrated babies with diarrhea and shaved heads, attached to IV lines running into scalp veins, infants with pneumonia and meningitis, and young children with high fevers.

The Ethiopian tolerance for suffering constantly amazes me. Without frustration or complaint, Ethiopians sit with quiet dignity for hours in hot, dirty hospital rooms, only to receive far from optimum care. I turned to my colleague and explained that this was a typical evening in the emergency ward. He shook his head in disbelief.

A Hospital in Disrepair

We stepped out of the pediatric emergency room and walked down a long corridor into the hospital's inpatient section. "Can we take the elevator?" my colleague asked. "We're at 7,500-foot altitude and I'm new in the country."

"Impossible," Mesfin replied. "As you can see, there are three elevators, but usually one or two are broken. By elevator it would take us ten minutes to get upstairs." We slowly climbed to the 7th floor.

As we walked, Mesfin described the hospital's situation. "Outpatient clinics are always crowded. You pay 2 birr (about 32 cents U.S.) to open a file, and then you're seen by a doctor. Patients begin showing up at 4 A.M., hoping to be seen the same day. Follow-up cases are charged 5 birr (about 80 cents) per month."

Mesfin continued, "People often wait for weeks to be admitted into the hospital. A friend who needed orthopedic surgery went to Black Lion every afternoon for five weeks until he was admitted. Once he got a bed he waited ten days for his operation... There are three classes of care here: a first-class, private room costs 30 birr per day (about $4.75); a second-class, two-bed room costs 11 birr ($1.75); and a bed on a ward with 8 to 16 other people costs 2.2 birr, or about 35 cents U.S.

A Boy Fighting for Life

We walked into a ward — all poor people. A nurse immediately spotted me and called me over. "You're a cardiologist," she said.

"You'll be interested in Bewoket. He tells us he walked from Gojjam Province, about 300 kilometers away."

She led us into a room with nine beds, each occupied by a child. The nurse pointed to her right. "This is Bewoket." I saw a boy of about 12, wearing a torn hospital gown and a cross upon his chest. He was sitting straight up, attached to a tall oxygen cylinder, breathing rapidly.

There are no facemasks for oxygen delivery, so a piece of used IV tubing is attached to the oxygen valve on one end, and the other end is taped into a nostril. He was in obvious distress, and appeared to be chronically ill.

"He has rheumatic heart disease," she explained. "I don't know which valves are involved, but he has very bad valves...and a very bad x-ray."

She reached over and took the x-ray from its rusting metal bedside stand. I held it up to the light and saw that his heart was taking up at least 75 percent of his chest, while the upper normal limit is about half. This child was clearly in severe heart failure.

"How long has he been ill?" I asked.

"Five or six years," the nurse replied. "He was hospitalized a few times in Gojjam and it helped a lot, but this time he got sick and his family decided he should just stay home and die. He tells us he walked to Addis Ababa instead."

I found it difficult to believe that a boy who could barely sit up in bed had walked 300 kilometers to the capital.

I borrowed a stethoscope and briefly listened to his heart and lungs. "As I see it," I said, "the problem is all in the mitral valve." From my exam, it was obvious that he needed aggressive treatment.

I checked his bedside chart. He was getting a variety of tablets: digoxin (which strengthens contraction of the heart and slows it), quinidine (to correct the abnormal heart rhythm), lasix (diuretic or water pill to get rid of excess fluid), and antacids.

"He is on the wrong drugs at the wrong doses and the wrong method of administration," I told my colleague. "Patients like this have poor absorption. See his edema? It's probably like that inside as well. If you're going to get the excess fluid out, you have to give the lasix into the vein. His doctors are afraid of overdosing him, so they're keeping him on a low-dose of oral lasix. He should be urinating heavily, but now he's so overloaded with fluid that he has to sit bolt-upright in bed just to breathe.

"And why is he on quinidine? In a new case of atrial fibrillation, quinidine may convert a person back to normal sinus rhythm. But he's probably been fibrillating for a couple of years; he'll never convert."

"Doctor," the nurse said, "why don't you send him to America for surgery?"

"It's far too late," I said. "His heart has so much damage at this point that he would be at extremely high risk for surgery. If he did survive surgery, he'd still have a very limited life span. The only thing that will help at this point is a transplant. And that's impossible — he's not American, and he has no money. We have to be realistic. In the best case, he'll be stabilized, discharged, and live for a couple of years. Worst case — he'll die very soon."

His suffering is my suffering, too. It is painful for me to look into his eyes. I grieve, not so much because he will die young, but because he's been robbed of the life he had while still alive. He had few joys to balance his sorrows.

I held his hand and we sat together quietly. I wiped a tear from his eye and then from my own, and simply said *"Aizo,"* an all-purpose word meaning "Be brave; do not fear." I was speaking to myself as well as to him.

Saving One Small Child

I checked back at the hospital daily. I was able to sit with Bewoket and get a more complete history. I learned that he is from a poor family in rural Gojjam. His father is a farmer. He complained that he had little to eat at home and that he was forced to pay for his own school fees. But he had completed third grade.

His heart condition was the result of rheumatic fever, which itself is due to infection with the bacteria streptococcus, "strep throat." He had been hospitalized a few times in Gojjam. Each time he improved significantly, but when his family decided he should give up and die, he summoned all his strength and came to Addis Ababa to get treated.

He collected food that had fallen on the sides of the road, and resold it to passersby. It took him two months to save 16 birr ($2.50). He paid 2 birr to ride on the top of a truck to get to a bus station. At the bus station, he learned that the bus to Addis Ababa cost 18 birr. However, someone took pity on him and agreed to sell him a ticket for 14 birr. He rode for two days, without any food. At night he slept on the dirt floor of a "hotel" room, for which he paid his last half birr (7 cents). He arrived in Addis Ababa penniless and knowing nobody. Luckily, someone at the bus station saw him and brought him to Black Lion Hospital.

I asked to review the chart for a moment. I found an echo result, which read: "Dilated left atrium and right atrium with evidence of mitral valve disease." I then checked where the echo result had been copied into the chart. Inexplicably, it reported the opposite: "*without* evidence of mitral valve disease." His doctors were unaware of the echo's existence, as well as the discrepancy in the chart.

A few nights later Bewoket looked even worse. His neighbors reported that he was not eating anything all day, and he was breathing more rapidly. He was coughing up blood-streaked sputum, a sign of pulmonary edema, fluid in the lungs.

I was afraid he would not live through the night, so I tracked down the doctor on duty and suggested Bewoket be put on IV lasix to help his kidneys excrete the extra fluid in his body.

"But there is no IV lasix in the hospital," he replied.

"Give me 15 minutes," I said. I ran to my car and drove a few blocks to the International Medicine Shop, a high-priced private pharmacy that tends to have a better supply than other pharmacies. I bought ten doses for 10 dollars, and drove back to the hospital. "I recommend 40 mg IV right now," I told the duty doctor.

"40 mg?" he said doubtfully.

"I'm sure that's what he needs," I said. "Minimum. If it doesn't work, I'd go up to 60 mg."

"Okay, for now one dose of 40."

I thought how in the American system, a consultant physician is treated with respect and their recommendations usually followed; here I felt like a peasant trespassing on the nobleman's territory.

And here sat 12-year-old Bewoket, hundreds of kilometers from his family, being cared for in a filthy hospital by overworked and under-supervised physicians.

Turning Point

I felt that Bewoket needed much more aggressive care, and I asked the nurse to encourage his doctors to give him more lasix.

This proved to be a turning point, and every day after that Bewoket was at least slightly better. His appetite improved. I visited him daily. This was the high point of his day. As I walked in, someone would say in a loud voice, "Bewoket, your father is here." I'd walk over and shake his hand, then place my hand on his shoulder. I'd ask about his health, and then do something to try to make him laugh and lift his spirits.

There are a couple of things that can make these kids laugh. Ethiopians have only one given name; the concept of a family name does not exist here. To their names they add their father's given name, and their grandfather's given name. (In the Ethiopian system, my name would be Richard Elliot Philip.) I ask Bewoket his name, to which he answers, "Bewoket."

"Bewoket who?" I ask.

"Bewoket Sintayehu," adding his father's name.

"Sintayehu who?"

"Sintayehu Abebe," he responds. At some point, often after six or seven generations of names, he will respond, "Alawkum," which means "I do not know" in Amharic.

"Alawkum who?" I ask, as if Alawkum is simply another name.

Another thing I ask kids is: "How many belly buttons do you have today?" When they say, "One," I answer, "Oh, that's right! Ethiopians have only one."

"How about foreigners?" they ask.

I run my hand slowly across my lower abdomen and answer, "Yesterday I had three; today I have four and a half." After several days, most of the children catch on and claim to have several belly buttons themselves.

The hospital provided injera, a pancake-like bread made of a local grain, teff, and a spicy bean sauce, but Bewoket missed eating meat. Every few days I would give him 5 birr (about 80 cents) to buy roast lamb. When I did this, I'd tease him that he must use it to purchase pork or hyena meat, both strictly prohibited by Ethiopian Christians who follow the dietary laws of the Torah. The room would erupt with laughter at the suggestion.

On my way out, I'd always gently "slap him five," and have him slap me in return. Then I'd briefly pray for his recovery.

Mother Teresa's Mission

I had to leave the country for a month, and upon my return, I found that Bewoket had been discharged from the hospital and sent to Mother Teresa's Mission in the north of the city. I went to visit. The mission is a series of low buildings filled with handicapped, deformed, mentally retarded, ill, and dying people. Some had AIDS. They were the poorest of the poor.

Bewoket was in a room with about 30 other people. He had food. The nuns were giving him his medicine. The room was clean, with a cement floor. I listened to his heart. He had reverted back to sinus rhythm. My confident prediction that he was stuck forever in atrial fibrillation was wrong.

But Bewoket was depressed, not eating and very unhappy. He told me he missed me and wanted to live at my house. One afternoon, he escaped and ran to me at the hospital. I promptly took him home and put him to sleep on cushions on my living room floor. The following day I returned him to the mission. But we cut a deal: Once a week he could sleep at my home.

Last Friday I stopped into the mission. Bewoket was in bad shape. A nun from Slovakia said to me, "Doctor, he is in a deep depression. He will not eat anything. We are feeding him with a feeding tube once or twice a day. But he's 12 years old and weights

24 kilos (53 pounds). You made a big mistake to attach yourself to him so much. Now he feels he can't live without you."

I was not convinced I had made a mistake. I decided to take Bewoket home at once. He was too weak to step into my car, so I lifted him and placed him in the front seat. He spent the day at my house. As soon as he arrived, he was a different person. He sat up, ate, smiled, walked around a bit, and played with my dogs. I told him that if he would eat well at the mission on Sunday, he could spend Monday at my home.

Postscript

Bewoket had an amazing course. He made it out of the hospital and was living part-time at Mother Teresa's Mission and part-time with me. We used a combination of medicines to stabilize his heart. He developed active tuberculosis and was treated with 4-drug therapy and did well. He then went to near death from chronic hepatitis B (very common in Ethiopia where about 10 percent of the population are hep B carriers).

Based on a small study in the *New England Journal of Medicine*, I treated him with lamivudine, one of the AIDS drugs which was reported to have activity against hepatitis B. To our great surprise, it cured him. He went from being too weak to walk up the two small steps to my house, to being able to walk a half-mile. His liver shrunk to normal size and his liver tests normalized. Then I sent him to Atlanta where he had open-heart surgery to repair his mitral valve.

He is back in Ethiopia, living at my home, taking six drugs a day including coumadin to thin his blood. He is in third grade and walks three-quarters of a mile to school every day. He feels pretty well, but because he's on blood thinners, has to restrict his activities. This is sometimes not so easy for him, but thank God, he is doing quite well.

Yet there are many kids like Bewoket. What hope do they have? Very little. In this country, where the annual health budget is about 50 cents per person, and the prospects for controlling "strep throat" (the cause of so much heart disease) are low, it is likely that things will continue as is. Economic development, medical education, and expanded primary health care may improve things after a while. But it will be years or decades before real changes occur.

In the meantime, I'm just trying to do my part.

DARKNESS & LIGHT

NESANEL SAFRAN

Faith Healing

A t first, I thought he was a hallucination. He was a big black man, maybe 6-foot-5. He looked both ancient and futuristic in his loose-fitting, pale blue hospital fatigues. That morning after the longest sleepless night of my life, I could have been seeing anything. At first, his size and the suddenness of his appearance made me judge him as menacing. But soon it became clear that before me (or rather above me) stood a gentle man of sensitivity and simple depth.

I had been crying. My eyes were still red and teary from the marathon session of reciting Psalms and sobbing over my baby's bed, or should I say, his space capsule. He was lying there strapped-in and motionless, wired from head to toe. He was wearing only a see-through plastic loincloth where his diaper should have been. Most of the night, it was just he and I, spending a Shabbat night,

NESANEL SAFRAN graduated Brandeis University, then embarked upon a worldwide, intercultural research tour. He eventually landed in Beitar, Israel, where he currently resides with his wife and children. In addition to writing Aish.com's popular weekly column, "Family Parsha," he teaches and studies classical Hebrew and Aramaic texts of Jewish spiritually. He is presently at work on his first full-length novel.

his first on earth. He with his injured brain, and I with my broken heart.

So when I saw my visitor, I could only look up, yield, and prepare to accept whatever was to come. When he placed his giant hand on my shoulder, I didn't flinch. I was too tired to care.

"The child's going to be fine," boomed his voice like a French horn. "Man, you just gotta have faith and he's gonna be just fine."

His reassuring message seemed to lift me up, for just a moment, into a warm place — a place where light was permitted to shine again. I could only nod a wordless "thank you" as he moved down the hall with his cleaning cart, like a temple priest purifying the corridors from their terrible night, preparing them to accept the new sacrifices of the emerging day.

While I will always be grateful for his good intentions, the giant's prophetic-sounding words did not come to pass, and my son, Yisroel Nachman, was not to be fine. But for me, his brief life was my introduction into the world of faith.

Faith Is Learned the Hard Way

Although I had imagined myself as a seeker of spirituality since having begun studying Torah several years before, faith had been a topic that eluded me. I simply didn't know what to do with it.

The rise and fall of Yisroel Nachman, of blessed memory, changed all this.

I was soon to realize that the Torah view of faith is quite different from the one I grew up with. The latter was expressed by my well-meaning hospital angel-janitor, as well as countless old Jimmy Stewart movies, i.e., "If you believe strongly enough, it will happen."

Although our thoughts can and do affect our perception of the physical world, this is not faith.

The Torah view of faith, called *emunah*, has an entirely different starting point.

God, the Higher Source of all being, is in active and intimate contact with everyone and everything. His guidance is based on His knowledge and loving desire to bring about that which is in our best interest, for our ultimate good. Our faith is that — as Creator and Designer of all — He knows what is good for us... better than we do.

There were many times that I fought, at least inwardly, against this perception of faith, against the Torah that taught it, and against God. It seemed like cruel and unusual punishment to bring a person to the threshold of happiness — the happiness of holding my newborn son — and then smash a person down only a few days later in so shocking a manner. As one relative put it, "If that's what happens when you become religious, who needs it?"

Part of me wanted to agree. I had been pushed to the brink, placed at a crossroads where there was no standing still. My choice was clear: either claim my faith, or abandon it. I felt I understood a little better what is said about Holocaust survivors. They either came out with their faith strengthened or abandoned, but nobody came out from the camps the same as they went in.

Faith Is a Choice

Before me lay two paths: Either declare that life has a purpose, or it doesn't. The decision was painfully easy. I had seen too much in my life, too many miracles with my own eyes to ever claim with honesty that life was without purpose. I found myself stuck, as it were, with the conclusion that yes, life had a purpose. Yet I couldn't see a purpose for this comatose baby lying in front of me.

Wearily, reluctantly, I felt compelled to dig, claw, and scrape to try to find "meaning despite the pain." Or perhaps because of it.

Ironically, one thing that gave me strength was another tragedy I had experienced seven years earlier — my mother's untimely death after a long, painful struggle with cancer.

In retrospect, it had become crystal clear to me that the pain and confusion I had experienced then had directly resulted in my receiving a precious gift — an inner awakening that had brought me to a more spiritual perception of life, and a lifestyle much deeper and more real than I had known before. I reasoned that this present suffering must also have hidden within it a gift. But what?

I tried to let my intuition guide me. I found myself drawn, for the first time, to the many teachings of the Torah that speak of *emunah*, of faith. I was drawn to the men and women who lived it. Words of *emunah* became a balm for my aching soul. Not an anesthetic that just covers up the wound, but a true and deep inner healing — a kind of "faith-healing" that was beginning to make everything feel whole.

Strength Comes with Acceptance

I discovered a sort of patient, bittersweet acceptance and even love of life, and an inner strength that comes with the realization that we don't control reality. All we can do is respond in an elevated manner to the challenge before us.

Slowly, slowly these feelings began to take root within me. People sensed it and would comment.

There was the time when my wife and I were beside Yisroel Nachman's bed in the intensive care ward and a very prestigious neonatologist exclaimed, "I've never seen parents react to this in such a balanced way. How do you do it?" I calmly replied: "It's in God's hands. We don't know what's best."

Indeed, everything does work out for the best, and we are not left alone to wander in a random universe. We are on a "guided tour," personally tailored to direct us to our spiritual perfection, to our ultimate good. For the Jew, faith means putting forth our best effort and then accepting whatever results occur. Everything is for the best even when we don't understand why. In the World to Come, all will be revealed.

In his brief lifetime, Yisroel Nachman introduced me to this path, and for this I owe him eternal gratitude. He taught me a lesson that I still struggle to learn. Not only that in the end everything will be just fine, but despite appearances to the contrary, everything is really fine right now.

ELANA ROSENBLATT

Life Is Beautiful

About two years ago, we had an unplanned growth in our family — a large cancerous tumor. But the growth I want to talk about is how the cancer affected me emotionally and spiritually.

When I first felt the lump, I was sure that it had everything to do with nursing my baby, born six months earlier, and nothing to do with cancer.

I live in England and I was soon going to America to see my parents, so I put it to the back of my mind. When I came back, I could tell that the lump had gotten bigger. The time had come to see the doctor.

"Don't worry," he said. "If it's still there, come back in two weeks."

I came back in two weeks, and it was close to Rosh Hashana. The doctor said, "I'm sure it's nothing, but I want you to have a clear mind for the holidays, so I'm sending you to a surgeon for an evaluation."

I went to the surgeon, who sent me for a mammogram and a

ELANA ROSENBLATT passed away, tragically, on August 8, 2001 (19 Av 5761). May the soul of Elana Golda bas Yisroel Mordechai be bound in the bond of eternal life.

biopsy — again, just to be sure it was nothing. Nobody wanted to believe that a 27-year-old, new mother could have breast cancer.

So I waited.

A couple days before Yom Kippur we returned to the surgeon. We sat in his waiting room for about an hour-and-a-half — waiting and waiting and waiting. It seemed like eternity. Finally, we were called in.

He looked at me and said, "It's metastasic cancer."

It was like being struck by a bolt of lightening.

After quite a long pause, he said, "Do you think you're going to die?"

I was scared — but I said, "No." That "no" resounded through the coming months, over and over and over again.

Life Continued

Indeed, life continued. That day it was my turn to drive carpool. So my husband Shaul and I went straight from the surgeon's office to my daughter's school. We were quite late, and my carpool kids were all waiting in the principal's room.

I went in to get them, and I figured since the principal was going to have to know sooner or later, I might as well tell her now. When I told her, I saw such love and care in her eyes. She said, "Anything you need, we're here for you." She was someone I hardly knew, as it was my daughter's first year in the school, but the love that I felt from her was absolute. This was my first taste of so many things to follow.

We brought the kids home, and I dropped them off at unsuspecting friends. Now my husband and I had a chance to talk.

It was a very emotional time, and we both had a lot that we needed to say, but there was one idea that kept coming up over and over again: God does not do anything that is not perfect.

I can't prove to you that pain is good. Or even that pain can be good. But I do want to try to show you that life really is beautiful.

Our lives are a puzzle. We add the pieces of the puzzle one by one. And as we do, the picture of our lives becomes clearer. Sometimes we're not sure where to put a piece; we can't even imagine how it's going to fit. We hold it up and turn it over in our hand, and we feel sure that someone must have made a mistake — surely this piece does not belong to this puzzle.

There is no mistake. This piece belongs. As we put together this jigsaw puzzle of our lives, the pieces fit together so beautifully that the seams between the pieces seem to disappear and an awesome picture emerges.

I began to see this puzzle coming together.

Support System

Ever since I'd married and moved to England, my family had only been able to come for short visits. But one month earlier, my little sister decided to take six months off from college and come to London. Clearly, God was making my life a bit easier in this most difficult situation. Not easy, but as easy as it could possibly be.

My in-laws, who are amazing, usually come to London twice a year, for the High Holidays and for Passover. I had been diagnosed right before Yom Kippur, which meant that my in-laws were still with us.

I had a tremendous support system that normally wouldn't have been there.

Two hours before I lit Yom Kippur candles, we got a phone call. At first the doctor had been only 99 percent sure that the cancer was metastatic. Now she was 100 percent sure.

I was able to see this call also as a blessing. After all, I had found this out before Yom Kippur and still had the opportunity of Yom Kippur before me. This is the day that God is closest to us, the day we have the most special relationship with Him. I felt that my fate was not yet sealed.

Sukkot came four days later. On Sukkot we leave the sturdy walls of our home and go out into a flimsy shack. A Sukkah has rickety walls and a roof of branches; it doesn't even protect us from the elements. Sukkot is about understanding that it's God Who is our protection, not the material world. During Sukkot, I started chemotherapy. The timing could not have been better. It was so real to me that my only security was in God.

During Sukkot, a time of *simchah*, joy, the calls and e-mails —
literally hundreds — came from every continent. The love, the
care, the overwhelming concern — all that was healing in itself.

Mary Poppins Arrived

A few months earlier, right after I'd had the baby, I put out a
call for help in the house. I sent out e-mails, advertised, and called
everyone I knew. I came up with nothing. This time I put out
another urgent call, but I really didn't have much hope. I wanted
someone who would understand, both physically and spiritually,
the needs of my children. Shaul sent out an e-mail to everyone we
knew and the next day we got an email back — from someone I
don't even know so well in Toronto. She wrote, "I have a Jewish
Mary Poppins for you!" And she did.

Our new helper was a reflexologist, with a degree in nutrition,
and incredibly creative. She immediately developed a special
relationship with my children, and with the whole family. Once
again, supernatural!

This young woman had been on her way to learn in a Jerusalem
seminary. But when she heard about my situation, she decided it
was a bigger mitzvah to help me than to study Torah in Israel. You
may not believe in fairy godmothers, but I had a live-in one.

As time went on, the puzzle was making more and more sense.
But there are always pieces that don't fit right away.

There is a reason why we might have missed a train, or why we
lost the letter on the way to the mailbox. Even if we haven't figured
out the reason yet, just knowing that there is a reason is incredibly
empowering.

We human beings don't mind pain, as long as we feel it is
worthwhile. Nietzsche said that man can deal with any "what," as
long as he has a good enough "why." Let's say we're working out to
get fit. Our muscles are killing us. We're stretching to the breaking
point. But we persevere — because it means enough to us. We're on
a diet and have to say "no" to our favorite ice cream. It's painful,
but it's worth it. The "why" overcomes the "what."

This is pain that we choose. But what about a situation in

which we can't control the pain? What about when the pain is coming from the outside?

Training for the Olympics

I have a little analogy:

There are three runners whom I'll call A, B, and C. They are training for the Olympics. The Olympic trainer has A and B running ten miles a day. But he has C running 30 miles a day.

Not only does C run 30 miles a day, he also has to be up very early in the morning, follow a strict diet regimen, and lift weights two hours each day. You look at this and think, "Why is the trainer putting C through so much torture? He must really dislike C." But the trainer is not putting C through torture; the trainer knows that C has the potential to win. The trainer wants to bring that potential out into actuality. He's not so sure about A and B, but he knows that C can do it.

In *Pirkei Avot* (Ethics of Our Fathers), it says that God tested Abraham with ten tests to show how much he loved Abraham. These hardships were a gift of love. Our forefathers were spiritual giants, and yet we see that their lives were filled with trials. Murder, kidnapping, rape, famine — you name it, they endured it.

Our forefathers were God's Olympic athletes. And He wanted to make sure they won only gold medals.

Not one thing that ever happened to them was an accident. Not one thing was unnecessary — on any level whatsoever.

This is why I know that when I go for chemotherapy and it takes them six tries with a needle to find a vein, not one of those times was an unnecessary discomfort. Each jab was exactly perfect for what I needed. There are no accidents, and there is no lack of control. God is in control.

Everything is perfect. Certainly not easy, but perfect nevertheless. Beautiful.

Worry Is the Enemy

But if God is constantly making our lives beautiful, what makes life "not beautiful"?

Worry.

Worry is a personal spiritual barometer. It indicates where we're holding spiritually, personally. When I say "personally," I mean that we can't compare one person to another. One person might naturally be more of a worrier, and another person less. It doesn't mean that the one who is less of a worrier is on a higher spiritual level. But you can use your own relative degree of worry at any time in your life as a personal spiritual barometer.

When we worry about our future, we're out of touch with the reality that God is in control. We're out of touch with the reality that nothing is an accident. We're out of touch with the reality that all is exactly perfect.

Worry, not pain, is our enemy.

There are two things I do to strengthen myself.

First, I make a list of all the worries that never came true. All my worrying about things that were never actually anything to worry about was just a waste of time.

Secondly, several times a day, I go over different aspects of my special relationship with God. Sometimes I forget; some days I don't do it. But I try to remind myself several times throughout the day so that I'm one step ahead of the doubt. And one step ahead of the fear.

Prayer is part of this relationship. Will God answer my prayers the way I want them answered? I can't know. But I believe that if I remember to ask for God's help, the outcome will more likely be something easier to accept as beautiful, as opposed to something harder to accept as beautiful.

Thank God, I've been feeling well. Cancer is a very funny disease. You can have a cold and not be able to get out of bed, while you can have cancer and do just about everything.

Cancer Is Very Serious

But cancer is also very serious and sometimes, "Mommy's not feeling well." The way I look at it, though, my situation is really no different from that of anyone else. None of us knows what's around the corner. We all pray that it should be something good and easily recognizable as beautiful. But who knows what tomorrow will bring?

That's how I deal with the children. I haven't said to them, "Cancer can be fatal," although there are people on the block who have died from cancer and they know it. They have me around today, thank God, and I'm so appreciative that I can be a mother to them.

Tomorrow is another story — and it would be even if I didn't have cancer.

It's not easy. In fact, it's incredibly difficult. On one hand, I wish I was runner A or B. But at the same time, deep down, I know that runner C is the only one who will win the gold medal. The "what" of cancer pales in comparison to the "why" of the growth I am getting.

There have been moments of anger. I've never been able to come out and say, "Thank you, God, for giving me cancer." That's a tough one. I've tried to be very, very real with my anger, and not to push it back down. I've really tried to face it head-on.

And I found that when I accepted the anger and didn't let it fester, the anger became less of an enemy. The same is for fear. Sometimes I have to say, "Okay, I'm scared." But I am not going to let that fear get the better of me.

I wasn't like this three years ago. I'm two generations from the Holocaust. My grandparents lost almost their entire families in the Holocaust. For many years I was angry with God. My relationship with God was not one of love; it was one of fear. When my kids would say, "Mommy, when I'm ten..." I would think to myself, "God willing, you should live to be ten." I wasn't the most positive person. I wouldn't say these words, but I certainly thought them. I wasn't one of those people who had perfect faith that God is in control and everything will be fine.

But I've grown since then.

When I thank God for the little things, it helps me know that God is with me for the difficult things. I thank God for my food and my arms and my legs...and when I go to the hospital — though it's the last place in the world I want to be — I thank God for that, too. I know He's there with me.

My husband's rabbi taught us an exercise to do. Every Friday night, we ask the kids (as well as ourselves) to think of a serendipitous event that happened during the week. The kids come up with ideas like, "I knocked over my cup, but I'd just finished my drink," or "I didn't want to go to kindergarten yesterday, but I went and they had a birthday party, and I would have missed it." It really helps keep the family focused. And if you know you'll be asked to tell a story on Friday night, you make sure to notice during the week.

I try to take pleasure in the good instead of focusing on the bad. When I go for chemotherapy and the nurse smiles at me, I try to take pleasure in that. She could walk in with a scowl on her face and make the experience a lot worse.

It's up to us. What is our focus going to be? Worry and fear, or blessing and knowledge of perfection, even if we don't feel it?

Life Is a Train Ride

Life is like a train ride. The nice thing about this train ride is that everyone has first-class tickets. We often see many people, even ourselves, riding third class. Why is it that, if we all have first-class tickets, so many of us are riding third class?

Circumstance is never the problem. It is what we conjure up with our imagination that really hurts us. Often the physical pain and the emotional anguish, in any given situation, is relatively easy to deal with. It's the worry that torments us.

I was in remission for a while, but I have cancer again. It's not easy. There's worry, there's fear. But that's my challenge to overcome. Cancer is not a third-class ticket. Cancer is a guidebook to what first class has to offer.

I've gotten a big wake-up call, and I'm slowly waking up. Anything else is worry.

Life has so much to offer. Let's not allow worry to take away from the incredible goodness that we're blessed with. Let's not ride third class, when we all have first-class tickets — no matter what our circumstance. Life really is so beautiful. It's up to us to enjoy it.

RABBI SHAUL ROSENBLATT

Seeing the Light in Darkness

The following article was written ten
days before the author's wife passed away.

As with all good things in life, trust in God does not just happen. You don't go to bed one night feeling that God is out to get you and wake up the next day confident that you can rely on Him — no matter what you take.

If you want to trust God, it is going to take conscious effort to develop and maintain the emotion.

My wife has metastatic breast cancer. If you are *au fait* with cancer jargon, you will know that the situation is pretty bad.

At the time she was first diagnosed, I realized that I had many options. I could hide in a corner and block out the world. I could pretend to myself that everything was okay. I could accept the "inevitable" (as doctors would say) and enjoy the time we had left. Or I could develop a sense of trust in God and allow myself to feel that we are in very good hands.

The last option seemed the most appealing (and the most reasonable). So I set out to try to develop an emotion within myself that was, until that time, pretty dormant. I still have my bad

RABBI SHAUL ROSENBLATT is originally from Liverpool, England. He is the founder and executive director of Aish UK.

moments. It's not so easy to trust in God when you get bad news after bad news after bad news. Not so easy, but equally not impossible. My pain is usually short-lived and I can quickly reactivate a confidence that God is here with me and I have nothing to fear. Each new development brings with it a test that I cannot be sure I will pass, but so far so good. If anything, as the situation has worsened, my trust has been growing.

I want to share with you the lessons that I learned, from a number of wise people, in terms of how to develop a feeling of trust. I guarantee that if you put in the time and energy, it works. And it's worth it. You can put your time into fitness and be rewarded with a healthy body. You can put your time into business and be rewarded with material success. Put your time into trusting in God and you will be rewarded with tranquility of heart and mind for eternity.

Two Prerequisites

So how do we do it?

Let's begin with two prerequisites.

First, trust is a feeling. You can intellectualize all you want, but if you don't "feel" confident that someone will catch you at the bottom, you aren't going to jump.

There is the old story of an atheist who falls off a 2,000-foot smooth cliff. He grabs onto the one twig 1,000 feet down. He looks up to Heaven and figures it's worth a shot.

"Is anybody up there?" he asks.

"Yes, it's Me, God," comes the response.

"Thank God for that," the atheist replies. "Please God, help me. I'll do anything."

"Of course, my son. But I have just one request to make."

"Anything, God," replies the atheist.

"I will save you, my child," says God, "but you have to trust Me first. Let go of the twig and I will catch you."

The atheist looks down at the rocks 1,000 feet below and looks up again.

"Is there anybody else up there?"

The point is clear. You can know there is a God intellectually, but that doesn't mean you will trust Him emotionally. A person can switch from being an atheist to one who knows there is a God in a moment — if he or she were to have a clear experience of God. But trusting in God is a very different matter.

Knowing God Exists

The second prerequisite is that if you want to trust God, you have to first know He exists and loves you. We have a dangerous ability to feel emotions that are intellectually unsupported and unsupportable. People can feel "love" for a person who has none of the qualities required in order to love them. It's called infatuation. People can find deep meaning in something that is utterly meaningless (Timothy McVeigh felt it was deeply meaningful to kill hundreds in Oklahoma). And people can have faith in something that, intellectually, is clearly false — the Moonies and other cults prey on this constantly.

So too, people can trust in God without being sure that He even exists. It's very possible, but dangerous and incorrect in Jewish thinking. It's dangerous because it's mindless. And wherever there is mindlessness, there is escape from Godliness. And where there is escape from Godliness, there cannot be deep-rooted trust.

Trust cannot be a crutch. It must start with the mind and spread to the emotions. Otherwise, it is a castle built on sand.

So how do we go about feeling trust in God in a seemingly dark and lonely world? How do we get in touch with the fact that there is a God, whom we can rely on, when at times He seems so distant and impersonal?

The following steps are predicated on the intellectual belief in God's existence. If you've got that, then this is how you can go about getting yourself on the road to trusting Him.

According to the 10th-century classic *Chovot HaLevavot*, (*Duties of the Heart*), there are seven elements involved in trust in God. If you feel all seven, you will feel trust. I am using an order put together by Rabbi Noach Weinberg. I will explain how I personally relate to each one in the context of my wife's illness in order to make them more practical and relatable.

1. Tell yourself that: God loves me with a love that is deeper than any parent has ever loved any child. He loves me as a unique individual. I am His special, sweet little baby.

I personally try to imagine God holding me in His arms, smiling at me, as I do with my children, enveloping me with His love.

2. God knows my every need, my every challenge, and my every problem. He knows what I feel, what I think, what concerns me, what worries me. He knows exactly what's on my mind and He knows it constantly. He doesn't forget about me, not even for a moment. Nothing slips past Him. He "thinks" about me and my problems 24/7.

He knows the location of every cancer cell in my wife's body. No rogue cell can slip by His notice and start growing on its own. He is fully aware and cognizant of all that is going on. He also knows what I am worried by. He knows exactly what I am feeling, exactly what I want. He hears every one of my prayers.

3. God has the power to do anything. There is nothing I need that He cannot provide. Nothing I am lacking that He cannot give me. He is able to solve all my problems and solve them immediately. He is able to prevent any problem arising.

He is able to take away every cancer cell instantly. He can change the whole situation around in a moment. And it's not difficult for Him to do so. My wife could jump out of bed tomorrow, free of cancer, as though nothing ever happened.

4. Nothing else has any power. There is nothing that works independent of God. Nothing, no matter how small, can or does happen without His full approval. He does not give over His power to other forces. He remains in full control at all times.

There is no cancer; there is just God. There is no chemotherapy; there is just God. Cancer cells do not grow by themselves; God makes them grow. And there is not a single one that can grow without God's express desire for it to do so. God and cancer are not adversaries. They are partners.

5. God has done so much for me until now. He has given me life. He has given me free will. He makes my heart beat. He makes the blood run through my body. He gives me air to breathe, food to eat. He provides warmth. You name it, He has done it. He has a track record of complete and utter goodness. Anything I need or want is like asking my father for a dime to make a phone call. I have no doubt that He will give it to me because He has already given me so much. Anything I could possibly want is so small compared to His goodness to me so far.

Taking the cancer away is nothing compared to making my heart constantly pump just enough oxygen to my brain for the past 35 years. And He did that without my even asking.

6. God's love is unconditional. It is not dependent on my actions or my way of life. Like a good parent, He loves me no matter what. Even when I stumble and make a big mistake, He still loves me. Even when I completely ignore Him, He still loves me. His love is with me no matter who I am or what I do. Despite all my imperfections, I can feel secure that God is backing me.

God would like me to be great. His expectations for me are massive — because of what I can accomplish with the soul He has given me. Nevertheless, I could waste it all and He might still make my wife better, just because He loves me.

7. Like any good parent, God will always give me just what I need. Life will not always be exactly what I want it to be. He might not give me what I think will be good for me. But He will always give me what is really good for me. No matter what I am going through, it is exactly what I need to be going through.

Whatever God might have in store for me, the road this illness is taking us down is a road we need to traverse. And wherever that road might lead, its destination is where we need to be.

For me, this final point creates the greatest sense of trust and security. No matter what I am going through — no matter how "bad" or painful it may seem — I know that it is for my ultimate good.

Try feeling each of these elements a number of times a day.

Don't spend too much time on each one — you may find it frustrating. Taking one minute to focus on these points a few times a day will make a significant impact.

Working on feeling these seven elements has been very powerful for me. It has brought a tremendous sense of security into my life. Spending a few minutes a day is a small price to pay for the dividends that can be reaped from developing trust.

I am praying for my wife's recovery. Only God knows what will be. But there is one thing I do know. God is giving us, and will give us, just what we need.

RABBI NOAH WEINBERG

The Madness

September 12, 2001 — The entire civilized world stands in shock at the terrible tragedy that has struck American targets.

We mourn for those lost and pray for the recovery of the injured.

The enormity is staggering. The pain and grief is indescribable. So many lives, so many families shattered forever. To put this into perspective, terrorists in America killed ten times more civilians — in one day — than have been killed by all the terrorism in Israel over the past 30 years. How fragile is our existence. How quickly our lives can turn to turmoil.

With Rosh Hashana upon us, we search for understanding amidst this senseless horror.

Fighting for a Cause

Our precious world is threatened by twisted minds who think the way to heaven is to murder innocent civilians.

RABBI NOAH WEINBERG is the dean and founder of Aish HaTorah International. Over the last 40 years, his visionary educational programs have brought hundreds of thousands of Jews closer to their heritage.

We have only one chance to live a normal life. We have to look this evil in the eye and defeat it. Not passively and sluggishly. But with the same degree of passion, and the same level of commitment, that the evil is being waged against us.

Every human being has a personal responsibility to fight this epidemic.

Concretize your feelings about the World Trade Center tragedy. Say out loud: What did I learn from this? What I am going to do about it? And if I'm not going to do anything about it, why not?

Pledge yourself to fighting for good, for justice, for truth. Look around and see the problems facing us today. Ultimately, we are each committed to a cause. Whether it's world peace, political reform, or fighting racism — everyone is dedicated to something.

In some sick, misguided way, even the terrorists are fighting for their cause.

Choose your cause. Carefully. Figure out what you are willing to die for. And when you indeed live for that cause, you will have unparalleled power and purpose.

Once you have answers, make a plan to implement positive change into your daily life. Start slowly, taking one small step at a time, so not to be overwhelmed. Keep your eye on the goal and gauge your progress every day.

Life on Track

On Rosh Hashana, two books are opened in the heavenly court: the Book of Life and the Book of Death. Every moment of existence we are choosing one or the other: awareness or numbness. Clarity or doubt. Reality or illusion.

Each moment can be lived to the fullest — or wasted into nothingness.

Imagine what you could accomplish if you were clearly focused on the goal. You're not even scratching the surface.

My friends, we have the power. Don't underestimate yourself. Stop looking at who you are. Instead, look at who you can be. You can solve humanity's problems, instead of just suffering with them. You can build the entire world.

The time to begin is now. Rosh Hashana is upon us, the day of judgment, when we're asked to justify our own existence. To articulate why we should be granted another year of life.

The prophet says: *Kiru levav'chem, v'al big'deichem* — "Tear your hearts and not your clothes" (Joel 2:13). Don't wait for another catastrophe. When you see the first indication, pay attention. If you're sick in bed, imagine being carried to your funeral. Don't wait until the funeral to regret everything you "could have done."

We've had wake-up calls before. In the 1993 World Trade Center bombing, a 50-foot difference would have produced disastrous results. Then bombs were discovered that would have blown up the Lincoln Tunnel. Then armed gunmen were ready to slaughter hundreds in Times Square.

We all have a clock ticking and don't know how long it's going to run. How many years do you figure you have left? Life is not open-ended. Someday you will have only one year left. And someday you will have only one day left. Plan for it now. This week, the shofar is blowing. The World Trade Center is our wake-up call.

RABBI YAAKOV SALOMON

The Day After

Septembereptember 12, 2001 — Can you write a song without music? Can you construct a house without concrete, wood, and steel? Can you build a relationship without feelings?

And can you write an article without words?

Today is forever to be known as "The Day After..." and my soul compels me to write about yesterday. But it isn't easy without words. The words, you see, have not yet been created to properly depict events and emotions that no one dreamed he would ever see or feel.

And yet, millions around the world listen to media analysts, scan the radio waves, read the tabloids, and surf the web... searching, exploring, desperately hunting for the description that will connect with their sentiment or soothe their pain.

Which nouns and adjectives do you relate to?

"Shock?" "Devastation?" "Senseless?" "Unspeakable?"

Does "horrifying" suffice, or would "ghastly" come closer to home?

Perhaps the prophet Jeremiah, in his epic requiem, Lamentations, said it best. In lamenting the fall of the Jews and

See biography of RABBI YAAKOV SALOMON, page 63.

Jerusalem over 2,400 years ago, he used the simple word, "Alas!" It is more of an utterance than a word. It is a cry. A wail. A guttural expression that goes beyond the limits of any finite definition. Real words just don't capture what has happened to our world. Alas.

Personal Action

There are those whose intense pain may lead them to the feeling that speaking about action, in the wake of immeasurable grief and bereavement, may be insensitive or even disrespectful. I can understand that, but I cannot agree. "Response" is not a contradiction to loss. It is its evolvement.

In truth, if ever there were a time when the saying "actions speak louder than words" was appropriate, this would seem to be it.

Certainly the actions of the heroes in the ongoing Herculean rescue effort, speak volumes about the value of human life...and death. And certainly the actions of the thousands who waited in lines for hours to donate blood, speak clearly about caring for others. And certainly the military response that must surely follow, will speak loudly about the lessons that need to be learned and taught.

But cataclysmic events also call for actions of a different strain. Actions of a very personal nature.

I'm not alone in feeling numb, while I struggle and contemplate what it is I could possibly do now. Despite my full realization that language is inadequate to encapsulate the enormity of this calamitous nightmare, I find I am no different from most. I too scour the articles and websites in my own frantic pursuit of some literary balm. The journey is fruitless, yet fixating at the same time. I suppose this is all part of the "healing process," as they taught us in graduate school.

But one observation emerges. After all the pundits have concluded their conjecturing and meandering, they seem to land on the same finish line — more or less. No matter how you size up the particulars, they say, one conclusion is clear: "Our lives will never be the same again."

And then something strange happens. The more I read it, the less I understand it! "Our lives will never be the same again."

What does that mean? Is it something positive or negative? Are they referring to a state of fear and chronic insecurity, or to a dazed impetus toward resolution and self-improvement?

Sound the Alarm

Shocking events of mammoth proportion contain within them colossal potential for serious contemplation. Nothing gets you moving faster than the rage of a five-alarm fire! Which is probably why God sends one in the first place!

But the real shock is what happens afterwards — after the blaze is doused, the smoke has cleared, and the embers cease to smolder. More often than not, the fire is gone. Daily life resumes — as well it should. But when it does, it often extinguishes the inspiration and passion that could have brought about real and lasting changes. What seemed so important just a few days ago suddenly appears trivial, grueling, or just out of reach. The event, so traumatic and packed with vitality, actually fades into the permanent recycle bin. The "wake-up" button becomes the "snooze" button.

Yes, there are exceptions — plenty of them. But most of us somehow fall prey to the clutches of complacency. The promises fade and the perseverance all but vanishes. We forget...we deny...we rationalize — and sadly, we stay the same.

There are no magical ways to avoid this plunge into neutral gear. The conviction necessary to forge ahead must come from within. Only a relentless surge of zeal and enthusiasm can forestall the avalanche of resignation. It takes real muscle to remain steadfast in your new resolve. It also helps to start as close to the event as possible. Sometimes a great start can give you the momentum you need.

I can't tell you the specifics of what these days of apocalypse should catapult you to do. The action we each need to take is very personal. Only you know, deep down, the changes you need to make.

I can tell you one thing. No matter how dreadful and alarming the current situation may seem, even a catastrophe as virulent as this one is subject to the very same perils of complacency.

The analysts are wrong. The tragedy today is not that "Our lives will never be the same again." The tragedy is that, in all likelihood, our lives will actually be very much the same again.

You know what to do.

Do it now. You may never get the chance again.

Alas.

SHERRI MANDELL

Thanksgiving Blessings

On Thanksgiving we are supposed to give thanks.

But what does it mean to give thanks?

It means being grateful for what you have and not dwelling on what you don't have.

It means being humble enough to accept what we are given.

When my kids were babies, I was grateful to have survived another day. It was so much work taking care of little kids. They wore me out so much that sometimes I would put them in the car just to drive around and get them to sleep.

Now I am also grateful to have survived another day. But it is because I live with pain as my companion.

When my 13-year-old son Koby was suddenly killed, stoned to death by Arab terrorists, I was sure my blessings were over. But life always surprises you. During the week of *shiva*, a woman I know who has ten children came to me and said: "Your son blessed you in life and he will continue to bless you."

SHERRI MANDELL is the author of *Writers of the Holocaust*. She made aliyah five years ago and lives in Tekoa. She and her husband are founders of The Koby Mandell Foundation, dedicated to creating and funding programs that help children and families struck by tragedy or trauma heal their emotional wounds and improve their quality of life.

Her 18-year-old brother had died as a soldier in the Yom Kippur War. She told me that her mother had suffered, but had also received gifts from her brother's death. I didn't know what she was talking about, but I wanted to believe her.

And now, now that my son has been dead almost five months, I am beginning to understand what she meant.

I am forced to reconsider the whole notion of blessing. If the Torah tells us we are blessed, what does it mean for me? When Isaac blessed his children, "His eyes were dim so he could not see." We are also supposed to close our eyes when we bless our children. The reason: We are supposed to see our children as whole, to overlook their faults, not to see anything wrong with them.

The Lazy Prince

Blessing doesn't mean that we get what we want. It can mean letting go of what we think we want, so that we can recognize the gifts we are given.

Discovering blessing starts with accepting imperfection, both our own and others'.

Since Koby was my oldest child, my battle with imperfection usually rested on his shoulders. I found it much easier to accept the other kids, but much more difficult to accept him totally because he was more of a challenge in many ways.

For example, Koby could choose to be magnificently lazy, like a prince. He never felt rushed or hurried. The moment was so precious to him that he didn't want to risk spoiling it with chores or studying.

He wasn't always lazy, though. Once I came home and found that he had cleaned out a year's worth of caked-on ice from the freezer. He would take care of his younger brother whenever I asked him. He would run to go pick up a pizza. He could skate miles on his roller blades.

He chose when he wanted to move.

Not easy for a mother to handle.

Getting ready for holidays was especially frustrating. To get him to help was very difficult. I would get angry at him, especially when I saw all the neighbor children helping like little worker ants.

And then I would get even more upset, because I felt his laziness showed me as an inadequate mother.

And in fact, now that I think about it, the reason he upset me so much is because I too am lazy, in just the same ways he was lazy.

A Full Life

But now, as we get ready for Shabbat and holidays and I don't have Koby to yell at to help, I realize: Just when the pain of missing him is a constant knife to my heart, his laziness is a gift to me. Because as we go through the holidays, I can't think, "If only Koby were here to help us." Because I know that he would be lazing in his bed eating chips and salsa and I would be yelling at him.

What I perceived to be my son Koby's faults have turned out to actually be attributes. What irked me so has been transformed into a blessing.

Mind you if he were to come back, alive and well, and tell me: "I went for a walk. I'm not really dead," I would serve him like a king for a couple of days, maybe months, or even a year. And then, I would still work on getting him to help us. But I wouldn't feel angry about it.

Because now I see his laziness in a different light. I recognize something I wasn't ready to see before: There was also a positive part of his unwillingness to get up and work with me.

I could have learned some things from him: how to be in the moment; how not to care what other people think; how to enjoy life; how to relax.

In short, I could have accepted his nature more. I could have been grateful that I had a kid whose biggest problem was what I perceived as a messy room.

Now the fact that he didn't help, helps me. Because it forces me to remember him as a real person. I cannot romanticize him or put him on a pedestal.

Miraculously, I have begun to understand how we should bless the bad as we bless the good. What used to drive me crazy seems so trivial now, so meaningless.

And I wonder, will I also one day be able to accept my life, a life without my eldest beloved son?

I already see glimmers that I will learn to accept the life that I've been given, to be able to bless it, to put my hands on my life and close my eyes and see it in all its wholeness.

This article originally appeared in The Forward.

ROSS HIRSCHMANN

Reality Knocks

I'm cruising in my car on the streets of L.A. It's six o'clock. I'm off work. I turn on the radio. It's an "all-'80s evening." Perfect. Thomas Dolby is singing how she blinded him with science. Great tune. All's well with the world. I'm happy. Now it's time to go help the poor and unfortunate. Time to deliver food to needy Jews for Tomchei Shabbos. Time to be a hero. I turn up the radio and smile as I head down La Brea. I'm feeling pretty good about myself.

I arrive a few minutes late. No problem. Heroes can be a little late. I load up my car with the boxes to be delivered. Man, these people consume a lot of food! The car is packed to the brim. I get my list. Four addresses. No problem. I can handle that. Be done within an hour. Just in time to tune into Vin Scully's golden voice and listen to the Dodger broadcast on the way home. But first I've got to get rid of all this food. First, I got to be a hero.

First stop: an apartment on a small street. You'd think it could've been better marked, for heaven's sake! Drove past it once

---

ROSS HIRSCHMANN graduated from UCLA and earned his law degree from the University of California Hastings College of the Law in San Francisco. He currently works in the field of pharmaceutical sales, and lives in the Los Angeles Aish community with his wife and two daughters.

already. I park and exit the car. This should be easy. Grab the box, ring the bell, drop off the food, get a big "Thank you," and then I'm off to be a hero somewhere else.

But God has other plans for me this night.

I walk up to the door, whistling as I go, and ring the bell. No answer. Great! Easier than I thought! I'll just leave the box by the door. This hero stuff is a cinch! Then a voice, "Just a minute! I'm coming, but I don't move so fast!" I peer in the side window. An older lady with a walker moves methodically and with great difficulty to the door. I stop whistling. She opens the door and musters a big smile. "Please come in!"

I enter and look around. The apartment is old and messy. She doesn't have much in the way of possessions. And it's hard for her to stand. "Could you put the boxes on the table for me, please? It's hard for me to lift things."

I am stunned by her and the whole scene. Not what I expected. The reality of her life situation hits me like a punch in the stomach. I am barely able to reply. "Of course. No problem," I somehow mutter.

As I place the boxes of food on the worn, weathered table strewn with newspapers, mail, and other unknown documents, I notice photos on the wall. They are old, all in black and white. They are of a handsome young man and his wife. The couple is nicely dressed, circa 1960. They look happy with big smiles. I wonder who they are.

"Who are these pictures of?" I ask gently.

"Oh," she says, gaining a sparkle in her eyes, "that's me and my late husband. He was the love of my life! We were married only six years. Then he died suddenly in 1962. I've been alone ever since."

She still smiles at me. But how? Alone since 1962? Losing the love of your life after only six short years of marriage? How can she smile?

"Do you have any children?" I ask.

"No," she says, looking down for the first time. "But he sure was something else, my husband. Swept me off my feet!" She's smiling again.

I don't know what to do, but I want to do something for this poor lady whose Camelot came to an unexpectedly quick end. "Is there anything else I can do for you, ma'am?" is the only thing I can muster.

"Oh, please!" she says. "You've done so much already! Thank you so much! And may God bless you with a long and happy life filled with love and many children!"

Tears now well up in my eyes. She is blessing me? She who lost so much and lives so alone still has it in her to bless others. At that moment, I realize she is one of the most remarkable women I have ever met. "Amen," I say to her blessing. "And may God bless you, too."

As I turn to leave, she says joyfully, "Have a good Shabbos!"

I turn back and manage a smile. "Thank you. And good Shabbos to you, too."

The Lucky Ones

The rest of the evening is no less painful and just as poignant. A woman bedridden by cancer, getting chemotherapy at home. She has no family and is painfully lonely. As I prepare to leave, she too blesses me. As I leave her small apartment, I turn back to see her turn away and quietly sob.

After that, a man who can no longer make ends meet, yet has too much dignity to feel comfortable accepting charity. He stands proud in the doorway as I deliver his food. And of course he blesses me, too. They all bless me.

I am driving home at night on the streets of L.A. It's 8:30 P.M. I have just made my last delivery for Tomchei Shabbos. I stare out the windshield lost in thought. The radio is not blaring, and Thomas Dolby is not singing about how she blinded him with science. I am not singing, either. Instead I am thinking about how I was blinded by reality.

But mostly I am thinking about how I am no hero at all — not even a little bit. Those people who I met tonight have endured and continue to endure hardships, and still have it in them to bless me. They are the real heroes.

Me? I'm just another one of God's kids, no better, no worse. But now a little more humble after tonight. I am one of the lucky ones. I am in good health, my Camelot of my wife and two beautiful daughters is still going, thank God. And I can still make ends meet.

I am also lucky because God let me meet these people, learn from them, and in some small way help them. God bless each and every one of them.

Cancer's Gift

My wife always struggled with the concept of suffering. It really bothered her. She just could not reconcile the Holocaust and other tragedies with the concept of God being a loving father. She even said at times that she felt angry with God for making people go through such pain and hardship.

Then she was diagnosed with cancer and all her anger went away. Almost immediately, she began to feel that God loved her very deeply. It was quite amazing.

We were both shocked at this response. Neither of us understood how it worked. How can it be that you are upset that God makes people go through pain, and then when He makes you go through pain you suddenly feel that He loves you? The response seems to be a complete non sequitur.

We asked my teacher, Rabbi Noah Weinberg, and he gave an explanation that made a lot of sense to both of us.

He said that we often get so caught up in the pettiness of life that we don't allow ourselves to appreciate God's love for us. We get frustrated that the car won't start, that we're not earning enough money, that our relationship with our spouse is not that of

See biography of RABBI SHAUL ROSENBLATT, page 143.

Prince Charming and Sleeping Beauty, that there's nothing decent to watch on TV tonight...

We get caught up in petty, silly things, and by so doing we make our world petty. It's hard to feel excited by a petty world, so we get frustrated with God that life is not exactly how we want it to be. We feel that life is too difficult and challenging. There is too much pain, suffering, and tragedy. So we get upset, even angry, with God.

Then you are diagnosed with cancer and suddenly life is not so petty anymore. Life is very heavy. Mortality stares you right in the eye and you realize that life is truly something special. You don't want to die. You want to live. It's a wonderful world and it's very much worth living for. The pettiness goes and the value of life is suddenly plain to see. And who cares if it's challenging? Who cares if it's difficult and painful? Who cares if it has its share of sadness and tragedy? It's worth it. Life itself is so good that it's worth it all.

That's on a macro level, but it happened to us on a micro level also. Six months before my wife became ill, we had our fourth child. The last two were born within 20 months of each other, so we had two babies. It was really hard for us. The challenge of four young children, including two babies, really wore us down. We never thought to limit the number of children, but suddenly the thought of having more was very imposing. Did we really want to go through the challenge of five, then six...? We had a conversation about it and we both felt the same way.

And then Elana was diagnosed with cancer.

It became pretty clear from the outset that, even if she survived, we wouldn't have any more children. Then gradually our attitude changed. We desperately wanted more. Each child was so precious. Each one so special. Each one of such infinite value. We had been so caught up in the pettiness of what a hassle it was to change a diaper that we had lost track of what an incredible blessing children are.

Sometimes we need shocks to shake us out of our pettiness. And when we awake from our pettiness, we begin to appreciate just how incredible life is.

On the holiday of Sukkot, we move out of our homes into a little shack for an entire week. We move away from the material world, the petty and silly world that so easily distracts us from what we know to be important.

Sukkot is called the holiday of joy. We move away from our pettiness for a few days in order to understand and experience true joy. Yes, if we can lift out of our self-imposed smallness, we can appreciate just how much God loves us, and feel the joy that life has to offer, every moment of the year.

MIRIAM LUXENBERG

Pulling the Plug

What does one do when the smallest flame of human life, a baby, is snuffed out?

I'm not the first person on earth to lose a baby. In times past, a mother could lose her entire brood to sickness, plague, frostbite, or starvation. Death was part of living, and while it wasn't less painful, it seemed more inevitable, and bearable somehow.

Nowadays, with advanced medicine and high standard of living, we have pushed death to the outer reaches of our consciousness and are absolutely shocked when it comes roaring in.

Losing a baby is a heart-rending experience. When our first baby was three days old, he simply stopped breathing in his crib. The paramedics were able to resuscitate his heart, but his brain was long gone. He lay in a coma for five months, and died alone in a hospital in a city far away.

Many painful issues arose in the face of this trial. One of the

MIRIAM LUXENBERG was born in New York City and attended the Bronx High School of Science and Hunter College. She now lives with her family in Israel.

most vexing centered around the doctors' consternation as to why we were not "pulling the plug." They thought we were out of our minds for putting ourselves through such suffering.

Part of me agreed with them wholeheartedly. Nothing in my tender existence had prepared me for such gut-wrenching pain. As our baby lay still, day after day, week after week, I thought I would go mad. No one held out hope, and I felt like a drowning person gasping for air. A baby's entire essence is permeated with hope and potential. When that hope is extinguished, it's like the roof being blown off the house. You can't have hope without a chance for life. It just doesn't work.

Moral or Not?

As time ticked by, the doctors became more persistent about our moral and ethical obligation to "relieve" his and our suffering. This moral dilemma became one of the foremost sources of pain and uncertainty. We were haunted by the thought that we may be somehow acting cruelly by allowing our baby to live, and perhaps suffer needlessly. Yet on the other hand, to "play God" and decree an end to our child's life was too heavy to handle.

For a while we simply stalled for time, hoping against hope for a miracle to heal our son and put an abrupt end to the entire matter.

To the doctors it seemed a simple matter. The right thing to do was to pull the plug. But as my husband said after one particular grueling encounter, "This guy is ten years younger than me and probably took one short course on ethics in med school. Does that make him an authority on what's moral or not?"

We felt that the answer might lay in the Torah. We had become more Jewishly involved and had found the timeless wisdom of Torah to be an invaluable guide in many difficult situations. But this was literally life and death.

Our rabbi deeply empathized with our plight. He assured us that the Torah did indeed offer clear guidance on the subject, but humbly admitted that the answer was beyond his expertise. He gave us the name of a rabbi in New York who was an acknowledged expert in these questions. "If there is anyone in the world who can guide you through this, it is him," our rabbi assured.

That evening, my husband nervously dialed the number we had been given. I heard him describe the whole situation, going into great medical detail, prompted by the rabbi's thorough questioning. Fifteen minutes later my husband hung up the phone with a look of relief and certainty on his face that I hadn't seen since our whole ordeal had begun. He looked at me and said, "Miri, it's clear. As long as the situation remains as it is, the right thing to do is not to pull the plug."

As he repeated to me the rabbi's rationale and other details, it became clear that this rabbi was medically knowledgeable and sophisticated. That put me at ease. But what stood out the most and inspires me to this day is the way he viewed my baby's life with such depth and sensitivity. He explained that whether we could see it or not, every drop of life has value and purpose in God's vast cosmic plan, and we had no more of an ethical license to end it than we have to end any other "normal" life.

The dignity with which he related to our baby's life brought tears to my eyes, and cut a sharp contrast to the often indifferent and disposable attitude we had encountered from many of the doctors. I felt so grateful that we hadn't bowed under the hospital's pressure to pull the plug. And I realized that it wasn't going to be easy to keep going, but at least we had a clear direction. And I felt strangely calm and resolved knowing that we had a 3,500-year ethical tradition backing up our decision.

When the time came to transfer our baby to a long-term care facility, the doctors, sensing our clarity, pulled us aside one last time. "We've never seen anything like this. We've never seen parents in your situation keep their baby alive, and conduct themselves with such dignity. How do you do it?"

We tried to discuss with them briefly our ideas about faith and belief in a power greater than ourselves. (Luckily they didn't see me screaming into my pillow every night.)

Shining Souls

Our baby died naturally, soon after we transferred him. We had moved him to an out-of-town facility because the hospital where he had been needed the bed space, and we had not yet relocated to the city where he was. We received a phone call in the middle of the night, a hasty funeral was arranged, and I assumed this chapter in our lives had come to a sad but definitive end.

What I didn't realize, however, was that while my baby had left the world, a part of his soul remained attached to mine, very much like when we had been physically attached. He never left me. Even though we buried him, I could not forget him.

Every experience I faced afterward included him. Every door I opened admitted him. Every pain or suffering I felt was compared to him and left wanting. In a sense, I became both more vulnerable and more insensitive. Losing a child is like losing a limb that will never grow back, and yet you continually sense its presence long after it's gone. You learn how to function without it, yet life is never the same.

As the years passed and our family grew, I was surprised to find my pain increasing rather than decreasing. As the children got bigger, and I grew so fond and attached to them, I appreciated more what I lost when my precious firstborn left the world. I hadn't realized what having a child meant or what being a parent entailed. It was all theory.

Now, with these beautiful, shining souls blossoming before me like a wild poppy field run amok, I was shocked again by my loss. Every milestone left me thrilled and drained at the same time, as I experienced everything twice: once for the live child before me, and once for the potential child that was not meant to be.

I worried more than the other mothers. I never left a child unattended for even a moment and devoted myself completely to the task at hand of mothering.

And yet, I also found myself subject to a curious detachment. "Wait a minute," I told myself. "These little guys could come and go." I sensed at any moment they could be snatched away, and I didn't want to get too close. I never had that easy, almost careless rapport some mothers have with their kids because, for me, there was just too much at stake.

Anchor in the Storm

I try to imagine what my life would have been like if I had to face it without the knowledge that God was watching over me every moment and orchestrating the symphony that is my life down to its last detail. What would there have been to hold on to? Who would have been there to guide us?

Looking back, it does seem rather amazing that we were able to withstand such pressure. So much was at stake: the baby's life, our lives, our parents, our new marriage. Everything was hinged and teetering. The doctors and social workers made it clear to us that our marriage could easily fall apart, as many do in this situation. But Jews don't fall apart so easily.

I can clearly see in retrospect that the decision to follow the Torah's guidance was a major turning point — an anchor to get us through the storm. I saw how the sensitive yet unequivocal stance of Jewish law saved a precious marriage that could have easily collapsed beneath the weight of an unbearable burden. And I discovered that Jewish law — halacha, which literally means "the path" — doesn't merely stop at the pages of the legal codes. It extends itself deep into the human heart.

Knowing we were following this path gave us the strength to withstand our test, thank God.

THE INNER STRUGGLE

SARA YOHEVED RIGLER

It's So Hard!

For 45 years Rebbetzin Devorah Cohen lived in a house with only an earthen floor, without running hot water, and without a bathtub or shower. During those years, she raised numerous handicapped and retarded children whose parents had abandoned them on her doorstep.

"It must have been hard," I remarked, sitting across the table from her for another of the interviews I subjected her to for the sake of the book I'm writing about her.

"No, it wasn't hard," she replied simply.

"Of course it was hard," I insisted. "At one point you had seven handicapped children you were taking care of, all by yourself, when your husband was away half the year. It must have been very hard."

She shook her head. "It wasn't hard," she repeated.

I was annoyed. The rebbetzin had this maddening habit of turning my reality upside down. I wasn't going to let her get away with it this time.

"You had to cook for them, bathe them by heating up water on the stove, change their diapers before there were disposable

See biography of SARA YOHEVED RIGLER, page 17.

diapers, even change the diapers of grown children, keep them from hurting themselves and each other..."

"And do the laundry," she chimed in.

"Yes — the laundry! How could it not have been hard?" I asked petulantly.

"For meals I would just take a big pot, fill it with vegetables or chicken or noodles, and cook it up," she chuckled. "It wasn't hard."

Aha! I had done my research, and now I had her. "Isn't it true," I asked like a wily lawyer, "that Hindele, who lived with you for 14 years, had to be spoon-fed? It wasn't just a matter of cooking up the stew and calling, 'Come and get it!' You had to sit and spoon-feed her."

"Yes, I spoon-fed her," Rebbetzin Devorah admitted.

I continued my cross-examination. "Were there other children who had to be spoon-fed?"

By now her face was shining and she was smiling broadly as she remembered those years. "Yes," she replied simply.

Checkmate! "You had to feed seven handicapped children, and spoon-feed more than one of them. Then it must have been hard!" I proclaimed triumphantly.

"No," she shook her head, and repeated, not insistently, just matter-of-factly: "It wasn't hard."

I left her house in a state of total cognitive dissonance. "How could it not have been hard?" I asked Rebbetzin Tzipporah Heller, my occasional companion for these interviews.

She thought about it for a minute and replied: "Imagine an athlete, like a tennis player playing his fourth match of the day. The sweat is pouring out of him, he is working every muscle to capacity, he's almost out of breath. But he would describe it as exhilarating rather than hard, because he appreciates that all this effort is his way of actualizing his maximum potential as an athlete. For Rebbetzin Devorah, spoon-feeding and changing the diapers of adult children was exhilarating, because it stretched her full capacity as a human being. Didn't you see the light pouring out of her face as she remembered it all?"

Labor and Ease

We live in a society that values ease. It started with the sensible (and blessed) "labor-saving devices." Why go through the back-breaking labor of washing sheets and towels by hand if you could use a washing machine?

No one quite noticed when the "labor" we were so determined to save gradually became any movement of any muscle which took more than half a minute. Today no one even questions spending millions of dollars in R&D to develop a "better" product whose only advantage over the previous version is that it saves a few flicks of the index finger.

Who hasn't rejected a worthwhile undertaking only because it was hard? When I was a psych major in college, I expected to go on to graduate school and become a clinical psychologist. Sometime during my sophomore year, I discovered that a prerequisite for grad school in psychology was the deadly Statistics 301. As I, Ms. Unmathematical, listened to horror stories of the difficulty of statistics, I cowered. Finally, standing in line for course registration for the final semester of my senior year, I decided that I didn't really want to become a psychologist anyway. I registered for 17th-Century English Religious Poetry in the statistics time slot, and breathed a sigh of relief. My fear of tackling statistics changed the course of my life.

The mantra "it's so hard" can be heard everywhere. Some people choose not to have children because they are daunted by the prospect of the 24-hour workday. Some people who would love to start their own company cop out because of the major effort required. Some people walk away from the opportunity to help others in significant, life-changing ways, not because they can't afford the time or the money, but because they can't envision themselves crossing the comfort divide.

Rabbi Shimon Green taught me that it's a mistake to think that great people do great things. In truth, people who do great things become great people.

No wonder I couldn't understand what Rebbetzin Devorah

was talking about. When faced with an undertaking, my inner question is: How hard is it? Her inner question is: Does God want this of me? That's why I see her life as full of hardships, while she sees her life as full of opportunities. For her, it's like winning the grand prize of 30 minutes in the supermarket with all you can grab for free. She would run down the aisles, reach for the top shelves, bend for the low shelves, and work up a sweat moving as fast as she could. And not for a moment think it was hard.

And that's why, at age 76, light shines from her face brighter than any gilded medieval picture of a saint with a halo.

Le Chambon

Some years ago I saw a documentary about a whole village that stepped into Rebbitzen Devorah's mentality.

During World War II, in a French village named Le Chambon, the Huguenot inhabitants decided to save Jews. For the duration of the Holocaust, they hid 5,000 Jewish children, more than the entire population of the village. In other words, an average family of six took in seven Jewish children and "hosted" them for a period of five years.

Let's leave aside the issue of the tremendous heroism that these French villagers exhibited. Some people are capable of the great heroic act in a given moment. But think about the effort required to pull this off. The day in and day out effort of feeding, clothing, bathing, and caring for these Jewish children that had to be sustained for five long years. Think about the laundry that number of "guests" generates, when undoubtedly not one family in Le Chambon owned a washing machine. How many of the children would wake up the whole household for nights on end with nightmares of their final parting from their parents? How many childhood diseases needed to be nursed? How many psychological traumas borne? Think about the fear of being found out and annihilated that they had to wrestle with daily.

One of the Jewish children who was saved made a documentary film about Le Chambon. Bill Moyers interviewed the filmmaker and asked him how did this entire village muster the resolve to do what they did, and to keep doing it for such a prolonged period?

His penetrating answer is etched in my memory:

"The villagers of Le Chambon understood that effort does not deplete a person. It completes a person."

RABBI CHAIM LEVINE

Mud on the Soul

*I*t's 9:15 A.M. You're more than a little late. The traffic is thick and you're still a long way from the office. The driver in front of you stops to speak to a pedestrian. You watch as they chat away. You wait another 20 seconds. You tap your horn lightly. The driver turns to give you a dirty look.

That's it. You fly into a rage, slamming your horn and yelling. You consider ramming him from behind, and calculate the projectile. You start grabbing and searching for a sharp object to throw. People are watching and you don't care. Then the pedestrian turns and looks at you quizzically. You notice he has a dog. It is a seeing-eye dog. You stop honking your horn.

You have just had another encounter with your ego.

Your ego, referred to in Hebrew as *yetzer hara*, is the self-centered, immediate-gratification-at-any-cost, destructive part of your personality.

RABBI CHAIM LEVINE, a former high school wrestling champion and rugby player, attended Macalester College in St. Paul, Minnesota, where he studied anthropology and philosophy before coming to Aish HaTorah in 1989. In 1995 he received rabbinical ordination in Jerusalem and is presently the executive director of Aish Seattle.

The mystical sources say the *yetzer hara* covers your essence like mud on a windshield. It's given to you at birth and dies along with the body. In the interim, it wreaks havoc. It speaks to you in the first person, saying things like:

- "If the other guy gets more honor and recognition than me, I'll die!"
- "I don't really have to prepare for the meeting, maybe I'll just catch a movie."
- "Just one more piece of double-chocolate cheesecake and that will be it."

The ego has no compassion for others, and it's always there when you are stressed out, angry, or upset. When you look back at all the stupid, rash decisions you made in life, be assured that your ego was doing the talking.

Giant Mirage

The job of the ego is to make problems seem bigger than they actually are. Why? In order to challenge the soul to strengthen itself — and to make the ego disappear.

The secret of overcoming the ego is having clarity that it is only an illusion. The Torah says that the ego is like a giant holding a battle-ax, standing at the crossroads. A fool will be frightened and run for his life. The wise person looks closely, sees that the giant has no legs, and walks right past him.

That's the ego: all bark, no bite. To the degree that you recognize the ego as a giant virtual mirage, you will be able to see through the mirage and increase your life experience as a soul. If the ego is mud on the lens of the soul, then this clarity is the water that washes it away.

Soul's View of the Universe

The ego is driven by all things external. All the complexes that land you in a therapist's office come from ego thinking — fear of failure, fear of rejection, identity crisis, etc. All these fears are expressions of the ego as it tries to trick you into believing that you are defined by something outside yourself.

Pay attention to the thoughts your ego feeds you. You'll probably hear something like this:

- "Success is in your paycheck."
- "If I fail, then I am less than worthless."
- "The one with the most toys wins."
- "I'm fat and everybody knows it."
- "S/he forgot to call, and it means s/he doesn't love me."

The ego also does something more subversive, more sinister, more corrupting, and ultimately, more painful: It tries to convince you that your well-being and happiness are completely dependent on your surroundings. It tells you things like "He made me angry!" or "My job is getting me depressed." These statements make it seem like circumstances are controlling how you feel. The result? You are constantly bounced from feeling to feeling — from stressed to relaxed to depressed to happy — depending on what is happening around you.

The next time you lose a sale, blow an exam, or miss an opportunity — and then start to entertain thoughts of depression and failure — ask yourself, "Are my circumstances causing me to feel this way, or is it how I am relating to those circumstances?"

If you think circumstances are causing you to feel depressed, ask yourself why it is that others in the same boat seem to shrug off failures like water off a duck's back. How is it that some people — no matter what misfortune comes their way, or no matter what negative comments others make to them — always keep their well-being and happiness intact?

If, God forbid, you became a paraplegic, it would be reasonable to suppose that you would become seriously depressed. Yet there are paraplegics who go through life happy. Although they cannot walk or perform the simplest physical functions on their own — eating, getting dressed, washing, or sometimes even breathing — they are truly happy.

Soul-Thoughts

Does happiness depend on your circumstances? Your ego would have you think so.

You might be asking, "Wait a minute, are you telling me that all circumstances are neutral and it's only how we think about them? What about when a person gets cancer, or loses a loved one? What kind of feel-good, fluffy nonsense is this?"

Of course some circumstances are objectively difficult. But you can think soul-thoughts to gain understanding and perspective. For example, with the loss of a loved one, instead of feeling guilt, anger, and blame, the pain of loss can be accompanied with deep feelings of gratitude and understanding of the cycle of life.

The Jewish custom of "sitting *shiva*" (a seven-day mourning period after the burial) is designed to help one go through the mourning process from the perspective of the soul. For seven days, people disassociate themselves from the material and focus on appreciating the gifts the person they lost gave to those around them.

The soul understands that the only thing determining happiness is what goes on inside your head. If you fail a test, the soul understands there will be many more tests to pass and many more opportunities. When you fall, the soul softly whispers that if you dust yourself off and get right back up, you will grow nothing but stronger.

A righteous person is actually defined by the fact that he keeps getting up. As the wise King Solomon said: "A righteous person can fall seven times and rise..." (Proverbs 24:16).

Anyone who spends time with toddlers knows they have the ability to be happy no matter where they are. What is the secret of their self-esteem? They are living their natural essence, living via the soul.

Small children don't go around asking questions like "Gee, I wonder if I'm tall enough?" or "If I can't figure out how to use the potty, I'll never be successful." Children walk around happy and buoyant simply because that is their natural state of being.

Remember: You were once a small child and walked around in this state. You still have the ability to walk around smiling and you can even do it without drooling. If your ego is constantly looking for outside confirmation that you are good enough or successful enough, steer your consciousness toward your soul. Be aware of the ego's attempts to define you according to your circumstances.

When we can understand that the ego's skewed view of the world only leaves us as happy as our last success (or as depressed as our last failure), then we are sitting on top of a mountain.

Making It Real

Want to catch the ego at its illusionary game? Try these exercises:

Sit back and spend five minutes observing all the thoughts that come into your head. Notice that it is a continuous process that just keeps going.

Notice what feeling you get with each different thought. The more intense the feeling, the more real the thought seems to be.

Ask yourself at any given time: "Where is this thought coming from — my ego or my soul?" If it's from your ego, see that it is distorting reality. Choose to doubt its validity.

Notice how many times you blame circumstances for how you are feeling. What you are thinking in your head at the moment is what truly defines your experience.

Write down three things in life that are bothering you. Then think of the people you know, and ask yourself if everyone would have exactly the same reaction. Try to figure out why that is.

You have the ability to determine whether your experience is the ego just doing its thing, or a depiction of real life. Just because your thoughts and feelings appear real, doesn't mean they need to have any greater impact than a bad B movie playing in your head.

To be human is to be a chooser. Choose the clarity of your soul and experience what your life can truly be.

RABBI YITZCHAK BERKOWITZ

The Process of Change

Everyone gets inspired at one time or another to change. We look at our lives and, dissatisfied, we resolve to become great and fulfill dreams. It's a new beginning to finally do those things we've always sensed we were capable of, but never followed through.

Every resolution starts off with the same high expectations — that there will be a whole new world and things will never be quite the same again. Unfortunately, the initial enthusiasm all too often gives way to a somber reality; enthusiasm tapers off and we end up not too different from how we were before we started. Of course, we do grow slowly, year after year, but the big breakthrough — becoming the person we know we can and should be — never seems to materialize. It remains an elusive dream.

How do we take all the initial goodwill, enthusiasm, and excitement — and parlay it into significant and lasting change?

RABBI YITZCHAK BERKOWITZ is director of Aish HaTorah's rabbinic ordination program, and is the co-author of *Chofetz Chaim: Lesson a Day* (ArtScroll).

Prepatory Plowing

The Sages say there is a heavenly voice (*bat kol*) that reverberates, saying, "Plow the fields, don't plant for the thorns and weeds." There are of course many layers of Kabbalistic meaning here. But the most straightforward explanation is that if we don't properly plow a field beforehand, no matter what we plant, the garden will eventually be overrun by weeds.

Therefore, the key to a successful transformation is to properly prepare — i.e., consider what seeds we wish to plant.

How does a person "plow" himself, to ensure that everything he accepts upon himself will develop the way he wants it to — so that a few months down the road he doesn't regard the resolution as wishful thinking?

Our desire to change is clear. But what causes us to change? The key is to understand oneself ("the ground") — how we function, how we grow, and what motivates us.

Mature Changes

The story is told of a young man in the yeshiva of Rabbi Meir Chadash. He was a lazy student who never learned, did whatever he pleased, and seemed ready to drop out completely. Then one day the student did a 180-degree turnabout. He was the first one in the study hall in the morning, and the last one out.

The next day, Rabbi Chadash approached him and said, "You're so immature. When are you going to grow up already?"

The message was clear: We don't change overnight from being irresponsible and apathetic, to being the most responsible and consistent person around. And if you try, it's a fake. We may succeed for a few days, thinking we've accomplished it all, but how long can that last? That's not "growth," it's immaturity. True growth is gradual. We have to know what the next step is, understand ourselves, and be honest.

We have to decide what to accept upon ourselves that will make a difference — e.g., lighting Shabbat candles, buying kosher food, or dedication to becoming more caring and sensitive. These seeds all have tremendous potential...if we prepare the ground first.

We need to look deep inside, get good advice, and above all, be realistic about what is possible to achieve.

Realistic and Appropriate

What about the actual process of teshuva, of "spiritual return"? The first step is recognizing our mistakes — understanding what we've done wrong and how we could have done better.

To do this, we have to know our specific capabilities. Otherwise we'll make the mistake of trying to change things that are beyond us. This is insidious, because when we "regret," we don't really mean it — since deep down we always knew it was unrealistic.

True teshuva and regret means articulating the fact that at our particular level we could have done better. It's important to do this in a way that we'll hear it and believe it.

Understand what our issues are today. If they're beyond us, they're not "our" issues. Deal with what's realistic and appropriate. If we don't, we'll plant seeds year after year — and be left with nothing but weeds. Of course, don't pervert this idea as an excuse to continue making mistakes. Rather, realize that drastic change often backfires.

Don't move into a dream world. The Torah doesn't want us to be "unnaturally pious." Assess what aspect of your character is "off," and then start to change it — gradually.

Cheering You On

"Preparing the ground" means discovering what motivates us and recognizing what you have to do now. Ultimately, the final major change may be years away. But don't be discouraged. The Sages say that once we've put ourselves in a position that will get us somewhere, as far as God is concerned, we've actually arrived. Once we've sincerely resolved to do something, there's an elevation of the soul. In the metaphysical world it's considered as if it were already done. The "soul" has arrived; it's just that the "body" still has to go through a lot of steps.

One more thing. To be inspired to teshuva, we have to realize that God loves us — even in light of all the mistakes we've made. Realize that God understands us, that He's "cheering us on" and wants to help. Don't feel guilty; any mistakes we've made are part of a growth process to get where we are today.

God doesn't want us to suffer. On the contrary, if growth is what God created us for, then even the hardships involved must be the best thing for us. God is not the "big bully in the sky." He's on our side. If we don't realize this, we'll never do teshuva.

Think big and have long-term goals — but be realistic. Take things one step at a time. But keep up the momentum. True teshuva demands maturity, realism, and honesty.

CHANA HELLER

Confessions of a Worrywart

*I*f you're like me, then you wake up every morning with some anxiety. I feel it right in my stomach. It's a little knot of ten- sion, which has tremendous power to pull me into a terrible trap of worry.

I worry about a lot of things: the quality of our kids' education, my mom's health, paying the bills, whether I am doing my job well enough, sick people in the community, you name it. I just read that kids growing up in the smog-filled air of Los Angeles have only 75 percent of the lung capacity of kids growing up in healthier environments. So now I worry about that, too.

Add to these more global concerns such as the security situation in Israel and the general state of the Jewish people, and I could be a wreck before I've even brushed my teeth.

We all know that worry is a bad thing. It has no constructive purpose and is associated with many physical and emotional maladies. And yet, most of us spend considerable time and energy

CHANA HELLER, M.S.W., is the mother of five children. She works for Aish HaTorah Los Angeles as the Director of Women's Outreach and has taught Jewish parenting workshops for eight years. She is married to Rabbi Dov Heller, also of Aish L.A.

ruminating about all the things that could go wrong in our lives.

Let's not confuse worry with concern. Worry wastes valuable resources of time and energy; it can even become crippling. Concern has a more positive focus. When I am concerned I feel empowered to do something constructive.

How do we win the battle against worry? Here are some key tools.

Saying Thank You

My first tool is to say the *Modeh Ani* prayer in the morning. The first words out of a Jew's mouth upon awakening, before beginning conversation with anyone else, are supposed to be: "Thankful am I before You, living and eternal King, that You have returned my soul within me, with compassion. Abundant is Your faithfulness." This prayer gives me the focus I need to start my day without anxiety.

Thankfulness is a good focal point for worriers. Instead of going into the worry spiral, I focus on all that is going right in my life. I say this one-line prayer and add few of my own thank-yous: Thank You, God, for giving me a good husband, beautiful children, health, and a new minivan. Thank You for giving my friend a baby after ten years of marriage. Thank You for giving me the opportunity to be a constructive member of my community. Thank You that we can live full Jewish lives without fear of persecution. The list is endless.

This routine is more than just counting my blessings mentally. Through the act of verbalizing, I feel more of the reality of there being a Listener. It affects me much deeper than if I was merely engaged in a mental exercise.

Once I start the day with a few thank-yous, I open myself to the possibility of being overwhelmed by all that is going right. I am straightening myself out to start the day rooted in reality. The knot of tension begins to loosen, and feelings of calm and gratitude start seeping into my system.

Sure, there is still some worry, but I can start my day feeling that life is very good. What's right far outweighs what's not.

Trusting In God

My next best anti-worry tool is reviewing the "Gate of Trust" in the classic *Duties of the Heart* by Rabbi Bachya Ibn Paquda. He begins by listing the ideal qualities a person should have in order for others to trust him completely.

1. One should be compassionate, sympathetic, and loving.

2. One should not overlook any requests of others; their concerns should always be on his mind.

3. One should be capable of fulfilling the requests of others and not be overwhelmed by them.

4. One should know what is inherently good for others, and discern the difference between that which is truly good and that which only appears to be good.

5. One should have a great track record.

If we analyze these requirements for trust (this is not the full list), we find that it's a nearly impossible level for human beings to attain. My best friend may love me dearly, but if I tell her all my needs she is likely to become overwhelmed, and she surely isn't capable of fulfilling even a few of them!

By contrast, God fulfills this entire list. God loves me, cares about me, and listens sympathetically to my concerns. He knows me intimately and knows what is good for me. He has the power to do anything. And He has a great track record.

When I worry about meeting next month's bills, I say to myself, "Has God let you down yet? Have you gone hungry? Or a day without shelter? Or a sick child who you could not buy medicine for?"

I think of my parents and how much they cared for me day after day, providing for my every need. Did I worry as a child that maybe one morning I would wake up and hear them say, "Sorry, we decided not to take care of you today"? They had such a great track record, it was unthinkable to worry that they wouldn't be there for me.

So how can I doubt that God, Who is most worthy of trust, will let me down?

Trust in God does not mean that I am sure He will feed and shelter me every day just because He has done so in the past. Maybe He won't. But it does mean that whatever happens, I know it comes from a loving God, Who knows my needs intimately and will always do what is best for me and my growth.

The Magic Wand

Last Friday night at our Shabbat table my husband asked our guests, "If you were offered a magic wand to use whenever you wanted to change anything in your life — no more financial woes, difficult relationships, or health issues — would you take such a magic wand?"

Would you want to have that type of power over your life? Would you trust yourself to make better decisions for yourself than God is making for you now? Choosing the wand would be tantamount to saying: I trust myself more than I trust God.

If I had the wand, I would make myself rich so I wouldn't have to worry about money. I wouldn't have to work, but, of course, I would volunteer because I need something useful to do with my time. I would use my wand to make the troubled happy, the poor wealthy, and the sick healthy.

After a day of wand work, the world would already look very different. Everyone would be so blessed with everything that no one would need each other for anything. We'd all be independently wealthy, healthy, and happy, so much so that there would be no volunteer work for me to do. No one would need my services for anything. I'd end up poolside with a tall glass of lemonade, a nanny, and nothing to do.

No, I don't think I would trust myself with that wand. Thinking I was doing good, I would really be checking out of the challenges and difficulties of life which force us to grow and reach our potential.

When I start to worry, I think about the wand. "Okay, Chana, do you really want the wand so you could wish it all away?" I refocus and feel thankful that God is in control. I try to shift from unhealthy worry to positive concern. I strive to make whatever effort I need, and leave the rest in God's hands.

The person who trusts God submits to Him contentedly and surrenders himself to God's judgment. I am not there yet, but using these tools helps me feel happier in the moment, and happier in my general life circumstance.

We are all familiar with the saying that if we were given a choice to have our troubles or our neighbor's, we would chose our own burden hands down. As Rabbi Bachya Ibn Paquda says, "In worldly matters, [the person who trusts in God] will not favor one thing over another, or wish he was in a different situation than the present one. As one who trusted God said, 'I never arose in the morning in one place and wished I was someplace else.'"

Try saying "thank you" to God out loud for some of the blessings in your life. Feel the presence of God, Who loves and cares about you, and is more deserving of your trust than anyone you have ever known. Review His track record with you, and try to see your life as a tapestry of opportunities for growth.

Above all, use your energy to find creative solutions for what you can change...and let God worry about the rest.

SARA YOHEVED RIGLER

Real and Enduring Freedom

T he ballroom of Jerusalem's Plaza Hotel was filled with 250 well-dressed young Americans, Englishmen, South Africans, and Australians. The occasion was the 20th anniversary of one of Israel's institutions that teach a sophisticated level of Judaism to adult Jews. The attendees were all college graduates and professional people who had become observant and had relocated to Israel.

The guest speaker, Minister of Immigrant Absorption Yuli Edelstein, was shifting uncomfortably in his seat. As he surveyed the crowd, all of whom had moved to Israel from affluent English-speaking countries, he wondered what he would say to them. He himself had made aliyah from Russia, after years as a refusenik and three and a half years of hard labor in the Gulag. What could he say to these spoiled Westerners? When he finally did rise to speak, however, he surprised even himself.

Mr. Edelstein began by admitting his qualms in addressing a crowd whose background was not fraught with the hardships he had faced. He told how, when he was first imprisoned by the KGB, he did not have with him his tefillin (the black leather boxes

See biography of SARA YOHEVED RIGLER, page 17.

containing scriptural verses which the Torah bids a man to bind on his arm and his head every day). His wife brought his tefillin to the prison every morning, but the KGB refused to give them to him.

When his official interrogation began, Yuli refused to talk. He explained to his KGB interrogators that he could not speak because he had not recited his morning prayers properly, because he did not have his tefillin. Within an hour, his tefillin were brought to his cell.

On the day the investigation ended, a group of KGB thugs came to Yuli's cell, ransacked the place, and found his tefillin. While two men held him, a third broke apart the tefillin, tearing the sacred parchment scrolls to shreds in front of his anguished eyes.

"How could I not come to Israel?" Mr. Edelstein now asked us in an impassioned tone. "They tore up my tefillin! I had no choice to stay in such a country. But you," he said looking directly at our rapt faces, "none of you had to make aliyah. Nobody tore up your tefillin. Yet, you chose to leave countries where you were free. It is my privilege to be in your presence."

Real Freedom

According to Judaism, human beings have free choice, but only in a circumscribed area of moral choices. Every human being has, as Rabbi Dessler describes in his book *Michtav M'Eliyahu*, a unique "choice box" — a specific area of moral choice where he or she could truly go either way. This is the total locus of our freedom.

Most likely, the decision to murder or not to murder is not a viable choice for anyone reading this essay. Although the commandment "Do not murder" is one of the Ten Commandments, when we stand at the threshold of the Next World, most of us will not be rewarded for our assiduous obedience to this mitzvah. Given the society in which we were raised, and the parents who trained us in basic values, murder is not a real option for us (even when someone cuts us off in traffic). In not murdering, we are not exercising free choice.

At the other end of the moral spectrum, few of us are on the exalted level of altruism where we would donate our entire life savings to pay for a life-saving operation for a child we don't know. Nor would most of us seriously entertain the option of donating a kidney to a stranger. Such decisions are above our "choice box." They are not viable courses of action, given who we are today.

In exercising the moral choices within one's unique "choice box," a person fulfills the very purpose for which s/he has come into this world: to change and to grow.

This is what the Sages mean when they say that at the end of life, we will be judged only according to our choices. A person born with an altruistic nature, raised in a family where doing for others was the norm, will not be highly rewarded for volunteering weekly at the local hospital. "Doing what comes naturally," to the extent that it means maintaining one's spiritual status quo, is a cop-out on one's life mission. We are here to struggle and stretch ourselves and become more than what we started as. All true choice implies struggle.

Prime Value

Recently, a friend of ours, an elderly widow, lost her only brother. She wanted to sit *shiva* in our neighborhood in Jerusalem's Old City, where all her friends live, and inquired about renting an apartment here. My husband and I immediately decided to invite her to sit *shiva* in our home. To us it was unthinkable that she should sit *shiva* alone and have to pay rent for it.

Our response was immediate and automatic, a product of the kind of homes we came from — where hospitality and helping others was a prime value — and the compassion we had learned through 50-plus years of life experience. Our decision to invite our elderly, bereaved friend was an instinctive expression of who we were. It was no longer a matter of free choice.

For our teenage daughter, on the other hand, the question of whether to invite this elderly woman was complex and challenging. She was the one who would have to share her bedroom and bathroom. With a teenage girl's sense of privacy, she did not particularly like the stream of guests who had so recently shared her room over the holidays. Even less did she like elderly people who ask (what she calls) "prying questions."

My daughter sat across the kitchen table from me, struggling between her aversion to sharing her room with this woman, and her attraction to doing a mitzvah of kindness. That's what the process of free choice looks like. (Yes, she chose to invite the woman.)

It is not how good we are, but how good we have become, that is the measure of the person. Moral upward mobility is our only expression of true freedom.

The Tower Went Down, but the Person Went Up

The day after the collapse of the World Trade Center, *The New York Times* reported the story of a woman who could walk only with the aid of crutches, who worked on the 64th floor of Tower 2. Fellow employees tried to carry her down the stairs. "They had me over their shoulder for five or ten flights, and just couldn't do it," she later reported.

Another coworker she knew only as "Louis" came upon the struggling group, lifted the woman to his shoulder, and carried her by himself, she said, adding that "the temperature in the stairwell was at least 90 degrees."

Louis carried this woman down 54 flights of stairs, and did not leave her until she was safely inside an ambulance.

The Louis who fled from his office on the 64th floor was not the same man who emerged from the building. Somewhere between the 54th and the ground floor, Louis exercised his free choice and chose good. It may not have happened on the landing of the 54th floor when he picked up the woman and hoisted her over his shoulder. At that point, he may have been acting from an innately altruistic and heroic nature. He may have been constitutionally incapable of ignoring the incapacitated woman without at least trying to help her.

But somewhere in the smoky stairwell of the World Trade Center, when his muscles started to hurt, and the heat got to him, and the weight on his shoulder slowed him down more and more, and hundreds of panicked people pushed past him fleeing for their lives, somewhere — perhaps on the landing of the 34th floor or the 24th floor — instinct gave way to choice, and Louis chose to save this woman at whatever cost to himself.

The *Times* article related that around the 15th floor, a rescue worker told Louis that the woman was out of danger, and suggested that he leave her there and evacuate the building by himself. One of Louis's inner voices must have echoed the proposal: "Surely, I've already done enough. No one else would have done half of what I did to save her. Even a professional fireman says it's good enough." Louis chose to heed the other voice which said: "She's not safe until she's in a vehicle which can take her away from here."

Minutes later, the building collapsed.

The Louis who had arrived for work that morning was a man with the potential for greatness. The Louis who emerged, sweating and aching from the World Trade Center, was a great man. Only moral choices sculpt us into the best we can become.

Choosing Up

We are living through difficult and fearsome times, times which confront us with greater challenges and more opportunities to choose. Each of us has the freedom to choose good. Our choices need not be on the scale of newsworthy deeds. Choosing beyond our comfort zone is intrinsically heroic. Stretching ourselves beyond who we are at this moment necessarily makes us bigger.

If you are a person who has no affinity with elderly relatives, right now call your great-aunt who lives alone. She's probably more frightened than you are by warnings of more terror attacks.

If you are a person who has been nursing a grudge against a friend or relative who treated you badly, right now forgive them. When life is uncertain, who can afford to take chances with what might be a last chance?

If you are a person who is too busy to invest time in old friendships, break out of your character mold and right now write a letter to an old friend. When letters are carrying deadly anthrax spores, why not send letters full of love and concern?

If you are a person who tends to give more attention to building your capital than building your family, right now make a daring reversal of priorities. When the economy is shaky, your only real assets are the people who love you.

If you are a Jew who has dallied with the idea of mitzvah observance, but never had enough time, knowledge or inclination to make it happen, right now commit to practicing one mitzvah — whether it's eating kosher, learning Torah for 15 minutes a day, or keeping one Shabbat a month. Every mitzvah forges a bond between you and the only eternal, immutable, omnipotent Reality in this frenetic world.

In the Torah, God tells us: "I have put before you today life and good, death and evil. Choose life."

Choosing good is choosing life. It is our only real and enduring freedom.

The Restriction Prescription

T hey installed a water meter in my home. Just like that.
This calamity happened about a month ago. The doorbell rang. The man spoke with authority. He had a clipboard with a dangling pen attached to it. "All your neighbors are getting 'em too," he said. "It's the law!"

Ninety minutes later it was all over. The meter was installed. I didn't cry, but I wanted to. "Now they'll know exactly how much water I'm using," I moaned.

Life, as we knew it, would never be the same again. No more 40-minute showers. No more dripping faucets that I could ignore for months. No more endless water fights for my kids with the driveway hose. Our long-standing, carefree lifestyle effectively came to an end on that fateful day.

A calamity? Indeed. But maybe it's more than just that.

Let's examine it from a very different angle. If we believe in God — a just God, a loving God, a compassionate God — then we also believe that God is only interested in providing for us, in giving to us. After all, if God is perfect, what could He possibly need or want from us? He has no needs or wants. Perfection, by

See biography of RABBI YAAKOV SALOMON, page 63.

definition, means that nothing is lacking! And if there is really nothing we can provide for God, then what is our purpose here?

If the only thing God "wants" is to give to us, our "job" is to find the best way possible to accept and utilize all the gifts He gives, and to get the most out of all we receive.

What is God's method of giving us the maximum fulfillment of every one of life's pleasures? What recipe did He impart to us, that guarantees we will enjoy and appreciate every avenue of satisfaction and happiness in this world?

In one word... restriction. In two words? Temporary restriction. Huh?

Surprising as it may seem, restriction is actually the single most important ingredient for humankind to enjoy every positive experience on this planet.

For instance, I like steak. I like it very much. Rib, fillet, sino, shoulder — you name it. Especially if it is medium rare. But try having it every night. It's just not the same, is it?

Enjoy the Beatles? Metallica? Bach? Just try to listening to them all day...every day.

What happens to your enjoyment level? Is it the same? Does it grow? Is that the premium method for experiencing the maximum amount of enjoyment from the steak? From a roller coaster? A sunset? A vacation? A great website? A hockey game? Sleeping late in the morning? (Alright, Salomon, now you've gone too far.)

When God bestowed upon us that great instruction manual for living, also known as the Torah, He included 613 regulations, also known as commandments. These are the ingredients which, when adhered to, comprise that total recipe for fulfillment on this world. But only 248 of them are positive commandments — things "to do." The other 365 are things not to do (symbolic of one each day, for every day in our solar year). Okay, call them restrictions if you like. Yet when adhered to, these "restrictions" comprise the blueprint for our greatest enjoyment.

So valuable is this formula, that you'd be hard pressed to find any pleasure in this world that isn't lawfully proscribed, at least temporarily. Why? Not to punish us, restrict us, frustrate us, or constrict our lifestyle. Quite the contrary. It is to make certain that we are pacing ourselves properly, so as not to overindulge on any single pleasure and dilute the excitement and appreciation of each experience.

Those experiences which potentially damage our bodies or souls are always prohibited — even though they might look enticing or fun. Again, because it would interfere with our game plan of getting lasting, maximum pleasure. But even the everyday stuff, which is given to us specifically to enjoy, is at some time made unavailable for us to experience.

Of course, self-regulation could work, too. But "legalized" restriction is a lot more effective (and therefore, more pleasurable). Suggesting to your kids that they "turn in early" for the next few nights, to help them "catch up" on their sleep, might not work quite as well as giving them a temporary curfew and sticking to it.

For example, not eating bread for a full eight days (Passover) may sound terribly oppressive to some. But anyone experiencing that first slice of P.P.P. (Post Passover Pizza) knows how indescribably memorable that can be. It's a fresh appreciation of something we easily become accustomed to.

Other pleasures are also temporarily restricted: music (during periods of personal or national mourning), comfortable shelter (Sukkot), eating (Yom Kippur and other fast days), and telephones, video, and computers (Shabbat).

A good parent knows all too well that the worst thing you can do to your child is to never say "no." Want a surefire way to get him to hate that new set of hyper, ergo-dynamic, jumbo, turbo, energized, jet-powered, alpha-omega, quantum, phaser-propelled, prismatic Lego? Let him play with it all day...every day. Then watch his interest fade into cyberspace (or wherever things fade into these days). Life without restriction is colorless, jaded, and uninspired. Setting limits only adds luster, passion, and vigor to the adventure we now call "life.com."

Don't misunderstand me. I do not love my new water meter. But I suppose there is something to say for moderation, accountability, restriction and eight-minute showers. Or am I just getting old?

Body and Soul

*H*ow does Judaism see the body, beauty, and physicality? Judaism, in contrast to most other religions, does not negate the physical world. Nor does it dichotomize the spiritual and the material. The Torah approach is that we should bring godliness to every aspect of life. God is no less present and accessible in the boardroom and bedroom than He is in our places of worship. Moreover, tradition teaches that it is God's omnipotent will and deliberate plan that we are in physical surroundings and not in a solely spiritual setting.

Recently, my husband and I celebrated our 40th wedding anniversary with a trip to Switzerland. The trip was at my urging (I don't want to say nudging). I based my reasoning on the Talmud which says that after 120 years of life on earth, when we come before the Divine tribunal for judgment, the Almighty will ask us if

REBBETZIN FAIGE TWERSKI of Milwaukee, Wisconsin has devoted her life to Jewish education and outreach, giving lectures worldwide on a myriad of Judaic subjects. She is a mother of 11 children, and has many grandchildren, whose number she refuses to divulge. She serves as the rebbetzin alongside her husband, Rabbi Michel Twerski, of Congregation Beth Jehudah of Milwaukee.

we fully enjoyed this world. We will be asked, I reminded my husband, "Did you enjoy My magnificent Alps?" (It's helpful to have a religious argument when you want a vacation with your rabbi-husband.)

There is a Torah imperative to notice, appreciate, and relish the beauty of our surroundings. They are God's gift to us and an expression of His love. As a means of heightening our sensitivity, we are instructed to recite blessings when we encounter fragrant trees, awesome storms (thunder and lightening), majestic mountains, and beautiful people. The Almighty's mandate is for us to bridge heaven and earth — the spiritual and the physical — though they might appear to us as opposite and conflicting dimensions of existence.

Tension of Body and Soul

The human being reflects this tension. On one hand, there is the body with its needs, demands, impulses, urges, etc. On the other hand, there is the spiritual aspect, the Divine soul, our essence, our very link to eternity. The requirements and needs of the soul are not as readily tangible as the needs of the body, but they are in fact much more critical. The well-being of the body has to be maintained as the vessel, the repository of our God-invested essence. This vessel has to last a lifetime — 70, 80, or 90 years, or as the expression goes, "May you live to 120!" In contrast, the soul is of eternal substance, and we have to nurture it so it can endure forever and ever.

Hillel, one of the great sages of Israel, was greeted on a Friday afternoon by a number of his students. He had what was the equivalent of a towel swung over his shoulders, sparking the curiosity of his students who questioned him about his destination. "I am going to the bathhouse, to take care of my host," he answered. Upon further inquiry, he explained that his body was the host for his soul for the duration of his journey on earth, and that there is a Torah obligation to treat one's host with respect, care, and concern.

The Torah recognizes that if one's body is neglected and in

disrepair, the soul will suffer.

In 19th-century Europe, Reb Avrohom was known as the *malach*, "the angel," because of his enormously pious and spiritually focused nature. He was a young man whose service to God was so intense that he often forgot to attend to his basic physical needs, such as eating and sleeping. When his father, Rabbi Dov Ber, the Maggid of Mezritch, was about to depart from this world, he called in his son. His parting words were "Avremele, Avremele, be very careful to give great care to your health. Because a small hole in one's body will create an even greater hole in one's soul."

The Challenge

The challenge of our existence here on earth is to successfully negotiate the tension between body and soul. While one must give the body its due, it should not become the exclusive or even primary focus. After all is said and done, the body is only the outside shell — the packaging that will die and be buried after exhausting its usefulness. But the human spirit — which is dependent on a lifetime of spiritual awareness and commensurate good deeds — joins other souls in a world of eternal duration.

How can we fathom eternity? Someone once explained that if we filled Madison Square Garden with sunflower seeds, and a bird would come once in a thousand years to remove a single seed, the time it would take for all the seeds to be cleared out would not even begin to capture a definition of eternity.

Yes, the body is very important. Our physical configuration — brain, heart, kidneys, intestines — are inspiring in their harmony and synchrony and serve as testimony to the presence of a purposeful Creator. The Torah commandment to "be concerned for yourself and greatly concerned for your soul" (Deut. 4:9) enjoins us not to do anything that would be injurious to our bodies. We must eat well, sleep, exercise, and seek medical attention — whatever will promote our health and well-being.

In addition, the Torah places value on an attractive appearance. Since the body is the garment of the soul, its presentation is a commentary on its bearer. The Talmud states that a Torah scholar dare not appear in soiled clothing. We understand this to mean that a person who represents a Torah standard must externally reflect what he personifies.

Moreover, traditional sources are replete with exhortations to a husband and wife to dress in a way that their spouse will find attractive. This is especially relevant in an open society where men and women interact constantly and freely. Opportunities and temptations out there are a constant challenge to every marriage. One of the antidotes to this reality is to enhance our vigilance to be appealing to our spouses. "Attractive but not attracting of others," as the saying goes.

At the same time, we must maintain a balanced approach, aware that there is much more to the human being than meets the eye.

RABBI AHRON LOPIANSKY

All the Rage

The Israeli tabloids graphically presented the situation — 12 snapshots of people remarkable for nothing except for their unremarkability. These people had been killed over a two-week span in various petty brawls and fights.

Jewish crime is typically white-collar crime and petty thievery. The idea that murder and violence could occur with such frequency in Israeli society was shocking. Even worse, it was murder for petty reasons — one was killed in a fight over a beach chair, another over a parking space, and yet another in a silly pub argument.

What caused this murder spree? The heat? The security situation? The economy?

All of the above were duly cited, along with appropriate jeremiads of our "becoming like Sodom."

But to call all murder by the same name is an over-simplification. True, morally speaking, all murders are wrong. But we must distinguish between the various kinds of murder,

RABBI AHRON LOPIANSKY is *rosh yeshiva* of the Yeshiva of Greater Washington. He is the author of *Timepieces* (Targum Press) as well as a number of scholarly works written in Hebrew.

according to their underlying causes:

1) Murder that displays a lack of respect for human life. This is the thief who plans to kill someone in the process of a robbery.

2) The murderer who gains pleasure in killing another person. This is psychopathic sadism — a deep perversion of the soul.

3) Rage murder. Someone is late for a meeting. He had a fight with his wife that morning. It is 98 degrees Fahrenheit outside and sticky as pea soup. He eyes a parking spot and at the last moment someone else cuts in and snatches it away. He storms out of his car, words fly, a gun is drawn, and someone is murdered.

Not an Issue of Morality

Can teaching children about the sanctity of human life prevent rage murder?

I think not. The problem is not the person's moral compass per se. An otherwise devoted, decent person may become swept up in rage and do things that would horrify even him. Many people are mortified at the crime they commit and can never forgive themselves. It is not murder that we are dealing with, but rage and frustration.

What are the roots of rage? How do we control it? What is the mindset that produces it?

A person is born with a very strong sense of self. He wants, he struggles, he acts, he accomplishes. As one grows up, the idea of "I accomplished" becomes identical to "I am." Eventually, failure of achievements becomes identical with failure of the person. If the person gauges a task as being within his abilities, but fails, the person is frustrated. He feels that his very self is constricted and diminished. It is more frustrating when the failure is caused by an object blocking his path, and worse still when the person himself is the obstacle.

Imagine someone racing to make an important meeting. The following jumble of thoughts runs through his mind: "I'm going to speed and hit the office at 9 o'clock. It will take me one minute to park, and another 90 seconds to make it up to my office. I know I can rely on myself in this tight situation."

Suddenly someone ahead of him is driving slowly. He furiously pounds on the horn. "Who is this idiot cruising in front of me?! Can't he move more quickly? What right does he have to restrict my freedom of movement?"

As the driver realizes he will be late for the meeting, the hapless person in front of him now becomes the direct enemy, striking at his self-image.

Frustration is the feeling of one's personality being hemmed in and choked. Rage is the reaction of desperate resistance to this emotional choking, akin to the reaction of thrashing to physical choking. "I am the master of my universe! How dare you obstruct me?"

Jewish Ideals

Living according to Jewish ideals engenders a different perspective. The global superstructure of the universe is a God who has willingly and purposely placed you in this world in order to bring out the best moral self. A person's life consists of challenges, aspirations, tests, and false leads — which all serve the purpose of developing the moral self.

Judaism does not preach a meek withdrawal or passive fatalism. Man is not an inanimate object, meant to "survive" various God-ordained events. Rather, he is a being with real freedom of choice, and in the words of Genesis, enjoined to "rule over the earth and conquer it."

But his ambition and freedom are only part of the picture. He does not know, a priori, which goals are attainable and which will never be his. He tackles all worthy goals with equal zest and drive. But after having done his best, if he fails, he is not frustrated or enraged. He puts it into perspective. They were meant to be tests of sorts. I did my best and that was sufficient. I have passed with flying colors, though I may not always be aware of what the test was.

Imagine a person taking an entrance exam at a prestigious university. The student discovers that the test is completely unfair and impossibly difficult. Extremely upset, he can react in a number of ways. He can cheat, or blow up in rage and curse the university administration, or get depressed and drunk.

Imagine the same student taking a test with the space agency NASA. As he is getting upset at the unfair test, a suspicion begins to sneak in. Perhaps they are not testing his knowledge, but rather his stamina, patience, and character. Maybe they are looking for people with qualities of endurance needed for harsh space-module environments. He decides to be a model of equanimity.

The Torah does not teach us to be simplistically resigned, "It's all for the best." Rather, it broadens our horizons by teaching that our personal perspectives are narrow and time-bound, while God's perspective is broad and timeless. Let's examine this idea.

Who Is in Charge?

One of the great figures of the 20th century was Rabbi Y. Z. Solovetchik. Known for his brilliant mind, he was a fastidious observer of Jewish law, and approached each decision with focused thought and extreme tension.

One of his hardest decisions came at the beginning of World War II, when German planes were bombing Warsaw, and he needed to choose the safest place for his community during the bombing. Thousands of lives depended on his decision, and the rabbi's tension while weighing the options was unbearable.

When the bombing started, everyone began trembling, frightened to the point of hysteria. Everyone but the rabbi. Someone asked him, "If you were so tense before the bombing, I would expect you to be a total wreck by now. And yet you are so calm!"

Rabbi Solovetchik answered: "Before the bombing, we were given the responsibility to make the right decision. The tension was unbearable. But once the bombing started, our responsibilities have been discharged. Now it is only God who is making the decisions. And my trust in Him is complete."

The rabbi was expressing the attitude of someone who lives within the world of God. As long as the baton of action has been handed to man, it is his total responsibility. No amount of effort or strain is excessive. But as soon as the baton is handed back to God, and man has no more course of action, then no matter what the result there is no need for frustration, rage, anger, disappointment, or even nervousness.

At this stage, such reactions show a lack of belief in the overwhelming Divine encompassing structure of the universe. As great as the rabbi's tension was beforehand — because at that stage he was in charge — so was he calm afterwards because God was in charge.

We may never reach the great level of trust exhibited by the rabbi in this story. But with focus and effort, we can begin to place our reliance for ultimate outcomes not on ourselves, but on the True Power directing life's destiny. And then, murder committed for the sake of a parking space would most likely fade into a memory of the past.

RABBI NOACH ORLOWEK

Turning Weakness into Greatness

E ach of us has a dominant personality trait that sets us apart. How we develop that characteristic decides, in the end, whether our lives end up in the red or the black.

No character trait is purely negative. Each has negative uses, but even the ones that seem purely bad can be channeled into positive actions. What counts is not which character traits you have, but how you use them.

For instance, someone with a hot-blooded nature will have a temper. It's in his makeup. But that doesn't mean he gets off scot-free. He can control that tendency by channeling it in a positive direction. He could get angry about "injustice" and persevere to correct it where others might give up.

An angry nature can be used to accomplish, or it can be used in a destructive way that will probably ruin his life. And so it is for all character traits. Even the so-called "positive" ones like kindness

RABBI NOACH ORLOWEK is a sought-after educator and counselor who lectures worldwide. He is the author of *My Child, My Disciple; My Disciple, My Child*; and *Raising Roses among the Thorns*.

can be used negatively — e.g., "smothering" someone with too much kindness.

Reward for Hard Work

In Jewish terms, who deserves praise? The one who works on himself and learns how to use the dominant aspects of his personality for positive, constructive purposes. You can't get credit for controlling a problem you don't have.

In other words, someone born with an easygoing nature does not earn credit for being "even-tempered" the same way as an angry person who overcame his fiery nature.

For the hot-blooded, the struggles he went through to create an even temperament gives his behavior an intensity and purity it would otherwise lack.

Conversely, the fiery person who never gets angry because he always gets his way, does not get credit for "controlling his temper." He still has a temper and an angry nature. He was just never in the position to overcome it or turn it to a positive use. It's still there, latent.

Try to control your negative tendencies and channel them in a positive way. That's true growth.

Where You Stumble Is Where You Gain

Ironically, the area in which you behave the worst is likely the area in which you can gain the most.

Pay attention to the areas you view as weakness, where you have a tendency to keep making mistakes. It signals an aspect of your personality that is a basic part of your makeup — and an area of potential strength for you.

There are two easy indicators of such traits: an intensity of feeling, and a frequency of occurrence. This is true even if only one indicator is present. But if you can identify an area where they coexist, then you've really found your spot!

For instance, if you're prone to gossiping, then you probably have a natural talent for communication and connecting with others — if you choose to use it that way.

Once you've identified an area to work on, stay hopeful. Knowing your weakness is a powerful discovery. It's like identifying the location of buried treasure. Once you know where the treasure — your defect — is, keep digging, even when it's difficult. That's where your success is going to be.

The best way to work on your problem may not be to attack it head-on. You may have to work on strengthening other areas to cause your defect to atrophy, to enable you to channel the tendency in a productive way.

Most importantly: Don't get discouraged. You can fortify yourself with the knowledge that you're not only uprooting that which drags you down, but identifying what can ultimately move you far forward.

The World's Worst Lawyer

This is an insight woven deep into Jewish history.

After the Golden Calf, God tells Moses that He is going to destroy the Jewish people — not because of what they did, but because they are "a stiff-necked people." God's anger is sparked not by the actions, but by the character trait that caused the actions.

In response, Moses asks God not to destroy them. Why? Because they are "a stiff-necked people."

What kind of a defense attorney is that? Moses is trying to use the exact same point that upsets the judge — in order to gain favor!

We see from here that the quality that causes God to be disappointed with us is the same quality that will save us. Being "stiff-necked" means to be stubborn — i.e., less likely to change or admit a mistake. A stubborn person doesn't listen. He knows what he knows and he's going to do whatever he wants despite what others might think.

But Moses understood the flip side to stubbornness: Once a stubborn person's loyalty is assigned, he stays true to it.

The Jewish people, the stubborn nation, stayed true to God throughout history. They didn't accept false messiahs. They didn't accept distortions of God's words. Throughout history, they died rather than abandon their relationship with God.

Other societies have changed religious affiliation as soon as they were conquered. But the stubborn nation of Israel wandered the globe, always faithful to God.

Moses understood that someone who is tough to convince can be a real pain, but once convinced, will solidly stand by you. Stand by us, Moses tells God, because we are the nation that will stand by You.

Our worst quality is also our greatest strength.

Get Up Again

The Talmud tells us that a righteous person falls seven times and gets up. The defining characteristic is not that he doesn't fall — but that he gets up. (And it's likely that the experience gained through falling and rising is precisely what made him great!)

When trying to refine your character, giving up is seductive. "It's too hard. I can't do it. I'll never succeed."

The righteous person knows that you have to be stubborn and keep trying. Once you've identified your area of weakness, you know you've found your strength.

When the Temple stood in Jerusalem, the state of highest spiritual impurity was removed by a ceremony involving the ashes of a red heifer — the symbolic mother of the Golden Calf.

The weakness itself provides the solution.

The true reward in life comes from using wisely what you have. You are born with a certain set of personality traits. What you do with them is up to you.

LOOKING FOR GOD

SARA YOHEVED RIGLER

Buddhism, Judaism, and the Great Cheerio Fiasco

For 17 years, I meditated, usually three times a day. My goal was to attain a state of elevated consciousness which the Hindus call *samadhi* — the experience of the total oneness underlying the apparent multiplicity of this world.

Sri Ramakrishna, the head of my ashram's lineage of gurus, used to say that the mind is like a pond. Because of the many ripples (thought forms), the surface of the pond cannot accurately reflect the sun of Truth. When the pond, or mind, is perfectly still (in meditation), the sun, or Truth, is perfectly reflected.

Once, during my 11th year of living at the ashram, a Hindu-style spiritual retreat, I actually experienced that transcendental state. Conducting the community's group meditation in the shrine room, I felt my consciousness rise out of my body. I left the world of time and space behind, and entered into a state of Total Oneness.

I was not aware that over an hour passed in that state, or that

See biography of SARA YOHEVED RIGLER, page 17.

the other members of the community had tiptoed out of the shrine room to begin their morning duties. When I finally, with great difficulty, managed to "come down" and open my eyes, it took me another 15 minutes just to reorient my mind to this world of form and motion.

The ritual worship over, I left the shrine, took off my *chuddar* (prayer shawl), and was engaged in folding it, when Sister Baroda approached me. I was the schedule maker, and she asked if she could switch her cooking day with someone else in the community. Up to that point, I felt like I had been descending to earth gradually, as with a wind-filled parachute, but suddenly, Sister Baroda poked a gaping hole in my parachute. I landed with a thud, and yelled at her for disturbing my rapture. Then I angrily stalked off to my room to escape the garrulous group of ashram members chatting frivolously over breakfast.

Bhu-Jews

A large number of Jews currently practice Buddhism. Rodger Kamenetz, the author of *The Jew in the Lotus*, says that "a third of all Western Buddhist leaders come from Jewish roots." Half of the participants in the Vipassana meditation retreat near Dharamsala, India, are Israelis. According to one estimate, three out of four Western visitors to the spiritual center of Tibetan Buddhism and the seat of the Dalai Lama are Jewish. Most of the street signs in Dharamsala have Hebrew letters.

A recent cover story of the *Jerusalem Report* profiled Jews who have been living in Dharamsala for years:

Tenzin Josh, formerly Steven Gluck of London, described his 253 monastic vows, such as dressing modestly and not sharing private space with women. He remarks, "It's not much different from being an Orthodox Jew."

But he is wrong. In fact, Buddhism is — in its essence and purpose — the diametric opposite of Judaism.

The Four Noble Truths, which comprise the foundation of Buddhism, are:

- This world is suffering.
- The cause of suffering is desire.
- The cessation of suffering is the cessation of desire.
- The cessation of desire is achieved through practicing the Noble Eightfold Path, which includes right speech, right action, right livelihood, etc.

The goal of Buddhism is to escape the wheel of birth and death. Since suicide leads only to reincarnation, the only effective way to escape this world is by attaining nirvana, a transcendental state of consciousness which serves as an exit pass from the wheel of birth and death.

As Tenzin Josh asserted in explaining his personal transition from a punk lifestyle in London to becoming a Buddhist monk: "Whether a punk nihilist or a Buddhist hermit, you just don't see a point in life and want to find a way out."

In the same article, an Israeli explained his post-army flight to India: "What hope is there when your whole life is one ceaseless fight for personal and national survival? I just wanted to run away and find some space for myself."

Religions of Heaven, a Religion of Earth

Judaism, by contrast, is a path of total engagement with this world.

The 613 mitzvot of the Torah are prescriptions for how to engage every part of one's body and every component of the physical world in consecrated action. Even a "mental" or "emotional" commandment, such as "Love your neighbor as yourself," has specific, physical stipulations, namely: concern yourself with your neighbor's physical welfare, show him honor, speak well of her.

The Talmud, that vast, 63-tractate compendium of the Oral Law, delves into picayune details as a way of including every imaginable physical object in its scope. Thus, in discussing which vessel is kosher to use for washing hands upon arising, the Talmud considers clay vessels, wooden vessels, animal skins, cracked vessels, etc. Nothing is too mundane to be dealt with, scrutinized, and either used or dismissed for holy action.

According to Kabbalah, every physical object possesses sparks of holiness. By using an object in the proper way, the sparks are released and can ascend. We are here in this world to elevate the entire creation.

Ironically, the lower the object or activity, the higher the sparks can rise. Thus, after using the bathroom, a Jew recites a blessing which includes the words, "It is revealed and known before Your Throne of Glory..." The Sages point out that the sanctification of this lowliest of activities gives one the potential to actually rise to the level of the Divine Throne. In this light, we can understand a puzzling statement by the Gaon of Vilna, the great 18th-century sage: Other religions are like the heavens; Judaism is like the earth.

The purpose of the other religions is to transcend this world. The purpose of Judaism is to elevate this world, and in so doing, perfect oneself.

Holy Union

Nowhere is the dichotomy between Judaism and the Eastern religions so pronounced as in their approach to sexuality.

Buddhism, Hinduism, and Jainism all mandate celibacy as the highest path, because indulging in sexual relations means giving in to the lower self. All the serious Bhu-Jews living in Dharamsala have renounced sex.

Torah, by contrast, regulates sexuality, and ultimately sanctifies it in marriage as the most potent way to unite with God in this world. The union between husband and wife is called by the Talmud the "holy of holies." Discipline is an essential component of sanctified sexuality. And it is a Torah obligation for a husband to sexually satisfy his wife (above and beyond the commandment of procreation).

Although Indian (both Hindu and Buddhist) Tantric tradition utilizes the energy of sexual union as a spiritual tool, Tantric sexuality is not supposed to be practiced with one's wife.

Preferably, it should be practiced with a stranger. This would be anathema in Judaism, where the highest union includes every aspect of the couple: emotional, mental, spiritual, as well as physical. That is why Judaism prohibits marital relations if either spouse is fantasizing about another person. The *Shechinah*, the presence of God, comes to rest only when the husband and wife are acting out total oneness, on all levels.

Purpose and Meaning

Another salient difference between Buddhism and Judaism is that Buddhism is a non-theistic religion. Although later Mahayana Buddhism virtually made the Buddha himself into a god, the historical Gautama Buddha (who lived in the fifth century BCE) never mentioned God. Thus, the existence of God and even the existence of an immortal soul are either denied or irrelevant in Buddhism.

Judaism, by contrast, centers totally on God. God is not only the source of all existence, but also the source of the Torah, the intricate system of ideal behavior for humankind. All wisdom flows from God's Torah, the instruction manual for living.

Further, God is not only the Creator of the universe, but continues to sustain it moment-by-moment, while supervising our participation in it. Living with the awareness of God's Oneness, love of God, and awe of God are three mitzvot that should be practiced on a constant basis.

According to Buddhism and Hinduism, this world is ultimately purposeless. Hinduism, which does posit a Divine creator, describes the Divine direction of this world as *lila*, "playful sport," with no more purpose and meaning than a game of ball.

According to Rabbi Aryeh Kaplan, "The foundation of Judaism and the basis of all true religion is the realization that existence is purposeful, and that man has a purpose in life. Both man and nature have meaning because they were created by a purposeful Being" (*Handbook of Jewish Thought*, 1:1–2).

It is the deep intuition of this truth which makes Jews such "meaning freaks" — always searching for meaning in life and events — unable to tolerate life as a couch potato. Ironically, it is this search for meaning which takes many Jews to the East. There they fasten on a purpose for their lives: to attain enlightenment.

Judaism maintains, however, that the purpose of life is not just spiritual consciousness, but primarily refined action. Therefore, that purpose cannot be attained by meditation alone, but through mitzvot — minutely prescribed, consecrated actions.

Of course, spiritual consciousness, or what Judaism calls *kavanah*, must provide the backdrop to one's actions. A mitzvah done without the consciousness that one is doing the will of God — in order to connect with God — does not actualize its full potential.

On the other hand, exalted consciousness which does not express itself in concrete actions is worthless.

The purpose of meditation — in which Bhu-Jews spend many long hours — is to clearly perceive ultimate Truth, in the universe and in one's own life. Unfortunately, one can be an adept in meditation, and still commit adultery, lose one's temper, and be bloated with pride. I have known great masters of meditation who succumbed to all three. Spiritual consciousness, in and of itself, does not lead to proper action.

The Human Mission

The sages of the *mussar* movement (a technique of spiritual growth articulated in the 18th century by Rabbi Yisrael Salanter) explain the human mission this way:

A human being consists of a soul together with a body. The soul is ever-perfect. We do not need to work on the soul. Rather, we have come into this world to perfect the body (which includes emotions and character traits). The body is like a child with which we have been entrusted. We are obligated to feed, bathe, and rest the body properly. We discipline the body — to get it to behave properly, to engage it in acts of kindness, to prevent it from hurting itself or others. The commandments of the Torah are physical because their object is to train the body. Judaism aims for more than an enlightened mind — for a sanctified body as well.

The spiritual work of a Jew is to train the face to smile at a nasty neighbor, to teach the hand to put a coin in the palm of a loathsome beggar, to restrain the tongue from making negative remarks, to feed the stomach only permissible foods, to drill the mind in judging others favorably, to educate the heart to love God, and to instruct the shoulders to carry a neighbor's load — especially that of an enemy.

The place for blissful contemplation of the Divine Oneness is not in this world but rather in the World to Come. The purpose of this world is to be a place of challenge and accomplishment. Although Jews, especially Israelis, may yearn to escape to a place of peace, our purpose in this life is better served by situations which stretch, test, and demand growth.

Judaism does not resign itself to a world of darkness. Judaism advocates jumping into the fray, facing evil head-on, struggling against one's own urges, and rooting out baseness — in the world and in oneself.

True, it is hard for a monk not to touch money and to live without the comforts of this world. It is even harder to labor to earn a salary and then give 10 percent off the top to charity, especially when you need every cent to repair your washing machine.

It is difficult to live in silence and seclusion. It is even more difficult to remain focused on God and one's highest ideals amidst the commotion and distractions of family life.

Cheerios and Enlightenment

For the last six months, I have been working on overcoming anger. During the 15 years I lived in an ashram and the 17 years I engaged in meditation, I never succeeded in controlling my volatile temper.

Young children provide an ideal environment to work on overcoming anger. They are irrational, contrary, famous for interrupting the sleep cycle, demanding, and do not clean up after themselves. They also make messes — usually right after the floor has been washed, and when their mother is at the lowest point of her biorhythm energy cycle.

I thank God every day for my beloved children. But I also yell at them — too much.

Now I am in a *mussar* group in which, using the techniques of the *mussar* teachers, I work to overcome my inveterate tendency to respond to stress by haranguing whichever culprit backed me into that corner.

Last Tuesday morning, my husband, a musical arranger, had an important recording session. Trying to model the ideal wife, I offered to prepare carrot sticks and humus to send for his lunch. He gratefully accepted, but, knowing my habitual tardiness, warned that he had to leave promptly at 8:30. "No problem," I assured him. In any case, my 6-year-old son had to be out the door by 8:20 to get to school on time. Ten minutes was exactly enough time to prepare the carrot sticks and package some humus in a smaller container. I was on top of it.

At 8:19, my son knocked over a box of Cheerios standing on the edge of the kitchen table. My jaw dropped in horror as hundreds of crunchy O's landed all over the kitchen floor.

My mental computer screen flashed a dozen red X's screaming Illegal Operation. The mess. The waste. The money (the Cheerios were imported from America). The time. My self-portrait as the ideal wife.

I couldn't get to the refrigerator to take out the carrots without pulverizing the blanket of Cheerios. If I took the time to clean it up now, I'd be late with my husband's lunch. My first instinct was to yell at my son and demand that he clean it up, even if it made him late for school. My second instinct was to lash out at my husband for his characteristic punctuality that put me under such pressure.

I didn't yell. I didn't get angry. In a calm tone, I sent my son off to school. Then I gingerly treaded over the Cheerios to the broom closet, got out the broom, pushed the mess over to one side, retrieved the carrots from the fridge, peeled and cut them as fast as I could, took the whole container of humus (it wouldn't be too much, I told myself), put everything in a plastic bag, and, with a beatific smile, handed my waiting husband his lunch at 8:33.

I felt a wave of ecstasy sweep over me. I had done it! For this time at least, I had overcome my anger.

It was a bigger achievement than *samadhi*.

LORI PALATNIK

Journey to the Next World

Are you a body, or a body-and-soul? Most people would answer, "I'm a body-and-soul." But do we mean it? Do we live our lives and make decisions as if we are not just a body, but a body-and-soul?

At certain times in our lives we reconnect with our souls. A wedding is a soul experience for the bride and groom, a new beginning through the spiritual union under the *chuppah*, the wedding canopy.

For many, going to Israel is a life-altering experience of connecting with the land, the people, and the legacy that is part of every Jew.

The birth of a child is a soul-stirring moment. We witness the miracle of creation, the wonder of a new life, and we feel the awesome responsibility of this priceless gift entrusted to the parents.

On a journey to the countryside, as we look up to a star-filled sky, we can truly see forever. A feeling of transcendence overtakes us.

LORI PALATNIK is a well-known speaker and Jewish educator based in Denver, Colorado. She is the author of several books, including *Friday Night and Beyond* (Jason Aronson), *Remember My Soul* (Leviathan Press), and *Gossip* (Simcha Press). She is the busy mother of five children and the proud wife of Rabbi Yaakov Palatnik. Contact her at: Lpalatnik@aish.com.

A near-death experience can be a dramatic soul encounter. People do not recover from such experiences without realizing they've been given another chance. Afterward, each new day holds new meaning, and even casual relationships turn precious.

Death itself puts us in touch with our souls. No one stands at a funeral and thinks about the menu for dinner that night. Everyone thinks, "What is life really about? What am I living for? Is there something beyond this world?"

We know that we are souls. When we look into the eyes of someone we love, we do not see random molecules thrown together. We love the essence of that person, and that essence is what Judaism calls the *neshama*, the soul.

"God formed the human out of dust of the ground, and breathed into his nostrils a breath (soul) of life" (Genesis 2:7). The soul is eternal, although the body's existence is temporary. When God decides that a person's time on this earth has ended, He takes back the soul, and the body goes back to the earth, completing the cycle of creation ("...dust to dust"). For in the beginning, the first person, Adam, was created from the dust of the ground.

When a loved one dies, the goodness and special qualities that they possessed, the part of them that made noble choices in life, performed good deeds, and touched the lives of others — their *neshama* — goes on to a world of infinite pleasure. In that world, physical suffering does not exist, and souls bask in the light of the Creator, enjoying the rewards for all they did here on earth.

Front-Row Seats

But what kinds of choices and deeds count? Those who saved the lives of others, who led armies to victory, who discovered medical cures? Yes, those people enjoy a place in the World to Come, but so do those who led simpler lives, who performed quiet acts of kindness and made a difference to those around them. Perhaps what they did wasn't front-page news, but small acts can also merit an eternity of deepest pleasures in the World to Come.

What we are experiencing now is called *olam hazeh* ("this world"), while the next world is referred to as *olam haba* (the

"World to Come"). We are all familiar with what happens here, but what goes on in *olam haba*?

Of course no one in Jewish history ever died and came back to tell us what happens in the world beyond. Yet we are assured there is another existence. Maimonides, the 12th-century scholar, includes this belief in his "Thirteen Principles of Faith." Our oral tradition speaks about it at length, and Kabbalah, Jewish mysticism, is replete with wisdom about the hereafter.

Olam haba, Heaven, is more easily understood when compared to a theater. Our Sages say that every Jew has a portion in the World to Come. This means that a seat in the theater has been reserved for each person's soul. But as in any theater, some seats are better than others. If God is "center stage," some souls will enjoy seats in the front row center section, others will sit in the balcony, and some will have obstructed views. But everyone will have a place. The seat we are assigned is based on the choices we make and the deeds we do in *olam hazeh*, this world.

We are told that we will be surprised who gets the best seats. We will look down and say, "What are they doing up front? They didn't accomplish much! They weren't so great!"

God will answer and say, "They are there because they listened to My voice."

We make a mistake when we think that only those who seem great, honored, and accomplished will merit a place before God. Each person is judged individually, and we don't know how one mitzvah, one act of kindness, will make a difference when God reviews a person's life.

Listening to God does not only mean obeying the laws of what and what not to do. Hearing His voice means that we see that life isn't ruled by coincidence, that we realize how events take place for a reason, and that we act accordingly. We may not know the Torah backward and forward, but if we have a relationship with our Creator, it can be worth a front-row seat in eternity.

Eternal Pleasure

Our Sages say that if we took all of life's pleasures, every one of them, and combined them with all the pleasures of everyone in this world, the total wouldn't be worth even one second in the World to Come — the pleasure of being close to God.

The Presence of God is a big deal. It may not have been uppermost in our minds in this world, but we know that if you were called to someone's home for a meeting, and following the meeting the host announced that God's Presence was about to arrive and wanted to communicate with you, you wouldn't say, "Well, sorry, it's late and I have to get up early tomorrow." You would be scared out of your mind, but there is nothing more important or more desirable than going before God, Creator of heaven and earth.

We can't imagine passive pleasure. For us pleasure is active. We go away on vacation. We ask for a raise and get it. We eat a big helping of the flavor of the month. Something happens and we feel pleasure. So how can sitting in one place be so overwhelmingly pleasurable? Because it is an earned pleasure — what we did in our lifetime on earth has yielded this result.

In *olam haba* we are sitting before God Who created us. He knows us inside and out. Every moment here on earth is His gift to us. He loves us more than our parents love us, more than we ever love or ever will love our children. And He calls us back to Him.

Of course people are not perfect and we all make mistakes. But those errors in judgment do not erase our good deeds. If we light candles on Friday night and then go to a movie, God does not look down and say, "Candles. Movie. We're back to square one." The act of lighting candles, of bringing in the Sabbath, is eternal. Nothing can take it away.

It is the same with every positive effort we make in life.

Of course we all make bad decisions and do things we deeply regret. What should we do about them? Ideally, we should take care of our mistakes here in this world. If we have wronged someone, we should make peace. If we are letting bad habits or bad character hold us back, we should work on breaking free and returning to the person we know we can be.

Judgment Day

What happens when our souls leave this world and go before God? We give an accounting, and a judgment takes place. Judgment is not something we look forward to. Who wants to be judged? But this is not just any judge. This is God, our Father in Heaven. A human judge might be biased. But our Creator gave us life and everything that happens in our lives. His judgment comes from love, and anything that derives from love is for our good.

Furthermore, His judgment means that our own "judgments" count. Life is not random; it has meaning and purpose. The decisions that we make in our lives count for something, and not just at the moment, but forever. The ultimate reward and punishment happen, but only in *olam haba*, the next world, not here in *olam hazeh*, this world.

But what about that bonus at work? I know God was rewarding me for giving charity. And that time my car broke down? That was a punishment for not driving my mother to her doctor's appointment.

This idea is a little bit right and a little bit wrong. It's right to realize that events happen in life for a reason and they are from God. But it's wrong to think that God "rewards" our good deeds and "punishes" our errors. What is really going on is that God is communicating with us. When we give charity or do anything that is right and good, God doesn't reward us, but He does give us more opportunities to do good.

The car breaking down is not a punishment, it's a message. Only you know what God is telling you. Get the message and learn from it.

Each year on Rosh Hashana and Yom Kippur, God judges us. He looks at the deeds and choices that we made during the year and decides what our next year will be like — based on our commitment to correct our mistakes. But at the time of death, after the burial, we go before God Who judges not just one year, but our entire lifetime.

Highway to Hell

The soul can go to one of two places: Heaven, which we have

discussed, or *Gehinnom*, Hell.

Do Jews believe in Hell? Yes! This may be surprising, because it is a subject not often brought up in Hebrew school or in synagogue. And growing up in a predominantly Christian society, Jews figure that if Christians believe in Heaven and Hell, then I guess we don't.

But we do. And the Jewish understanding differs somewhat:

Hell is the place that God created to help us take care of the mistakes we didn't correct in this world. It is called *Gehinnom*. But don't be afraid. It's not a place of devils and pitchforks, and it's not forever. If it is God's judgment that a person has to enter *Gehinnom*, the maximum amount of time spent there would be one Jewish year. A person can be there a split second, an entire year, or somewhere in between. That is the reason we say Kaddish, the mourner's prayer, for 11 months. We assume that our loved ones would never be there an entire year. Ideally, we want to bypass it all together.

A great rabbi was scheduled to speak on the subject of the World to Come at an "Executive Lunch and Learn" series in downtown Toronto. My husband picked him up at the airport, and on the way downtown asked him to "go easy on *Gehinnom*." He was afraid the rabbi would scare the audience.

The rabbi turned to my husband and asked, "Do you have hospitals here in Toronto?"

"Yes," he answered, confused.

"And," continued the rabbi, "are these world-class hospitals?"

"Yes," my husband answered again.

"Would you ever want to check into these hospitals?"

"No," said my husband.

"But if you need to, aren't you glad they're there?"

The rabbi explained that *Gehinnom* is a hospital for the soul. Going there will be painful. But it's from God's kindness, mercy, and love that such a place exists. We wouldn't want to check in even for a minute. But if we have to, we know it's for our good, and we hope our stay will be as short as possible.

The way to avoid *Gehinnom* altogether is to take care of our mistakes here in this world. This is not an easy task, but making a supreme effort in this world will ultimately avoid a much greater pain in the next.

Of Blessed Memory

Whether we are able to bypass *Gehinnom*, or we have to spend some time there, eventually we are able to enter the theater of *olam haba*. If we arrive and each of us is assigned a seat, does that mean that our share of pleasure is eternally limited to that particular view? No. The people we have left on earth can increase our share in the World to Come and enable us to earn better seating.

How does this happen? In memory of loved ones, people often give charity, name babies, learn Torah in their merit, and so on. These are not just good deeds. These are acts done in this world that have everlasting spiritual ramifications.

When we do something in someone's memory, we are saying:

Because of this person that I loved, I am living my life differently. He may be gone, but he is not forgotten. He continues to be a source of inspiration in my life. His life mattered, and his legacy will continue to make a difference.

What should you do in memory of a loved one?

My husband tells people to take a 30-day period, ideally the first 30 days after the funeral, which is called the *sheloshim*, and do something concrete in memory of the departed. For some it could be placing a coin in a *tzedakah* (charity) box each day and reciting a simple prayer.

Most people, after experiencing such a tremendous loss, feel a great need to do something to honor the departed. Souls in the next world have awareness of what goes on here. Doing good deeds in their merit will not only bring you comfort, but also add to the merit of the one you have lost.

Excerpted from Remember My Soul, *by Lori Palatnik*
(Leviathan Press — www.leviathanpress.com)

Is God Comfortable Here?

A chassidic tale relates that the Rebbe of Kotzk once summoned his disciples and challenged them, "Where can you find God?"

One volunteered an answer: "His glory resides in heaven." The rebbe frowned with displeasure.

A second disciple offered, "The entire world is filled with His glory." Once again, the rebbe shook his head in disapproval.

Anxious to understand, the chassidim implored: "Rebbe, please tell us where can we find Him?"

The rebbe said, "Wherever you invite Him!"

All of us at some point struggle with the need to make God a more integral part of our lives. As such it is imperative that we understand how the rebbe's counsel can be translated into daily reality.

Contrary to what we might think, making God a real part of our ongoing, moment-to-moment existence does not require an overhaul of our lives. It does, however, demand something that is very hard to come by in our hurried and driven society — focus and mindfulness.

See biography of REBBETZIN FAIGE TWERSKI, page 203.

Most of us move through life, day after day, in a predictable, robot-like way, hardly giving a second thought to what we are doing. To most of us, the words of the psalmist, "God is before me always," represent a remote and wishful goal — an ideal accessible only to the very holy and saintly of spirit.

Taking Stock of Everyday Life

Such, indeed, was my thinking, until a realization hit me like a thunderbolt.

When I took stock of my normal everyday life, I realized how very mundane it was. I would wake up, get the kids ready for school, serve breakfast, drive carpool, clean up, vacuum, make lunch, make supper, carry on with telephone conversations and familial interactions, help the kids with their homework, and get them to bed — all in the context of a typical day. How much spirituality could there possibly be in a day consumed by so many physical and material concerns?

The scariest part, I realized, was that things which are purely physical are limited, moribund, and perishable. They die, never to be heard from again. How could I justify a life where the majority of my precious moments would be relegated to oblivion?

Would the better part of my life be buried at its conclusion, like an animal? Would it be summed up with "been there, done that, and gone forever"?

In my heart of hearts, I knew it couldn't be. The moments of my life were too dear and meaningful — yes, even those spent baking, cooking, cleaning, and diapering babies — for me to consign them to nothingness.

The rebbe had advised, "Invite God into your life. He will come when He is invited." I came to realize that what it takes to transform a "mundane moment" into a "spiritual moment" is the presence of the Almighty.

As soon as one introduces God into the picture, His Eternal Essence transforms the moment into something immortal and timeless — into a moment that will never die, a moment that lasts forever.

Inviting God Inside

How do we do this?

Quite simply! Whatever it is that you're doing, stop for an instant to ask yourself: "Is God comfortable being here now?"

As I talk to my friend on the phone, I pause momentarily to reflect: Is the nature and the content of this conversation such that it invites His presence, or banishes it? Is my conversation gossipy or is it positive and uplifting?

As I clean, vacuum, and care for my children (all undeniably "mundane" activities), am I resentful, or do I recognize that these are necessary elements for a sacred environment, conducive to spiritual growth?

In other words, given my present attitude, would God be comfortable being with me or not? If the response is affirmative, then I have captured the moment for eternity.

Commerce is clearly another "weekday" venture. By applying the Torah's ethics to our business transactions, we can invite the Almighty to join us, thereby claiming these moments for all of time.

The same holds true of personal interactions and spousal relationships, if they are sufficiently sensitive such that God would relish being there.

When we sit down to eat, do we exercise our unique prerogative of choice to ask, "Is this what God would want me to eat? Does it meet His standards? Is it kosher? Is it healthy? Will it give me the requisite energy to fulfill His will? Is it the right amount? Did I remember to express my gratitude by reciting a blessing? Bottom line: Would the Creator be comfortable sitting at my table?

When applied to our daily lives, the psalmist's exhortation to have "God before me always" means focusing constantly on the opportunity for God to accompany us in everything we do. No moment of our lives need be written off as "time killed."

If you aspire to invite infinity into your finite life, all it takes is asking the simple question: "Is God comfortable here now?"

SARA YOHEVED RIGLER

The God Factor

"**W**omen your age have a 5 percent chance of becoming pregnant using In Vitro Fertilization," Dr. C. was telling me as I sat opposite her in a leading I.V.F. clinic. I was 45 years old, and since the birth of my first child at the age of 40, had been trying to conceive a second baby using every spiritual, medical, and alternative means available. Dr. C. continued: "Of those 5 percent, only half carry through to term and deliver a live baby. Thus, you have 2½ percent chance of succeeding."

I stared at the good doctor. I was thinking: "God runs the world. If God wants me to have a second child, I will. And if God doesn't want, I won't. It's my job to exert maximum effort, which I.V.F. is. Whether or not I succeed is up to God."

To Dr. C. I said: "In any case, I would like to try."

The first time I did I.V.F., it failed.

The clinic offered two tries for the same price. I tried again. This involved getting two shots of powerful fertility drugs every day for two weeks in order to generate as many eggs as possible; a minimum of three eggs was required to continue with the process.

See biography of SARA YOHEVED RIGLER, page 17.

Then the doctor would surgically extract the eggs from the ovary, fertilize them, and reinsert them into the womb.

The day before my scheduled extraction, I had an ultrasound to determine the number of eggs. The ultrasound doctor informed me sadly that I had only two eggs, not enough to even bother with the extraction. After all the effort, the drugs, the cost... Tearfully, I begged him to fudge the results and write that there were three eggs. "If God wants me to get pregnant," I thought, "He can do it with just two eggs." The ultrasound doctor consented.

When Dr. C. performed the extraction the next day, she found only one egg.

My chances of success slid from 2½ percent to zilch.

Since I was already on the operating table, Dr. C. humored me. She extracted and fertilized the single egg. Two days later, as she reinserted it, my non-religious doctor looked me straight in the eye and uttered a single word: "Pray."

I prayed and cried and made a vow to God. Two weeks later, I got a positive pregnancy test.

The next day, I saw Dr. C. in the clinic. I was jubilant. She was skeptical. Ever the meticulous scientist, she knew that a woman can't get pregnant with I.V.F. using only one egg. "I'll believe you're pregnant," she told me, "when I see an ultrasound with a heartbeat."

Three weeks later I ecstatically waved in front of her an ultrasound with a heartbeat.

At the end of nine months, at the age of 46, I gave birth to a healthy baby boy, may he live and be well, *bli ayin hara*.

Experts and Predictions

Ever since September 11, my e-mail has been full of predictions by experts regarding every possible aspect of war, bio-terror, and chemical warfare:

How many Americans would die in a smallpox epidemic launched by bio-terrorists.

What percentage of Israelis would survive if Saddam Hussein sent chemical warheads loaded with VX, an advanced chemical agent.

Why it is impossible to win a war in the rough terrain of Afghanistan (this before American allies ousted the Taliban).

All of these predictions, however, leave out one factor, the most crucial factor: God runs the world. Any equation which does not take into account the God factor is bound to come up with the wrong conclusion.

In 1967, as Egypt's Gamal Abdul Nasser was proclaiming the imminent destruction of the State of Israel, both political pundits and military strategists predicted Israel's defeat. The figures were formidable. The 19-year-old state was up against the impending combined attack of Egypt, Syria, Jordan, and Iraq. The four Arab armies together boasted 810 airplanes against Israel's 350; 2,880 tanks against Israel's 800; and 465,000 troops against Israel's 265,000. So convinced were the Israelis themselves of an inevitable bloodbath that the Rabbinate officially designated all of Jerusalem's parks as cemeteries.

Apparently, God had a different idea. Instead of defeat, Israel experienced a surprise victory. In just six days, Israel not only pushed back the Arab forces, but recaptured all the major Jewish holy sites, including the Temple Mount, the Western Wall, the Cave of the Patriarchs in Hebron, and the Tomb of Rachel in Bethlehem. The experts were left stammering.

My cousin Phil is a retired corporate executive, a highly intelligent, savvy pragmatist who keeps himself well-informed and draws clear-headed conclusions from the facts. In the 1980s, he predicted that the State of Israel would cease to exist by the year 2013.

At first, this doomsday forecast was based on the demographic threat: the Arab birthrate on both sides of the Green Line was staggeringly greater than the Jewish birthrate. The numbers were incontestable; by 2013 the Jewish state would have a majority of Arab inhabitants.

Barring the God factor, that is. In the Torah, God states His intention to bring the Jews back to Israel from the far corners of the earth. In 1990, the Soviet Union collapsed almost overnight, and through the tattered Iron Curtain half a million Jews exited to

Israel. Within a decade, the Jewish population of Israel had swelled by 10 percent, and all mention of the demographic threat disappeared from the media.

Now Phil, who dearly loves Israel, is convinced that we will commit political suicide. After the failure of Oslo and the aborted offers at Camp David, pro-Israel columnists in the American media warned that if the U.S. and Europe continue to push Israel into dangerous concessions, the map of the Middle East which appears in Palestinian textbooks — with Israel totally absent — may yet prove accurate.

I cannot argue with Phil's facts and figures, but I know that God is not bound by them. The story of Chanukah comes to teach us how history can take the most unlikely turns and produce the most improbable victors.

Chanukah Miracles

What would the experts of 167 BCE have said about the chances of the old priest Matitiyahu and his family and friends defeating the mighty army of the Syrian Greek empire? I can see their pronouncements now:

> *An ultra-Orthodox rabbi and his reactionary compatriots have raised the banner of revolt against not only the prevailing rule of the Seleucid Empire, but against all of modern Greek culture and enlightenment. This motley band of guerrilla fighters is outnumbered more than 4 to 1 by the Seleucid army, which boasts some 40,000 professional troops equipped with the cutting edge of military technology, as well as the ultimate weapon — a herd of elephants trained for battle, against which no warriors can stand.*
>
> *The Maccabees, as this reactionary rebel force is called, are opposed not only by the considerable Greek population on the coastal plain, but also by a large proportion of the Jewish inhabitants, who have, over the last century and a half, adapted to the worldwide hegemony of Greek language, culture, and religion. Thus, the Maccabees have initiated a civil war, targeted at their own progressive fellow Jews, who are*

*called Hellenists. As the Hellenists comprise the most wealthy
and influential segments of Jewish society, the effort to unseat
them is nothing less than preposterous.*

*In short, the attempt of the Maccabees to score a military
victory, overthrow the progressive culture which dominates the
whole world, and reestablish their antiquated religion on the
soil of Judea, is futile.*

The pundits would have been accurate in their analysis. After
all, who could have predicted that three years after issuing his
rallying cry, "Follow me, all of you who are for God's law and stand
by the covenant," Matitiyahu's followers would reconquer
Jerusalem, purify the Temple of its pagan desecrations, and
reinstitute the Temple service? Although the total victory was
hard-won — taking over 20 years and costing the lives of four-out-
of-five of Matitiyahu's sons, the Maccabees ultimately triumphed
over the Greeks.

The prayer to God that we add during the eight days of
Chanukah emphasizes the unlikelihood of the Jewish victory:
"You delivered the strong into the hands of the weak, the many
into the hands of the few..."

Chanukah celebrates the victory of the unlikely, the
improbable, the virtually impossible. It is the antithesis of the still-
prevailing Greek worldview which adulates logic and the laws of
nature as absolute. Chanukah proves that in a world run by God,
miracles can happen.

Maximum Effort

Judaism forbids relying on miracles. A Jew must always exert
maximum reasonable effort to effect desired results. The
Maccabees did not sit back and wait for a miracle to happen. But
they were not cowed by the odds, nor discouraged by daunting
prospects.

The rule of thumb in Jewish history has always been that when
we are threatened spiritually (as we were by the Greeks, who
wanted to exterminate our religion, not our lives), we fight back

physically, as the Maccabees did. And when we are threatened physically (as we were during the events leading up to Purim, when Haman wanted to exterminate every Jew), we fight back spiritually, just as the Jews of Shushan, at Mordechai's and Esther's behest, did teshuva.

Since we are today threatened physically, we must — in addition to the Israeli army's self-defensive measures — fight back spiritually.

The spears of the Maccabees are the mitzvot of today. Every time a Jew commits to keeping Shabbat or reaches out in friendship to a Jew of a different stripe, a spiritual force is produced which could make a terrorist bomb placed on a Jerusalem street fail to detonate. (The vast majority of terrorist bombs in Israel miraculously fail to detonate, or blow up on busy thoroughfares without injuring anyone.)

My cousin Phil accuses me of being passive. In truth, I am a spiritual warrior. I know that God will come through for Israel if I exert myself beyond my comfort zone to keep the mitzvot that aren't easy for me, and if other Jews do the same. If I overcome my urge to take revenge against my obnoxious neighbor, I have launched a projectile powerful enough to bring down Saddam Hussein's most deadly missiles.

The time has come to wage a spiritual war against our enemies. Every mitzvah is an infinitely more powerful weapon than anything in Bin Laden's arsenal.

So when you go to light your Chanukah candles, instead of thinking you are enacting a quaint custom of Jewish tradition, realize that you are fulfilling a mitzvah, and mitzvot are the spiritual antidote to whatever chemicals the bio-terrorists are brewing in their nefarious laboratories. God, who runs the world, expects us to exert maximum effort in doing mitzvot. The victory in this war, as in the Maccabean war we commemorate, will come from Him.

TZVI GLUCKIN

Shwarma: A Love Story

Most of my musician friends in college were either into heavy drug use or meditation. They were looking for a way to recreate the high of a performance in other areas of life.

I chose the spiritual route. I dug the Eastern flavor.

The problem was that too many years of serious coffee addiction had made it impossible for me to sit still for more than five minutes. I couldn't meditate. I bounced off the walls. My eyes flickered. My nose twitched.

But I wasn't willing to accept responsibility for my spiritual impotence. I blamed the world around me.

"I hate hippies," I told a friend of mine.

"Why? What'd they ever do to you?"

"They ruin my inner peace."

"How so?"

"It's that patchouli oil. Stinks the peace right out of me."

Deep down, I knew that meditation wasn't for me. I pretended to be into it because my friends were into it.

I kept trying. Years went by. I came to a point in my life where I

See biography of TZVI GLUCKIN, page 30.

was beginning to experience an ethnic Jewish awakening. I bought a book on Jewish meditation in an attempt to justify my growing interest in Judaism with a need to still look cool in the eyes of the art crowd. I tried gazing at letters of the Hebrew alphabet. I thought about various interpolations of the different names of God. I drove myself crazy.

"I can't find the space behind my head!" I confided to a friend.

"What are you talking about?"

"The book says 'focus on the space right behind your head.' I keep thinking about dandruff and male pattern baldness. This isn't spirituality, it's insanity."

I discussed my problems openly.

"Maybe God's a practical joker," I told a friend.

"Why?"

"The vehicles to transcendence are totally unnatural. Who in their right mind can sit around all day clearing their brain of static?"

"Maybe you're looking in the wrong place."

"Maybe. I'm always hungry."

Then a Middle Eastern friend turned me on to *shwarma*.

"Come, I give you an experience," he said.

"Great."

He took me to a greasy Israeli joint.

"It's kosher."

"Who cares."

The guy behind the counter brought out what looked like an overweight tortilla.

"*Laffa*," my friend informed me.

"What the heck is that?"

The guy behind the counter took the trouble to explain. "It like giant flat pita. You no stuff it. You roll it."

My friend slapped on a thick helping of crushed chickpea paste.

"Humus," he said.

"I know."

He loaded it up with chopped cucumber and tomato salad,

French fries, and a mysterious meat substance.

"Lamb," he said.

"Lamb?"

"Really turkey basted in lamb fat. Delicious."

He rolled it up and handed it to me.

I took a bite. Grease ran down my arm.

"This is unbelievable," I said.

"I knew you like it."

The feeling stayed with me for almost a week. It was in my head. It was on my breath. I knew I was onto something big.

I extolled the virtues of *shwarma* to everyone. It was all I talked about.

"What?! You haven't had *shwarma*? You haven't lived," I told people.

I ran into some of my meditating friends. "How can you spend your day sitting around like a lotus? There is *shwarma* to be eaten."

"We're into connecting to a higher reality."

"So am I. It's called *shwarma*."

I'd found it. I'd thought that in order to experience spirituality I had to do something "spiritual." I was wrong. True transcendence isn't about slipping off into an artificial world. It's about finding spirituality in the here-and-now.

I began to teach people about higher eating.

"There are two ways to eat *shwarma*," I began. "Way number one is to inhale the thing. Open wide and swallow, similar to the way a dog eats."

"Really?"

"Way number two is to pause a moment and say: 'Isn't it great to live in a world where I can experience the delicious pleasure of *shwarma*.' And then inhale."

"I don't get it."

"The first way is eating *shwarma* because it's *shwarma*. The second way is to use *shwarma* as a spiritual vehicle, to realize that this meal is an opportunity to connect to God, to plug in and experience transcendence. Why meditate only an hour a day? You can always be on the lookout for spiritual experience."

I had discovered the secret of higher living: Elevate the physical. All of life is a tool to connect to something bigger. Sure, sometimes we need to take time out to think about things, to meditate. But most of the time, we just need to eat something greasy.

SARA YOHEVED RIGLER

Spirituality without God

M elody died last week at the age of 42. Exactly 12 months ago, she got a surprise diagnosis: her throbbing back pains were caused by metastasized breast cancer.

Her prognosis was less than two months to live. Melody and her long-time boyfriend Kevin fought valiantly, using every weapon in the arsenal of New Age cures — including energy healing, acupuncture, rebirthing, visualization, diet, and contact with nature, in addition to radiation and chemotherapy.

Although I did not know Melody well, her ordeal touched me deeply. She had been a periodic member of the ashram where I lived for 15 years before I moved to Jerusalem and took the path of Judaism. The daughter of a Swedenborgian minister, Melody practiced a generic New Age religion, which embraced meditation, vibrational healing, positive thinking, and music. She played the guitar and sang beautiful songs of her own composition, songs about love and the spirit.

Kevin sent out frequent e-mails about Melody's progress, and eventual decline. In the spring she rallied, miraculously defying her prognosis. She started to walk again, gained weight, and was

See biography of SARA YOHEVED RIGLER, page 17.

featured on a PBS television special about alternative healing. A euphoric Kevin wrote to thank all the people who had sent Melody their prayers and healing thoughts.

Something was bothering me. I wondered why, in his long letter, he never thanked God.

Angels and Miracles, but No God

Throughout the year, Kevin wrote of angels, miracles, spiritual worlds, dreams, and the importance of sending Melody only positive energy. Many times he asked everyone to pray, but the more I contemplated his messages, the more I became aware of something I can only call "horizontal prayer" — the sending of positive, healing wishes for recovery not to God, but to Melody. In fact, in his first letter Kevin wrote:

"I've asked of all the Swedenborgian churches, that we performed at during the Peace Prayer tour, to offer prayers to Melody this Sunday morning."

I originally thought the "to" was a typo.

The last letter, written by Devipriya, one of our ashram friends, described Melody's passing. She was surrounded by fragrant flowers, with four of the ashram members chanting to their lineage of gurus, sending her off to complete her mission in the spirit world. During the transition, they devoutly followed the directions of a shaman and a Buddhist lama. Devipriya wrote: "The room was so charged, and so peaceful at the same time, like angels had come and lifted her from her body."

God was never mentioned.

Relationship, Not Religion

Reading that letter amidst my sorrow, I couldn't help but think how different is the focus of Jewish tradition, where a yearning for connection with God permeates every conscious act.

Rabbi Leib Kelemen is fond of saying: "Judaism is not a religion. It's a relationship." All the elements of Judaism work to further the relationship between the human being and God. Prayer is vertical: a one-to-one conversation with God. The mitzvot are to be performed in the same way that a lover does the bidding of his or her beloved. Therefore, Judaism without God would be like "Romeo and Juliet" without Juliet.

It is a truism that increasing numbers of people are not marrying because of their inability to commit to a relationship. One wonders if the predilection for spirituality without God derives from the same syndrome: valuing freedom and independence over a relationship which will often demand the total giving of one's self.

My teacher, Rebbetzin Tzipporah Heller, says that even when one is dealing with a situation in accordance with lofty principles and techniques, one must still ask, "Is God in the picture?"

For example, the self-help market offers dozens of books on how to control destructive anger. All these techniques may be useful. Judaism, however, would add that when faced with an anger-provoking situation, one must recognize that everything comes from God. That includes the phone ringing with a wrong number in the middle of the night, the spilled salad dressing on your just-washed floor, or the train you are running to catch pulling out of the station one minute early.

No matter which techniques you apply to bring down your blood pressure, if God is not in the picture, you are missing out on a custom-made opportunity to connect with the Divine.

What's wrong with a picture devoid of God? Quite simply: God is reality. Ultimate reality, and immediate reality. To live in this world oblivious to God is like being a fish oblivious to water. Maybe that's okay for a fish, but not for a person who aspires to greater consciousness.

Lost in the Shuffle

After two centuries engrossed in a materialistic vision of the world, the West is enjoying a resurgence of spirituality. The popularity of angels, psychic phenomena, faith healing, meditation, and near-death experiences testifies to a paradigm shift in our concept of reality. We have at long last begun to recognize that reality includes a spiritual dimension, which is not susceptible to scientific measurement.

But somehow God has gotten lost in the shuffle. It is rather like a lavish bar mitzvah party, replete with ten-piece orchestra, 14 tables of smorgasbord, six Viennese dessert tables, a troupe of jugglers and acrobats — and no glimpse of "mitzvah" in sight.

The materialistic worldview which prevailed in the 19th and 20th centuries denied the existence of God. The spiritual worldview gaining popularity at the threshold of the 21st century is too busy with psychic phenomena and personal growth to care about the existence of God.

It is no coincidence that the most popular Eastern paths in the West are derivatives of Buddhism, a non-theistic religion. Gautama Buddha, the fifth-century BCE founder of Buddhism, never mentioned God in his teachings. His Four Noble Truths and his Eightfold Way speak about escaping the inherent suffering of this world by transcending desire and practicing right action and thought. The entire thrust is on human consciousness, control of mind, and self-effort. This forms the prototype of most of the personal growth movements prevalent in America.

While Hinduism is a totally theistic religion, its American transplants emphasize their lineage of gurus rather than the deities of the Hindu pantheon (with the exception of the Krishna Consciousness movement).

The advantages of spirituality without God are obvious: One can choose one's own direction, methods, and goals without the intrusions of the Divine. The "inner voice," which functions as the CEO of most New Age enterprises, rarely whispers what one doesn't want to hear.

Judaism looks at things differently. The mitzvot, particularly those we find most challenging, are our straightest path to self-actualization. For they all derive from a loving God Who desires the most intimate relationship with all His creations.

SPIRITUALITY
& EVERYDAY LIFE

EMUNA BRAVERMAN

"You Incompetent Buffoon!"

"I can't believe the incompetent staff at Macy's!"
"Do you know how long I had to wait in line at the bank today?!"

"I wish they'd outlaw telemarketers. They're so obnoxious."

We all get frustrated with the way large corporations inconvenience us — Wal-Mart, Bloomingdale's, Bank of America, Visa — doing nothing but earning money and making our lives more difficult, more stressful. Sometimes these companies are to blame for being inefficient and overbearing. And sometimes they're not.

Either way, the target of our anger is usually not the CEO, the board of directors, or the shareholders — but some struggling minimum wage worker, doing his best to hold down two jobs, keep his family afloat, and put on a cheerful face.

Read Barbara Ehrenreich's *Nickel and Dimed*. She tried to survive at minimum wage, going out and imitating the life of a

---

EMUNA BRAVERMAN has a law degree from the University of Toronto and a master's in psychology from Pepperdine University. She lives with her husband and nine children in Los Angeles where they both work for Aish HaTorah.

hotel housekeeper, a cleaning service maid, a waitress. She was treated like dirt by employers, customers, and the social service agencies who were supposed to help.

Along the way, she discovered the most basic of truths: "It ain't easy."

Hurry Up and Load the Car

The minimum wage group doesn't get the press that the inner city does. Their plight is less obvious, their skin color not revealing. Yet they lead a tough existence, working hard, and barely eking out a living under frequently demeaning circumstances.

We certainly can't help all these people. Or can we?

True, we may not all be suited to teach in the Bronx. We may not be available to care for crack babies in Watts. And we can't all run after-school anti-drug programs.

But we can all be nice to the service people in our lives. And we don't even have to leave our neighborhoods to do so.

I've been in many homes where the cleaning help is treated as subhuman — ordered around, made to eat separately, severely criticized — by the same people arguing adamantly in favor of civil rights. Is that who we want to be? Is that what we want our children to see?

It's easy to be dismissive of the bag girl at the supermarket. After all, "I've got a lot to do and if they would only hurry up and load my car." A friend of mine recently stopped to ask the woman helping her how she enjoyed her job. "Grateful to have it," she explained. She had just moved to Los Angeles to start a new life after her husband was murdered and her restaurant went bankrupt.

My friend's attitude sobered. Instead of shrieking "Be careful with the eggs!" my friend warmly patted her arm. "Is there anything I could do to help you?"

Thank You for Calling

Isn't it embarrassing to be in a restaurant where a patron is yelling at the waiter? (No second date for him.) Aren't you humiliated by watching a customer screaming at the bank officer? Do you avert your eyes as the dry cleaner gets put down?

Do you ever behave the same way?

We are all employers. We have many "employees" serving us throughout the day. Do you remember that they're also human beings?

It's not always easy. Sometimes they really are annoying. Sometimes they're really incompetent. As I was writing this article, I received a phone call from a close friend. "I hate telemarketers," she began. "They interrupt us. They're trying to sell us something. They rattle on and on and on..."

And they're also real people with a mortgage to pay and children to feed. You don't have to purchase their product. But you do have to behave decently.

So what do you say to a telemarketer? (That we're allowed to print!) How about: "Thank you for calling. I see you're working very hard at your job. I appreciate your effort but I'm not interested right now. Thanks again."

And how do you keep from strangling the bank teller? "I realize it's not your fault. These computers can really be frustrating, can't they?"

Or in line at the department store (and you didn't bring a book): "It's so busy here. I see the staff is working really hard to serve everyone properly. These are great colors I picked out, aren't they?"

Or you could always try shopping online...

It's easy to condemn the cold-heartedness of big business, the callousness of large corporations. It's harder to turn the camera inwards. Maybe Xerox isn't the ideal employer. Or Microsoft. Or Federated Stores. But what about you?

RABBI YITZCHOK BREITOWITZ

Holy Money

M any have a mistaken idea of what is within the scope of Jewish tradition. People know that lighting Chanukah candles, observing Shabbat, and the laws of kashrut are the purview of rabbis. But many have an attitude that "If I don't tell the rabbi how to run his business, the rabbi shouldn't tell me how to run mine." Very often, we live fragmented, dichotomized lives where what we do in the office from 9 to 5 (or if you're a workaholic, from 8 to 7) is our own private affair, and then at home we observe the holidays and rituals of Judaism.

The Talmud discusses the questions people are asked by God after their deaths. The very first question — even before issues of religious practice — is *"Nasata v'netata be'emunah,"* which means, "Did you conduct your business affairs ethically?"

Throughout the Torah, there is constant juxtaposition between ritual commands and the ethical obligations of one human being to another. One verse may say, "Don't worship

RABBI YITZCHAK BREITOWITZ is the rabbi of the Woodside Synagogue in Silver Spring, MD, and a professor at the University of Maryland Law School. He is the author of *Between Civil and Religious Law: The Plight of the Agunah in American Society* (Greenwood Press). This article was originally posted on Jewish Law (www.jlaw.com), and modified with permission of the author.

idols," followed by, "Do not cheat, do not misrepresent, d engage in fraud" (Leviticus 19). Dichotomy between behavior and social behavior is foreign to Judaism, because they are all part of the same God-given morality, the same religious structure.

In business ethics, the ethereal transcendent teachings of holiness and spirituality most directly confront the often-grubby rat race of the marketplace. This is the acid test of whether religion is truly relevant, or religion is simply relegated to an isolated sphere of human activity. It is business ethics, one could posit, above all, that shows how God coexists in the world, rather than God and godliness being separate and apart.

Your Money or Your Life

We say in the Shema, "You shall love the Lord your God with all your heart, with all your soul, and with all your might." The reference to "all your might" is that we are enjoined to love God with all our money.

This raises a question: If the verse already says to love God with all your soul (even to the extent of giving up your life, if necessary), then why does it continue and say to serve God with all your money?

The answer, Rashi explains, is that some people prefer their money to their lives, and if the verse would simply say to "serve God with your life," we wouldn't necessarily infer to serve God with all our money. It's like the famous Jack Benny joke: Approached by a mugger who says, "Your money or your life," the guy says, "Let me think about it a bit."

What exactly is the concept of serving God with all your money? Certainly, God does not wish us to take oaths of poverty. God does not require us to renounce material wealth. So how does one serve God with money?

The short answer is: We serve God with the probity and integrity by which we amass those possessions. In the conduct of our business, in the accumulation of wealth, there is also a mechanism to serve God.

On Yom Kippur, we spend an entire day confessing our sins over and over and over again, and sometimes we don't even know what we've done wrong. Maimonides writes that we often fail to realize that every sin has many implications. For example, if you confess to God, "I'm sorry for the murders I've committed," you might think, "Well I haven't killed anybody." Yes, I didn't commit murder by shooting somebody, but perhaps I didn't take the steps I could have as a member of society to reduce the crime rate. And keep in mind, the Talmud says, that humiliating somebody publicly is tantamount to murder.

After a whole day of beating one's breast, we come to the end of Yom Kippur — the prayer of Neilah, the final moments of beseeching God. The Neilah confession (*vidui*) is only a few short paragraphs. But the one thing it stresses is theft. We ask God to forgive us for the appropriation of other people's property. As the Talmud says, while only a minority of people commit sexual offenses, most people sin in matters of theft.

Ancient Chutzpah

The Torah has 613 mitzvot, one of which is *Kedoshim tihyu* — "Be holy." What does that mean? Doesn't "be holy" simply come through doing the other 612 mitzvot? Or is there some extra dimension that this mitzvah entails?

The great commentator Nachmanides tells us that *Kedoshim tihyu* is a requirement not to just obey the letter of the law, but to obey the spirit of the law as well. Nachmanides posits that it is entirely possible for a person to be 100 percent observant, and yet be a "*naval birshut haTorah*" — a repulsive, disgusting individual within the confines of the law.

It's not enough to just obey the law. There is also the concept of "*Lifnim mishurat hadin*" — going beyond the law and embracing the ethical imperatives within that legal structure.

A Talmudic story illustrates this in the business context. The sage Raba Bar-Bar Chana once hired workers to transport barrels of wine. The workers were negligent, and as a result, the barrels broke, causing the rabbi a severe financial loss. He took the workers to court, suing them for the value of the wine.

The workers' only defense was, "We are poor and can't afford to pay you back."

The court ruled in favor of the workers.

Raba Bar-Bar Chana protested: "Doesn't the law entitle me to compensation for their negligence?"

The court said, "The letter of the law agrees with you. But as a righteous person, you have to take into account that these people are poor. Therefore, you must go beyond pressing your exact legal rights."

The story gets even better. In an ancient example of chutzpah, the workers turned around and sued for the wages they were never paid for that day. And again, astoundingly, the court ruled in favor of the workers. "These are people who need the money, and therefore you must go beyond the law."

Litigious Society

Judaism teaches us to live in this world, a world that is a mixture of good and evil. And it's a world where other people don't always play by the same rules. But the test of a moral person is not whether he behaves morally when others are behaving morally to him. The test of a moral person is whether he adheres to those values even if everyone else fails.

One problem in American society is that too many are obsessed with asserting rights to the fullest. Alexander de Toqueville remarked over 200 years ago that Americans are a litigious society, that we go to court over the smallest drop of the hat. We've become a "rights-oriented" society rather than an "obligation-oriented" society.

Judaism teaches, above all: Don't always press your claims to the fullest. Deal with the other person in a spirit of tolerance, acceptance, and compromise.

Through adherence to ethics in business, we create a peaceful world, a world where we're not looking after number one, a world where we have a shared sense of community. That paves the way for the ultimate redemption of humanity that we hope and pray for.

JEFF DUNETZ

Daddy on the Unemployment Line

T here were boxes everywhere, all filled with the tchotchkes that gave my office its personality. All the family pictures were wrapped in bubble paper and packed away. From time to time the phone would ring again, or somebody would call — I'd cry, they'd cry, and then I would awkwardly change the topic. Since my boss told me the day before that I was getting laid off from the best job I ever had, publisher of a popular children's magazine, my crying wouldn't stop.

First things first: I had to tell my family. I called my wife Lois as soon as I was told. She told me how much she loved me and how talented I was. She told me what a great job I had done — reminding me that just this past March the magazine had won awards for the job I did. In February the president of my division had introduced me to the chairman of the parent corporation,

---

JEFF DUNETZ is a 20-year marketing veteran and the married father of two kids who ask lots of questions about being Jewish that he can't answer. Jeff has been active in Jewish organizations since his USY days, and is presently on the board of trustees of the Dix Hills Jewish Center.

telling him what a great job I was doing. My wife kept reminding me that 500 other senior people also got laid off, so it had nothing to do with me. Consciously I heard her and believed her — but I didn't really. My wife loved me and she had to say these things.

My parents always taught me that if you work hard and do a good job, things would work out. My parents wouldn't lie. Now I was getting laid off from a job that I worked very hard at and won recognition for — so I must have done something very wrong. Even if I hadn't done something wrong, I was a failure; I was out of work and couldn't provide for my family. It didn't matter that my wife had her own business and we could live on that income. I am the father and I don't have a job, so I must be a loser.

I was worried about telling my kids. They loved having a daddy who worked for a children's magazine, even more than I enjoyed working there. Much to my relief, they took it in stride. My daughter gave me a hug and went back to her homework. My son gave me a confused look and asked if he could go back to his Nintendo. So much for the Robert Young, "Father Knows Best" approach.

I couldn't tell my parents yet because my last day at work was my dad's birthday, and my mom was about to go for a follow-up doctor's appointment for the heart surgery she'd had one week earlier. Eventually when my mother got the news, she asked me, crying, "Is there anything I can do? Do you need anything?"

"Well," I replied, "I could use some kasha varnishkas." (At 44 years old, food still equals love.)

Brand New Putter

The first week of unemployment was a blur. I remember going to shul one day that first week. I get real comfort from the davening — a feeling like whatever happens, at least I have God pulling for me.

Another reason I went is to see my extended family, the folks at the shul. They have shown me the meaning of the term "Children of Israel." As I have become more observant over the past few years, I have learned that Judaism is more than just a religion, or even a nation. What has really kept us going over these last few thousand years is that we are family of cousins, all descended from 12 brothers. When the chips are down, we stop everything and act like a family should.

At the shul, everyone wanted to help however they could. But I kept my public face positive. "Look at the bright side," I said. "Now I can get to minyan every morning."

But I was very sad. I wanted to work, I wanted to be productive, and I didn't want just another job — I wanted *my* job. I always said that if I ever left the magazine, they would have to throw me out. Well they did.

When I left my job, the management asked me to sign a separation agreement. I took it home and gave it to my wife (who is a wonder at details) to look it over before I signed. I wanted to sign it right away, subconsciously thinking that if I signed it fast, they would call me, forgive me, and let me have my job back.

Lois said that the document was a lot of legalese, which essentially said they would honor my contract, and in turn I would promise never to sue or speak badly about the company. In the meantime, I left it unsigned.

I came home one day and found a big box waiting at the front door. I opened the package and found a brand new putter. (I play golf every Sunday during the summer.) Attached to the putter was a note from my old boss. The letter thanked me for my hard work and passion, and attributed much of the success of the magazine to my leadership.

At first I was angry. If I was so good, why am I out of work? After a while I did calm down — he had only good intentions in sending me the gift.

Home Time

Around Thanksgiving, my son's class had to answer the question, "What are you most thankful for?" Perry answered, "I am thankful that my dad is out of work. Now he can play with me when I get home from school."

He's right. I got to watch my seven-year-old son take his test for a yellow belt in karate — which I wouldn't have been able to do if I was working at my old job. And now I get many more hugs.

By mid-December I had seen every recruiter in my industry. They all told me that I have a great reputation and an impressive resume; I will find something soon after the first of the year. Well guys, now it's after the first. What's going on? Why am I still here?

Everybody told me to settle into a routine, so I have. I help the kids get ready for school, job search until noon, and then go to the JCC where I spend an hour on the treadmill. On the treadmill I read the Torah e-mails that I print out each morning. In the afternoons I go back to the job hunt, until the kids come home.

And I do projects. I have cleaned out the garage, my home office, and the basement. I have brought my kid's leftover toddler toys and books over to the shul's nursery school. I rebuilt a computer for my son and one for my dad. I am doing stuff with the kids that I never have before — renting movies, building cars, and using power tools.

Last week I got a call from the president of my former employer. We always had a very nice relationship. When I heard his voice on the phone, I thought, "My boss must have gotten tired of doing both his job and mine, and now the president of the company is calling to offer me my old job back."

Well not quite. He called to see why I wasn't signing the separation agreement. I felt awful. It reminded me of those adolescent days when you get a call from your ex-girlfriend and you think she's calling because she misses you. But she's really calling to find out where you got the sweater you gave her for her birthday so she can return it. I was very angry — not at him — but at myself for not being able to get over it and move on.

Defined by Occupation

Though I still haven't gotten a job, I believe that God answers all my prayers. It's just that sometimes the answer is "no" or "not now." Maybe He has something else in store for me, or maybe He just wants me spend more time with my wife and kids. But He is listening. Hey, didn't He just get the N.Y. Mets a power hitter to bat behind Mike Piazza — something I prayed for all last summer?!

I've had a lot of ups and downs over the last two months — periods of anger, frustration, determination, and resignation. Lois says I'm so talented and creative, that I should just pick a new career. Every day she comes up with new ideas. The problem is that after two months of being unemployed, deep down, it's hard to believe her. I still think that if I were so talented, I'd be working.

As much as I would like to deny it, people are defined by their occupation. I was always introduced as Jeff who worked at the magazine, and before that I was Jeff from the entertainment conglomerate. But it shouldn't be like that. Joshua, who was Moses' right-hand man and given the job by God to conquer the Holy Land, wasn't known as Joshua the conqueror. He was simply Joshua the son of Nun. Joseph wasn't called the ruler of Egypt; he was Joseph the Tzaddik.

Why can't I be comfortable with Jeff the Dad, or Jeff son of Noach? I should be able to accept the fact that I am no longer Jeff the publisher. But there is a real high from being in the middle of the entertainment world. I suffer from withdrawal, still craving that fast pace.

All my life I have known exactly what I want to do next. Every life choice, every career option was made quickly and with confidence. Being laid off has left me confused and dazed. I am not sure what to do next, and that is very stressful. I guess when the time is right, with God's help, I'll figure it out. The right door will materialize and I will walk through.

RABBI NACHUM BRAVERMAN

Waking Up Is Hard To Do

*I*n the weeks that immediately followed September 11, many people found themselves paralyzed. No doubt some of this is fear. It is profoundly unsettling to read about anthrax in the mail, but a deeper aspect may be the unhinging of our accustomed worldview. There are a number of difficult lessons we've been forced to learn.

First, we're all going to die. Everyone knows this in the abstract of course, but there's a difference between knowing in general that people are mortal, and acknowledging that my own life could suddenly end.

The recognition of our mortality leads to the consequent discovery that most of what we care about is trivial and irrelevant. Our careers, clothes, and cars don't seem important.

The most recent catalogue from Saks Fifth Avenue arrived with a printed apology for inviting people to think about clothes and fashion. The *Economist* prefaced an extended discussion of globalization with two apologies for discussing an issue so peripheral as political economy. The *Wall Street Journal* interviewed a publicist unable to do her job. "I just can't call up the *Tonight*

See biography of RABBI NACHUM BRAVERMAN, page 26.

Show and ask whether they want to have Robert Redford as a guest. It doesn't matter."

We've discovered that many of the things we used to care about don't matter, and we haven't had time to understand what does matter.

Nothing has prepared us for the discovery that there is real evil in the world. We've dealt with crime, but to imagine someone getting up early in the morning and methodically planning the destruction of the innocent is totally outside our experience of living.

Most of those who've grown up since the Holocaust have never confronted real anti-Semitism. It is unsettling to go to bed thinking of yourself as a private person with private hopes and fears, and wake up in the morning to the discovery you've been designated as a symbol for all the world's problems.

Our philosophical mindset hasn't prepared us for these discoveries. "I'm okay, you're okay, everyone's got their own worldview, let's work on empathy" seems adequate for dealing with troubled adolescents; less so for confronting the apocalyptic vision we now face.

The Jewish Experience

These discoveries are difficult. Ripped rudely from our beds still drowsy, we have been shoved into a far more complex and challenging world than we ever knew existed. We have lived the sheltered innocence of childhood, our American experience anomalous in world history. Adulthood has been thrust upon us. Waking up is hard to do.

For 3,300 years, Jews had a worldview. It went like this: We have a covenant with God. That covenant gives our lives meaning, sanctity, and purpose. Anti-Semitism is a fact of life. It's not because Jews are rich — or else why were they hated in Poland, one step from starvation's door? It's not because Jews are different — or why were the assimilated Jews hated in Germany?

It's not a rational hatred. Many are unaware that until the Holocaust, the Papacy and church hierarchy were actively, aggressively, and consistently disseminating the view that Jews torture Christian children to death, then drain and drink their blood. (These days, that view finds frequent voice in the Arabic press.)

Jews accepted anti-Semitism as a consequence of the covenant. It was God's reminder of their stake in the world, and of the demands of the covenant. Much as the World Trade Center attack lifted America from comfortable apathy into groping for a deeper sense of community around a higher sense of purpose, Jews were moved by anti-Semitism to reexamine their relationship with God and with the covenant.

Rats in the City

Albert Camus wrote a novel called *The Plague*, as a metaphor for the German occupation of France in World War II. It tells the story of a terrible plague that occupies a town, causing death and disruption. In the face of death, everyone is forced to take a stand. Some become profiteers. Some lose themselves in mindless hedonism. Some try to heal the sick. Eventually the plague recedes. The people rejoice.

But the doctor, watching the celebration, "knew what those jubilant crowds did not know but could have learned from books: that the plague bacillus never dies or disappears for good; that it can lie dormant for years...that it bides its time...and that perhaps the day would come when, for the bane and the enlightening of men, it would rouse up its rats again and send them forth to die in a happy city."

The rats have come out again to die in our happy city. Each of us will be marked by the way we act and react. We will look back on this time as the period in which our goals and values were crystallized and defined.

It's time to pick a hill and take a stand, to characterize our lives by the way we face the challenges of life and death.

DINA MENSCH

Being versus Doing

W hen I was fresh out of law school and people would ask, "What do you do?" I would answer with great pride, "I am a lawyer."

I had graduated from a highly selective New England college and a top-five law school. At the end of an internship, a Wall Street law firm offered me a permanent position. This was after they had wined and dined me: cruises around Manhattan, outings at exclusive country clubs, and many trips to expensive city restaurants. (I also worked a little.) I felt on the top of the world. I had prestige, money, and connections. I also had a good family and friends. What else was there?

I started to become interested in Judaism during law school, where I had smart, accomplished friends who also actually enjoyed "quaint, ancient rituals" such as making kiddush on Friday night and not taking the elevator in the dorm on Saturday. So after I finished law school, I decided that for my obligatory pre-job, post-

DINA MENSCH attended Amherst College and New York University Law School, before continuing her higher education in Israel at Neve Yerushalayim and Eyaht Seminaries. She lives in Passaic, NJ with her husband and four children.

bar-exam trip across the ocean, that I would go to Israel and explore the strange world of Jewish observance.

While in Jerusalem, I became enamored of Jewish learning. During seven years of "top-notch" American higher education, I had never encountered such intelligence and clarity about ideas that really mattered. I was awed by the superior personal qualities of the observant people I met, and I was tempted to extend my stay in Jerusalem to discover what it was all about. However, the powers-that-be at my law firm said that I must return, or else...

Essence of Self

In my heart, I wanted to stay, to explore something that had meaning and the potential capacity for life-changing experiences. But in my brain, where all my previous experiences were stored, I was afraid that if I gave up the job that I had worked so hard to get, that I had so proudly bragged about to impress others, I would lose my very sense of self.

If I decided to let this great job slip through my fingers, for the more ambiguous, non-concrete goal of "learning about Judaism," who would I be? My self-esteem was directly tied to my professional and academic successes. I would be sailing without an anchor.

I struggled, because my identity was so tied up in what I was doing.

The question "What do you do?" is usually answered, "I am a ... (market analyst, administrator, etc.)." Although the question is posed with the verb "to do," it is answered by the verb "to be."

For many people, especially those who have invested heavily in their chosen professions, what we do to make money defines us in our own minds. After spending thousands of dollars to get through school, thousands of hours of study and practice to become competent, and 50-hour workweeks practicing our craft, it seems as if there is no room to see ourselves in any other light.

Sanctified Love

What happens when one gets fired, laid off, or fails in an undertaking?

Some people cope poorly in these situations because their self-esteem is undermined. Alternatively, one could experience the misfortune as a fact of economy or as a learning experience.

On a deeper level, the tying of one's self-esteem to professional success is not just practically unwise, it reflects an incorrect understanding of our humanity.

In Genesis, the Torah states that the first human being was created *b'tzelem Elokim*, in the image of God. This has always been understood to mean that the human being was created with a soul, which is a portion, or reflection, so to speak, of Godliness. This soul is what differentiates us from animals. It gives us the capacity to make moral choices and to carry ourselves with "human dignity," unlike a cow or monkey.

The fact that humans have a sanctified core is elevating and gives us intrinsic self-worth — because if God thought it worthwhile to create me, then I must have a unique purpose in this world!

Therefore, the point of my existence, and my self-worth, revolve around my moral choices, not my professional success.

Liberating Concept

This concept liberated me from the cycle of feeling good about myself when I was successful, and feeling bad about myself when I failed.

On a practical level as well, the ability to separate myself from my work gave me the necessary perspective to be able to leave a job or career when it turns negative, or when my personal or spiritual life should take priority, as mine did.

To the extent that a job or career drains an individual, or causes him/her to be dishonest or mean, it is surely damaging. Without separating "Who I Am" from "What I Do," one might never be able to objectively evaluate the effect that work has.

Fortunately, with the help of close friends, I found the courage to tell the law partners that I would be staying in Israel, and if they had to give my job away, so be it. I stayed in Jerusalem for over a year, discovered the wonders of Israel, the wisdom and beauty of the Torah, and the unlikely scenario that my soul mate was a rabbinical student, not an attorney!

I've had children, traveled, taught, written, volunteered, prayed, grown as a person, and even worked as a lawyer since. But my most liberating experience of all was the profound joy of hanging up the phone with the law firm that day.

My existence suddenly expanded, as if, like a balloon, my soul was pumped up by dimensions I didn't even realize existed. Not only was I not "sailing without an anchor," I was flying without a lead weight pulling me down! That anchor, my "work" self-definition, had confined me to a very narrow path in life.

Don't wait for a mid-life crisis to do a self-evaluation. Stage your "crisis" now and do some soul-searching. You may just be able to guide your career, rather than having your career guide you.

SARAH SHAPIRO

We Are What We Say

When I as a teenager was searching for truth as only an assimilated Jewish teenager can, one of the New Age disciplines I dipped into for a while was a system of self-study based on the teachings of a 19th-century Russian mystic by the name of Gurdjieff.

Gurdjieff's goal had been that people should "wake up" and become fully conscious human beings, rather than live out their lives as robots.

I joined a Gurdjieff group whose leader (he was Jewish, too, of course, as were most of the other members) took as his central premise this principle:

The behavior which most hinders an individual's psychological and spiritual awakening is the pervasive human inclination to put other people down. The study group's guiding maxim, therefore, was "Don't let a put-down pass your lips."

Following the Rules

At age 19, put-downs didn't seem to me like such a big deal,

See biography of SARAH SHAPIRO, page 109.

and I found it odd to have such emphasis placed on eliminating something that seemed such a natural part of life. Nonetheless, as a diligent and earnest young seeker, I took it upon myself to adhere to the rules.

Months went by, and something interesting started happening. This single abstention — inadequate as my sporadic practice of it proved to be — increasingly had the effect of casting a disconcertingly bright light onto all sorts of feelings that had previously been hidden from my view.

It seemed that this one gesture of self-restraint — that of denying myself the luxury of imposing my negativity upon others — was automatically getting me in touch with the much deadlier negativity I was unconsciously directing my own way.

Not much time passed before God in His wisdom plucked me up out of the sunny West Coast, and, much to my surprise, set me down — where else? — in Orthodox Brooklyn.

The cultural milieu could not have been more different, except, to my mind, in one noticeable respect. Just as put-downs had been strictly forbidden during my memorable stint at the self-study group — whose 40 or so members had waged a lonely, uphill battle against the socially accepted, casual denigration of one's fellows — here was an entire community that made *shemirat halashon* (literally, "guarding one's tongue") a pivotal, community-wide, institutionalized aspect of religious observance.

The Torah, apparently, had forbidden gossip, slander, and derogatory speech quite some time ago — at Mount Sinai, actually — well before the advent of California's Human Potential Movement.

A book published just about the time I arrived in New York, *Guard Your Tongue*, by Rabbi Zelig Pliskin, set forth for the English-speaking public Judaism's laws governing this area of behavior.

The Shortcomings of Goodwill

I learned that since human nature is such that we're all experts at rationalization and self-justification, goodwill is insufficient. The commitment to refrain from put-downs has to be buttressed by a subtle, comprehensive network of "halacha" (mandated behaviors) applicable in all the infinitely varied situations which arise in daily life.

The nuances were intriguing. Sometimes, divulging negative information can be essential — for instance, when it comes to a prospective marriage partner, or a business deal.

Ironically, under certain circumstances, saying something positive about someone is the wrong thing to do — for example, when it's likely to arouse a listener's jealousy or skepticism.

I was taken aback by this psychological realism in an ancient tradition which, tribally speaking, I could claim as my very own.

Aside from its vastly more comprehensive scope, there was an essential difference, however, between what I'd learned in the self-study group, and Judaism's concept and practice of this discipline. As understood in this observant Jewish community, the focus of *shemirat halashon* was not me or my enlightenment. At the center was my relationship with God.

Transcending Individual Quests

As legitimate, noble, and desirable as any given individual's personal growth may be, and as effective a tool as guarding one's speech may be along the way to that goal, I gradually learned that spiritual growth transcends any particular individual's quest for liberation.

Whatever I do, privately or publicly, is linked inextricably to the well-being of the community.

In fact, it's linked to the world beyond my own reach, and to worlds beyond human perception.

To the extent that my mundane daily speech is morally sensitive, and to that extent will it promote not only my own psychological well-being but the well-being of — dare I say it? — mankind, the little words I utter have infinite significance in the eyes of our Creator.

Refraining from putting people down, and from putting oneself down, is an aspect of our purpose here in the world — to come to recognize that each and every one of us is nothing less than the Creator's personal handiwork. To insult one of God's creations is to disturb our relationship with God Himself.

Community-Wide Dedication

Decades passed. I've long since been plucked out of that community in Brooklyn and set down here in Jerusalem, where the ancient traditions are far more deeply rooted than the tall old pine out my window. But I'm still surrounded, as I was back then, by Jews of all ages whose dedication to the goal of guarding their speech is as fervent and sincere as was mine when, as an innocent teenager, I first started looking for truth.

Recently, the annual city-wide seminar for *shemirat halashon* took place in neighborhoods throughout Jerusalem. An event organized by and for women, it consisted of classes held all day long on the meaning and practice of guarding one's speech, and a mass rally at night bringing together an estimated 10,000 people.

It wasn't the grand opening of a new department store, it wasn't a political party fund-raiser. It was a gathering of people who are trying to better utilize, in private and in public, the gift which is the identifying characteristic of our species: our amazing ability to speak.

There's a simple question that in general we can ask ourselves when in doubt as to whether a particular remark would be permitted: Would the person of whom I'm speaking be pleased or displeased were this comment uttered in his presence?

With a guideline as self-evident and straightforward as that, why should it be necessary to review the laws of proper speech on a regular basis? That is indeed a mystery of the human soul. But the good news is this:

If not for the powerful, ever-recurring urge that's implanted within us to speak ill of others, we wouldn't have this great opportunity to refine our characters, thereby joining God in our own creation daily.

When we curb that inexplicable urge to put others down, we start finding ourselves less frequently in the irritating company of imbeciles, ingrates, and sadists, and surrounded more often, much to our surprise, by fallible, vulnerable, striving human beings who resemble — how uncanny! — none other than you and me.

LISA AIKEN

Superwoman Juggling Act

Fifteen years ago I had a life that many people envied. I was the chief psychologist of a prestigious New York hospital, with teaching appointments at a medical school and two universities. I had a busy, interesting, and lucrative private practice. I had already authored two books, was working on a third, appeared on television and radio, and was interviewed by popular magazines. In my spare time I even managed to figure skate at Rockefeller Center several hours a week! How's that for having it all?

It took a while for me to admit that being this accomplished was taking its toll. I almost never finished dinner before 9:30 at night. I started getting heart palpitations when things went wrong, and my hair-split timing to see patients got thrown off causing me to run late for appointments. I found myself doing deep breathing to calm myself down when I got off the red-eye plane from Los

LISA AIKEN is a lecturer and clinical psychologist who specializes in individual and marital therapy. She is the author of *To Be a Jewish Woman; Why Me, God? A Jewish Guide for Coping with Suffering; Guide for the Romantically Perplexed*; and *The Hidden Beauty of the Shema*. She co-authored *The Art of Jewish Prayer* and *What Your Unborn Baby Wants You to Know*. She is available for speaking engagements, and can be reached at iramd@yahoo.com.

Angeles after a speaking tour, landed at Newark airport at 6 A.M., and had to be in my Manhattan office by eight o'clock to see the 12 patients I had scheduled for that day.

Of course, one of my specialties as a psychologist was teaching stress management, but I rarely took my own advice, thinking that I could always cram in one more interview, one more patient, one more lecture.

Why was I running at such a frenetic pace?

Running with the Pack

It's sort of like the frog that gets placed in a container of water that is slowly being warmed. At first, it feels really nice to be there, but by the time the frog realizes that it's far too hot, it's too late.

Living among yuppies in New York, it took a long time to realize that something was wrong with what all of us were doing. The men I dated were mostly working ten or more hours a day and often on weekends as well. Many women I knew were doing the same. Few people had hobbies, apart from the rare tennis buff, or the ones who worked out two or three hours a week. Almost no one took more than a week or two of vacation a year.

Most of us had been cooped up in graduate or professional schools for so long that we couldn't wait to pay back our student loans and grab the golden rings that were finally, after so much hard work in school, within our grasp.

What turned things around?

A combination of things, the first being a series of illnesses. I knew that the Torah mandates taking care of our bodies. But when? Who had the time? It took some dramatic wake-up calls for me to recognize that if I wanted to accomplish in the future, I had better slow down now. I had cherished a dream of becoming a professional dancer. The metaphor was clear. I knew that I needed to stop dancing.

God gave us bodies and a material world to enable us to fulfill our soul's purpose. I found it impossible to be consistently spiritual while running so fast. We all have our challenges. Some of my colleagues are obsessed with money, finding prestige, and being admired by others. I was driven to accomplish, *now*.

I decided to try to step away from myself to gain objectivity about my actions: why I was doing everything that I did, and whether it was good for me, and the world.

Living for Today

I was too focused on the short term. I was not living for today's pleasure, today's paycheck, today's power, today's comfort. I was, like many others, living on adrenalin and willpower, a spiritual and material overachiever.

Judaism teaches us to look at the long term. It tells us how to prioritize our time, our emotions, our efforts, and our money. It tells us to trust that if we make an honest, earnest, and realistic effort to earn a living and we give our fair share to charity, the real Master of the Universe will provide us with exactly what we need. Working ridiculous hours and following the stock market like a hawk will not land us a penny more.

It was a hard decision to make, but after having anxiety attacks, and dreading my hospital job, I decided to leave it. It was one of the best choices I ever made. I ended up making more money in private practice, working only two-thirds the time that I had before, and feeling much more fulfilled that my time was being well spent. Miraculously, I also got ten more hours a week for writing my Judaica books!

Of course God continually sends us situations that challenge us to make our spiritual pursuits more central than our material, self-centered, or hedonistic ones. A few years after leaving the hospital, I was offered $100,000 a year to work 20 hours a week screening patients for a clinic.

I could have taken the job, but it would have meant not having a minute to write any more books about Judaism. While I probably earn about $5 for every hour I spend writing books, and I hate writing (!), I knew in my heart of hearts that I could do far more good writing than seeing those 20 patients a week.

I told myself that if I took the job, the extra money might come in handy and I would give 10 percent to charity, but I certainly didn't need that much to live on. It would have been easy to convince myself that I could retire earlier if I had that money, but let's be real. Who ever says, "Now that I've made a million dollars, I can retire"? It becomes, "Now I need 2 million, or 5 million, or... I spent the extra money that I made, so now I need to work just as long."

Seeking Advice

When I discussed this dilemma with a spiritual mentor, she told me the following Jewish idea: Once we have enough money to take care of our basic needs, we should prioritize our time according to what we can uniquely do, and leave to others what they can do. If I didn't take the job screening patients, the clinic would certainly find someone else to do an adequate job helping them. But if I didn't write my books on Judaism, nobody else would.

I am now married, with two young children, and I often have to evaluate how to apportion my time and energies. Should I do what makes me feel best? Should I pursue my professional interests more fully, and let others take care of my children most of the day? One of the most important things that anyone can do is to raise good, moral, emotionally healthy children. If we physically bring them into the world, why should we entrust their emotional and spiritual upbringing to strangers?

Raising children has been unquestionably the greatest challenge of my life. It is far more difficult than getting a doctorate in psychology. Instead of measuring my self-actualization in terms of how much money I'm making or how many awards I receive, I now view it in terms of my spiritual growth. Was I able to control my temper today? Did I model patience and respect for others to my children? Did I make them feel that they are important and loved? Did I live today in a way that they will want to be like me when they grow up?

Supermom

Today, for me, being a superwoman means knowing that I

need to weather the challenges of raising a family, because that is what I can uniquely do. I may be less involved in the professional world than I used to be, but I make my contributions there as well.

I chose to give up writing for three years while I was having babies and constantly taking care of them. I was comfortable reducing my private practice to ten hours a week or less because I believe that I can uniquely mother my children while potential patients can find another capable therapist.

I teach Torah around the world, but we always travel as a family, so my husband and children don't feel that they're being neglected. Since I've resumed writing, I do so only after the children are in bed at night or before they wake up in the morning. I am also more involved with charity work than ever before, but I do it in a way that gives me a chance to recharge my emotional batteries, while including the rest of my family.

Torah teaches us that life is about growth. This is how I'm growing best right now. Check with me ten years from now and I'm sure that my juggling act will be different, just as it was meant to be.

EMUNA BRAVERMAN

A Beautiful Soul

She comes to our door for breakfast or dinner or for an afternoon snack. On blustery nights she sleeps in our playroom.
She comes with shoes and dresses to sell while she waits for a
Hollywood director to pick up her screenplay. She sings to my children and warns them of the monsters loose in the neighborhood.
Her name is Shaindel. She's schizophrenic and homeless — and a
fellow Jew.

I can't say that I always welcome her knock on the door; we
had to tell her that midnight is a little late to ring our bell! And
sometimes I get annoyed when she disdains our orange juice
because it isn't fresh enough. But I owe her a debt of gratitude for
opening up the hearts of our whole family.

While we can't cure schizophrenia, we can make her feel
loved. She knows just what families to go to for food or showers,
and sometimes calls to make a "reservation" for our back room.
She's a testimony to the power of community. I don't think there
were many psychiatric hospitals in pre-war Poland, but I believe
every shtetl took responsibility to feed, clothe, and shelter the
mentally ill in their midst.

See biography of EMUNA BRAVERMAN, page 255.

A Car and a Blanket

Shaindel doesn't want the risks to her physical health and the numbing of her psyche that come with most pharmaceutical interventions for the schizophrenic. She runs away and doesn't come back for months if we mention the "d" word — doctor. She'd rather be out on the street — laughing and dancing.

And laugh she does. Frequently at herself. If you poke gentle fun at some of her strange stories, she can see the humor. Sometimes contact with reality helps bring her back also.

Late on a Friday night, Shaindel knocked on our door. We didn't have any room for her to stay over. After a few minutes we heard our car door slam and my husband and I looked at each other. "I guess she's gone to sleep in the car. Leave her be."

A while later, she left the car briefly and our neighbors' dog began to bark. They called the police and our sleep was interrupted yet again. The police had dragged the hapless Shaindel out of the car and were standing at our front door.

"Did you give this woman permission to sleep in your car?" they asked.

Not wanting her to get in trouble with the law, my husband said "yes."

"Well then give her a blanket. It's cold!" admonished the officer.

Shaindel doubled over with laughter.

Conspiracy Theories

There have also been poignant moments. Shaindel scratched herself on a rusty nail and was concerned it may have broken the skin. We went to a private room in my house and I examined her. Thank God, she was fine. But I wasn't. I realized to my embarrassment, that previously she had not been quite real to me. She had been an interesting phenomenon (like the way some of our Shabbat guests look at us!), but not quite a full human being. Until that moment — when I saw her tremendous fear and felt her palpable relief. When I saw my own shallowness.

Shaindel can still frustrate me at times, like when she gives a very specific lunch order. I don't always have the patience to listen to her stories; she has intimate knowledge of suspicious FBI workings on our block. But I'm always grateful to her for teaching my children and me about true love for your fellow Jew.

Tradition has it that Elijah the Prophet disguises himself and goes from door to door, helping us refine our characters and providing opportunities for genuine giving. When I first helped out Shaindel I thought to myself, "What if she's really Elijah? I'd better not turn her away." Now I help her out just because she's someone I care about. Just because she's in need. Just because my kids love her. Just because I know I'm blessed to have the opportunity.

RABBI NOAH WEINBERG

World Repairs

*I*f September 11 taught us anything, it is that our world is in desperate need of repair. Divisiveness and violence must urgently be replaced by kindness and compassion. As the threat of terror looms, we need to find ways to make a positive difference in the world — to turn the pain into positive change, and to lead humanity back on the road to peace.

This is not just a global problem. It is a highly personal one as well. If someone spills ink on the floor and asks you to clean it up, you might say, "Hey, you made the mess — you clean it up." But when it comes to world problems, nobody will say: "I didn't cause the problem, so why should I do anything about it?" Everyone agrees we should try to help. If you knew how to cure cancer, you'd cancel your vacation. We're all responsible.

The Hebrew word *tzedakah* is commonly translated as "charity." But this is misleading. Charity implies your heart motivating you to go beyond the call of duty. *Tzedakah*, however, literally means "righteousness" — doing the right thing. A "tzaddik" is a righteous person who fulfills all his obligations, whether in the mood or not.

See biography of RABBI NOAH WEINBERG, page 149.

The verse says: "*Tzedek, tzedek* you shall pursue" — justice, justice you shall pursue (Deut. 16:20). There's a basic human responsibility to reach out to others. Giving of your time and your money is a statement that "I will do whatever I can to help."

That's the Jewish concept of *tikkun olam* — repairing the world.

Parameters of Giving

Aside from helping those in need, we have many other financial obligations — family, savings, even basic living expenses. So how much are we expected to help? Should we drop everything and run off to Africa to stop the famine?

The Torah recommends giving 10 percent. (Hence the popular expression "tithe," meaning one-tenth.) The legal source is Deut. 14:22, and the Bible is filled with examples: Abraham gave Malki-Tzedek one-tenth of all his possessions (Genesis 14:20); Jacob vowed to give one-tenth of all his future acquisitions to the Almighty (Genesis 29:22); there are mandated tithes to support the Levites (Numbers 18:21, 24) and the poor (Deut. 26:12).

Ten percent is the minimum obligation to help. For those who want to do more, the Torah allows you to give 20 percent. But above that amount is unrealistic. If you give too much, you'll come to neglect other aspects of your life.

Of course, don't just impulsively give your money away. The Almighty provides everyone with income, but it comes conditionally: 10 percent is a trust fund that you're personally responsible to disperse.

If you were running a humanitarian foundation, you'd make a thorough study of the best use of your money. It's the same with *tzedakah*. When you choose one project over another, you have to calculate why it is more effective than the other. God is expecting you to spend His money wisely. Consider it the "Your-Name-Here Save the World Foundation."

Put this money aside in a separate account. That way it's available when the need arises. And it's a constant reminder of your obligation to help.

How to Prioritize

There are so many possible projects: the poor, the sick, the uneducated, drug abuse, domestic violence, the homeless. Which one should you pick?

Tzedakah begins at home. If your parents are hungry, that comes before giving to a homeless shelter. From there it is concentric circles outward: your community, then your country. (For Jews, Jerusalem and Israel are considered one's own community, since every Jew has a share in the homeland.)

Once you've defined "who" to give to, what's the best method for doing so? Maimonides lists eight levels of *tzedakah* in order of priority ("Laws of Gifts to the Poor," 10:7). Many people think the highest level is to give money anonymously. Actually there's an even higher level: helping a person to become self-sufficient. This includes giving him a job, or a loan to start a business.

From here comes the Jewish concept of a free-loan fund, called a *gemach*. If you help someone start a business, he can feed himself and ten other people besides. As the old saying goes: Rather than give him fish to eat, teach him to be a fisherman. This represents a higher level of *tikkun olam*, because now the fisherman can go out and help others. You've really fixed something.

There's actually one higher level of *tzedakah*: being sensitive to someone before he's in trouble. As the Sages explain: It takes one person to support something before it falls, but after it falls, even five people may not be able to lift it (see Rashi, Leviticus 25:35).

Tzedakah is not only helping people financially, it's also making them feel good. If a hungry person asks for food, and you give with a resentful grunt, you've lost the mitzvah. Sometimes giving an attentive ear or a warm smile is more important than money.

You can also protect someone's self-esteem by giving even before he asks. The bottom line is that every person has unique needs, and our obligation is to help each one accordingly.

What if you offer someone a job and he's too lazy to work? Then you don't have to give him anything. The Talmud (Baba

Metzia 32b) suggests that if he doesn't care about himself, you're not required to care about him, either.

Get Organized

Beyond the 10 percent commitment of money, there's another aspect: a 10 percent commitment of time.

If you're really serious about fixing the world, you won't just mail a check. You'll join an organization. Many of the world's great revolutions have succeeded by strength in numbers: the civil rights movement, women's rights, or even save the whales.

What if no organization exists?

Then create it.

The Talmud (Baba Batra 9a) says: "Greater than one who does a mitzvah, is one who causes others to do a mitzvah." If you really want to be effective, wake others up to the problem, and mobilize their efforts.

Imagine a child is sick with a rare disease. If it's an acquaintance, you'd probably say, "Oh, that's terrible."

"So what are you doing about it?"

"Me?! What can I do about it?"

If you care, you could do a lot. If it was your cousin, you'd take some personal responsibility, perhaps researching information on the Internet.

If it was your own child, you'd leave no stone unturned.

I know a young couple — he's a businessman and she's a doctor. Their two young children were diagnosed with Gaucher's disease, a debilitating condition that is handicapping for life, and sometimes fatal. So what did they do? Together they founded an organization committed to finding a cure for Gaucher's disease. She conducted the medical research and he raised the money.

There was no guarantee of success. But inasmuch as it was their own children, there was no alternative but to try. And the Almighty helped them. After six years, they developed a synthetic enzyme which can effectively treat the condition — and their two children became the first in the world to have a hopeful prognosis.

Big goals, small goals. If you want to make a difference, it's possible.

All for You

Beyond the basic responsibility of *tzedakah* is a level called *rachamim*, "mercy" — caring about others personally and getting involved. You can walk around claiming to be a good person, but unless you feel it inside, you're not really there.

That's why the Torah juxtaposes the command to "love your neighbor" next to the prohibition "not to stand idly by while another is in need" (Leviticus 19:16–18).

Don't cruise through life as if it's some obstacle course: watch out, here's a human being, manipulate him, push him, score a point, one-upmanship! That's not the way. You have to share the burden.

The Talmud asks, "Why was Adam created alone? So that every person should say, 'The entire world was created just for me.'"

This is a recognition that everything — including the needs of every other human being — was created for you. We are all caretakers of this world, responsible to deal with the problems. Everything on earth, the problems as well as the beauty, offers an opportunity to connect and to grow. Everyone you encounter is there because you need it at that time. If someone needs help, it's part of your challenge, a message for you.

Look around at absolutely everything and ask, "What is this saying to me? Why was this sent as part of my path to perfection?"

Feel the victims of society. Feel the victims of crime. Feel the victims of terrorism. Feel the victims of old age. Feel the victims of discrimination. Feel the suffering of people you will never meet — the plight of strangers halfway around the world.

How do you become real with the suffering of others? To empathize with a blind person, for example, try blindfolding yourself for a day. Or go to the hospital and visit patients who have lost limbs. Share the burden.

Make the Difference

Every human being has a Divine spark that yearns to make a difference in the world. Ultimately, we are striving for universal perfection. We all care. We just need to focus our attention.

Tikkun olam means committing oneself to solving the world's problems. If everyone would give 10 percent, there would be no more problems — no hunger, no cancer, no homelessness.

Once you acknowledge that you are responsible, only one question remains: What will you do about it?

When you truly care, you will set priorities, organize, and make the sacrifice. And with the Almighty's help, you — yes, you — will change the world.

SARA YOHEVED RIGLER

Beyond Just Desserts: A Recipe for Thanksgiving

*A*lthough it was my second extended period helping out at this Calcutta orphanage, I still marveled at the standard of living of the girls. Growing up, I had my own room; these girls didn't even have their own beds. They slept on thin mattresses spread on the floor, two girls to a mattress, sharing a blanket and a mosquito net. During the day the mattresses were piled in a corner, and the room was used for play and doing homework.

Their only private space amounted to a box the size of a large shoebox. In this box each girl kept all her worldly possessions: the one of her two cotton frocks she was not currently wearing, two pencils, and a copybook. About 25 of the girls owned a pair of sandals, which they trotted out on special occasions. About a dozen girls owned a pretty dress, a gift from an impoverished grandmother. That was it. No other garments. No toothbrush. No crayons. Not one girl owned enough to fill her box. Yet they were the most cheerful and loving group of people I knew. I adored them.

The girls prevailed on me to teach them English. One day we

See biography of SARA YOHEVED RIGLER, page 17.

were on the lesson in our book about opposites: tall-short, thin-fat, rich-poor. After explaining the words in simple English, I would have one girl stand in front of the class and ask, "Is Bhavani thin, fat, or medium?"

The girls would raise their hands, and the one I picked would answer: "Bhavanai is thin."

The girls were smart and highly motivated. The lesson was proceeding well until I summoned Lakshmi to stand in front of the class. Pointing to the scrawny, barefoot girl in her plain white frock, I asked, "Is Lakshmi rich, poor, or medium?"

Two dozen hands flew up. I called on one girl. In loud and perfect English she answered: "Lakshmi is medium."

Obviously she didn't understand the words. Lakshmi, like all the girls, was abjectly destitute, a reality they all accepted with cheerful fortitude. I called on another girl. Eagerly, she replied, "Lakshmi is medium."

I again explained the meaning of the words "rich" and "poor," this time using their Bengali translations so there would be no further misunderstanding. Then I asked the whole class: "Is Lakshmi rich, poor, or medium?"

In joyful unison they all cried out: "Lakshmi is medium."

I was confounded. By what mental gyrations did these girls consider Lakshmi — and by extension themselves — as anything other than poor?

After the class, I repaired to my room (my own private room) and tried to figure it out. After all, the girls knew that most children, even in poverty-stricken Calcutta, had more than they did. They attended school with "normal" girls — girls who had parents and shoes and pretty colored ribbons in their hair.

Carefully I analyzed what exactly they did have. I came up with a list of just four items: a rudimentary level of shelter, food, education, and friends. That was it.

But what about all they didn't have? Not one of them had a dowry, without which prospects of marriage were slim. None of them owned a book or a toy. None of them had money to buy a treat or a trinket — ever. By what stretch of their imaginations — or their hearts — did they not define themselves as poor? The question simmered in my mind for a decade.

Just Desserts

Ten years later I was learning Torah in Jerusalem. The rabbi was explaining why the matriarch Leah named her fourth son Yehudah, a name derived from the word "to thank." Since the moniker "Jew" derives from the name "Yehudah," thanking is somehow integral to being Jewish.

But why did Leah wait until her fourth child to use this name? Wasn't she more grateful for her first child than her fourth?

The rabbi, citing classical commentaries, explained that Jacob's four wives knew prophetically that they would give birth to the 12 sons who would become the progenitors of the Twelve Tribes of Israel. Since there were four wives, each one expected to give birth to three sons.

When Leah gave birth to her fourth son, she felt she had received more than her fair share. So she named him Yehudah, saying, "This time I will thank God."

This teaches us something essential about gratitude. Gratitude is a function not of how much we have, but rather of how much we have relative to how much we feel we deserve.

When you've worked hard at your job, you usually do not feel flooded with gratitude when you pick up your paycheck. Even a holiday bonus may come to be expected as your just desserts and not elicit a great surge of gratitude — unless it is a far bigger sum than you feel you deserve.

The opposite of gratitude is a feeling of entitlement. The attitude of "I deserve it" turns every gift into a paycheck.

Recognizing Good

The Hebrew term for gratitude is *hakarat hatov*, which literally means "recognizing the good." The secret embedded in the Hebrew is that gratitude depends not on getting something good, but on recognizing the good that is already yours.

Thus, gratitude is totally a feat of consciousness. It requires a "back to basics" mentality, becoming cognizant of all the rudimentary things we usually take for granted. No matter how much we lack, no matter what difficult times we are passing through, every one of us can find a myriad of things to be grateful for.

If you've lost money in the stock market, but you still have your children, you can be grateful.

If you've lost your job, but you still have your health, you can be grateful.

If you can't move your legs, but you can still move your arms, you can be grateful.

The Object of Gratitude

In addition to recognizing the good and experiencing what you have as a gift not a paycheck, gratitude requires one more ingredient.

There is a fallacy which prevents many people from experiencing true thankfulness. Some think that thankfulness, like love, is a warm, fuzzy feeling inside, the way you feel when you've downed the second dessert of your Thanksgiving dinner. That good feeling, however, is not thankfulness, but satiation. It becomes thankfulness only when you realize that Aunt Rose toiled to make that apple pie, and then you direct your appreciation to her.

Both thankfulness and love must have an object. True gratitude implies that I am grateful to the giver of what I have received. Gratitude without an object is like one hand clapping.

From a Torah perspective, all human beings are creatures. Life — and every part of it, from the tiny hairs inside our noses to our thousands of enzymes — is a gift from our Creator. We are entitled to nothing. We should be grateful to God for everything.

A Recipe for Gratitude

Here, then, are the four steps to gratitude:

- Recognize the good that you possess.

- Acknowledge that it is a gift, not something you deserve.
- Identify the source of the gift, whether God or a human being.
- Express your thanks.

According to Judaism, gratitude is the basis of everything: faith, joy, awe, and love of God. Only when we recognize how much God has given us (and how little we deserve it) can we come to a place of faith and love.

Little wonder that a Jew is supposed to start every day with an expression of thankfulness for life itself, the recitation of the *Modeh Ani* prayer. To incorporate this small exercise into your life, here's how:

Upon first waking up, as soon as you've turned off your alarm, while you're still lying in bed, say these words:

"Modeh ani lefanecha, Melech chai v'kayam, she'he'chezarta bi nishmati b'chemlah, rabbah emuna'techa."

"Thankful am I before You, living and eternal King, that You have returned my soul within me, with compassion. Abundant is Your faithfulness."

You'll notice that this single sentence incorporates all the ingredients of gratitude. It expresses thanks for the most elemental gift of all, life itself, to the Divine source of life. There is no better way to start the day.

Once we are washed up and dressed, a Jew continues to thank God for things that might otherwise go unnoticed. The 14 short "Morning Blessings" focus our consciousness, in gratitude, on such elemental capacities as the ability to see, to stretch our muscles, to stand erect, and to walk. These blessings can be found at the beginning of any siddur (Jewish prayer book), which is readily available in any Jewish bookstore.

It is easy to feel genuine gratitude for some of the things mentioned in these blessings. We may be so oblivious to others of our "gifts," however, that we must be jolted into appreciation.

I personally could not relate to one particular blessing until the morning after I had emergency abdominal surgery. I was lying in a hospital bed groaning in pain when the nurse told me to get up and walk a little. I thought she was insane. Only when her gentle persuasion gave way to insistence, did I force myself to sit up and gingerly get out of bed, wrenching with agony at every movement. Standing up, the most I could manage was a stooped shuffle across the room. The nurse kept saying, "Stand up straight," but my abdomen hurt too much.

Then it was time for my morning prayers. Standing next to my bed like a hunched-over nonagenarian, when I got to the blessing, "Blessed are You, Lord our God, King of universe, Who straightens the bent," I almost cried. How had I never related to this blessing before? How had I so taken for granted the "simple" faculty of standing erect? Why did I have to lose this ability before I could appreciate it?

It has been exactly 13 years since that morning — 4,748 days of standing up straight — and I thank God every time I say that blessing.

The Talmud teaches: "Who is rich? The one who is happy with his portion."

My Indian orphans understood this. Feeling that they deserved nothing, they experienced the little that they had as a pure gift. No wonder they couldn't define themselves as poor. And they understood as well, that thanksgiving is too precious to be reserved for one day a year.

LAWRENCE KELEMEN

Elusive Holiness

At Mount Sinai, when God first hinted to us what it would be like to live Torah lives, He promised: "You will be a kingdom of priests and a *goy kadosh* — a holy nation" (Exodus 19:6).

Now, 3,300 years later, what adjectives most accurately describe our daily experience? Many might sum up their existential reality with terms like "harried" and "pressured." A few might describe their lives as generally "joyous" or "fulfilling." A tiny minority might go so far as to say that their lives are often "moral" or even "heroic."

But how many of us feel that significant chunks of our existence are *kadosh* — holy? Is it possible that we unknowingly live lives of *kedusha* — holiness — or are we a generation that has begun to lose contact with the very essence of what it means to be a Jew?

Defining Kedusha and Tuma

What exactly is *kedusha*? A superficial survey of Talmudic

LAWRENCE KELEMEN is professor of education at Neve Yerushalayim College of Jewish Studies for Women in Jerusalem. He is the author of *Permission to Believe; Permission to Receive;* and *To Kindle a Soul: Ancient Wisdom for Modern Parents and Teachers.* His website is www.lawrencekelemen.com.

sources lends the impression that *kedusha* is the opposite of *tuma* — spiritual impurity. However, this does not clarify matters much since we also feel difficulty defining *tuma* in any concrete or practical fashion.

Rashi offers an extremely helpful clue to defining both terms. In his commentary on Leviticus 1:1, Rashi reveals that God spoke to the gentile prophets using *lashon tuma* — impure language, but He spoke to Moses using *lashon chibah* — affectionate language.

Both *chibah* — affection — and *kedusha* are the opposite of *tuma*. Therefore affection and *kedusha* must be related. Perhaps *kedusha* is some sort of closeness or intimacy.

Rabbi Moshe Chaim Luzzatto (Ramchal) reinforces this impression in his classic *Path of the Just*. He defines *kedusha* as a state in which a person, "even in the midst of performing those physical acts necessary to sustain his body, never strays from the highest intimacy." According to Ramchal, *kedusha* is a state in which there are no distractions. It is an experience in which two beings become so fully united that all else is irrelevant. It is the state described by King David, "My soul clings to You" (Psalms 69:3).

The Troublemaker

If *kedusha* is intimacy, then its opposite, *tuma*, would be distance and disconnection. *Lashon hara* — speech that destroys relationships — is inherently *tamei*, impure, and during biblical times the act of impure speech produced visible leprous lesions requiring quarantine and ritual purification (Leviticus 13).

Similarly, whenever a human ovum or sperm is discharged separately, instead of coming together to form a new unity, there is *tuma* (Leviticus 15). At death, when body and soul part, there is *tuma* (Numbers 19).

In a comment far deeper than we likely comprehend, the 14th-century kabbalist Rabbi Menachem Recanati observed: "*Kedusha* is the preservation of the unity of the worlds, and *tuma* is the 'troublemaker who separates close ones.'"

The reference to a "troublemaker who separates close ones" is borrowed from Proverbs 16:28, and classical commentaries offer various interpretations. According to Rashi, this is a gossiper who separates himself from God. According to Ibn Ezra, this is one who inspires violence and causes a breakdown in all social relations. According to the Vilna Gaon, this is one who destroys a relationship between a man and his wife. According to all, *kedusha* is closeness and *tuma* is distance.

Creating Intimacy

Paradoxically, creating intimacy requires separation. First we must remove all potential barriers between us and our beloved. In Leviticus 20:26, God proposes, "Be My *kedoshim* — My holy ones." Rashi explains: "If you separate yourselves from the other peoples, then you will be Mine."

For marriage, a man draws a woman close through *kiddushin*, a process which forbids her to all other suitors. According to Ramchal, we take the first step toward personal *kedusha* by separating ourselves from those physical indulgences that would distract us from the One we love.

The common theme in all these initial steps toward *kedusha* is the removal of distractions and the elimination of interference. Absolute connection requires two surgically sterile surfaces.

Achieving *kedusha* seems to be a two-step process, however. Ramchal explains: "Its beginning is labor and its end reward; its beginning is exertion and its end a gift. It begins with one sanctifying himself and ends with his being sanctified."

By actively removing distractions, we create a space in our lives for real intimacy. All we can do is prepare the ground. The closeness that is *kedusha* — be it between man and God, between human beings, or between body and soul — the Holy One bequeaths.

Making Room for a Beloved

It is beginning to become apparent why we might feel a lack of *kedusha* in our lives. There is not a lot of space for intimacy. There is not a lot of room for closeness. Never has a generation been more bombarded with distractions, with troublemakers who separate close ones. In a word, with *tuma*.

Sometimes we allow technology to get in the way of *kedusha*. Once upon a time, women only had to battle the TV and newspaper for their husbands' attention. Today the Internet holds the attention of all but the most devoted spouses, and Palm Pilots routinely scan the stocks and headlines in the middle of meetings. Cellphones and pagers, ostensibly created to enhance connectivity, follow us into restaurants, the synagogue, and the most private quarters of our homes, shattering the intimate moments that make life worth living.

Sometimes we allow food to get in the way of *kedusha*. We "love" sweet things; we "love" fattening foods. We use that word without realizing the frightening truth it conveys. Too often we are so distracted by the chocolate chip cookies that we don't notice the spouse who made them for us. Too often we are so distracted by the myriad restaurants and products available to us — and the gustatory experience they promise — that we don't notice the real Chef behind the banquet.

Often we allow clothing, housing, career, and an endless list of other troublemakers to come between us and real intimacy.

Perhaps a normal Jew living in the 21st century can only experience *kedusha* by stepping back from these distractions. It is possible that the ancient formula for achieving connection — "*Kedoshim tihyu, perushim tihyu*" (through separation you can achieve holiness) — never deserved more attention than in this most modern of generations.

A Practical Plan for Achieving Kedusha

The sober reality is that we cannot have the best of both worlds. Selfish indulgence raised to the level of addiction interferes with closeness. Those involved in the treatment of alcoholics, narcotics addicts, and compulsive overeaters have long known this.

We need to create more space and time for those whom we want to love. We need to break modernity's mesmerizing stranglehold so that we can refocus on relationships. We don't necessarily have to make sweeping changes in our lifestyle tomorrow. Indeed, almost without exception, real spiritual progress happens in tiny but consistent steps forward. But we cannot allow ourselves to be distracted by the enticing onslaught of "progress" and expect to focus simultaneously on a significant other.

The pursuit of *kedusha* doesn't demand that we rid ourselves of cellphones and pagers, although it might require that we turn them off during certain crucial hours every day. If used intelligently, certain technologies — like answering machines and voice-mail services — can even help create the privacy and quiet time necessary for *kedusha* to flourish.

Breaking our food fascination doesn't require abandoning Chinese cuisine or Ben & Jerry's, but it might help to limit such indulgences to Shabbat, holidays, and other *simchah*s that help us focus less on the repast and more on God and our loved ones.

Many Jews already concentrate their clothing purchases in the periods around the holidays, and more rigorous adherence to this regimen would free us from ritual puttering around the mall and chronic rifling through clothing catalogs and advertising supplements during the interim months. Although we don't need to walk away from a successful career in order to live a sanctified life, we might need to make room in our professional schedule for prayer, daily Torah learning, and perhaps even dinner with the kids.

This is not an exhaustive or universally applicable list of recommendations; neither can all of these be instituted at once. But we could make it a family custom to take one small, practical step toward *kedusha* every year, perhaps on Rosh Hashana. The effects of such a custom over a five- or ten-year period are probably beyond anything we can imagine.

A Holy Nation

Several years ago, a secular, single woman had a Shabbat meal with my family. It was Friday night. She sat very quietly watching us talk, laugh, and sing. At the end of the evening, she turned to me and with burning seriousness asked how I managed to have such warm relationships with my wife and children. Like many people growing up at this point in human history, this woman had never seen *kedusha*, and it shook her.

The truth is that virtually every Jew has the potential for real *kedusha* in his or her life. We have Shabbat. We have holidays. During these special times, we withdraw from distractions and try to focus more on God and family. Kashrut limits our culinary indulgences.

The intricate Torah system creates time and space for closeness. God told us "You will be a kingdom of priests and a *goy kadosh*," and we often experience the fulfillment of that promise. Now we would just like to experience it a bit more.

If we make a courageous commitment today, perhaps next year we will look back and declare: "Its beginning was labor and its end reward; its beginning was exertion and its end a gift. It began with our sanctifying ourselves and ended with us being sanctified."